Follow the Money

Follow the Money

A Month in the Life of a Ten-Dollar Bill

Steve Boggan

Map: Rob Brooks

Union
Books

First published in Great Britain in 2012 and in the USA in 2013 by
Union Books
an imprint of Aurum Press Limited
7 Greenland Street,
London NW1 0ND
union-books.co.uk

This paperback edition first published in 2013 by Union Books

ISBN 978-1-90-852621-2

1 3 5 7 9 10 8 6 4 2

2013 2015 2017 2018 2016 2014

Typeset by SX Composing DTP, Rayleigh, Essex
Printed and bound in Great Britain by
CPI Group (UK) Ltd, Croydon CR0 4YY

For my father

Contents

Part II

Prologue

Several years ago, I took a phone call from Merope Mills, the recently appointed editor of the *Guardian*'s *Weekend* magazine. We had met briefly in her office a month earlier and I had been struck by her enthusiasm and her youth. She had the kind of energy and vitality that I vaguely remembered possessing once, a very long time ago. I had left feeling old and redundant. I doubted there was anything I could write that would appeal to her. At the time, my speciality was long and boring investigations that readers ignored and over which politicians often fell asleep.

'I have an assignment for you,' she said, 'but you don't have to take it . . .'

I knew I didn't. That's the whole point of being freelance. You choose what you do and, in return, you get to be poor and watch horse racing on TV. You are torn between wishing the phone would ring and disconnecting it. You spend too much time arranging lunch and convincing yourself that complete strangers with whom you get drunk could one day prove to be valuable contacts.

'. . . because it might be impossible.'

She had my attention.

'I want you to try to follow a ten-pound note for as long as you can. Keep tabs on it and watch it as it moves. Write about where it goes and the people who get it. Do you think it can be done?'

Instinctively, I knew who was behind this: Ian Katz. Katz was the editor of the *Guardian*'s Saturday edition, a handsome and clever workaholic who, in his previous incarnation as editor of the paper's *G2* features section, had landed in hot water for urging readers to try and persuade American voters in the marginal seat of Clark County, Ohio, to vote against George W. Bush in the 2004 presidential elections. Katz had bought a list of voters from the county for twenty-five dollars and suggested that *Guardian* readers write to those who described themselves as undecided, begging them to contribute to Dubya's demise. The project, called Operation Clark County, caused amusement in the UK, where it was regarded as a silly stunt, and uproar in Clark County, where people accused the *Guardian* of meddling where it had no business.

Katz finally pulled the plug on the exercise on 21 October 2004, after publishing a page of complaints under the headline: 'Dear Limey assholes'. This letter was typical: 'Have you noticed that Americans don't give two shits what Europeans think of us? Each email someone gets from some arrogant Brit telling us why NOT to vote for George Bush is going to backfire, you stupid, yellow-toothed pansies . . . I don't give a rat's ass if our election is going to have an effect on your worthless little life, I really don't . . .'

According to the online current-affairs magazine *Slate*, this letter-writer was right about the stunt backfiring. 'Nowhere . . . did more votes move from the blue [Democrat] to the Red [Republican] than in Clark,' wrote *Slate*'s Andy Bowers. In other words, the left-of-centre *Guardian* was responsible for a surge in right-of-centre voting. Bowers added, 'The *Guardian*'s Katz was quoted as saying it would be "self-aggrandizing" to claim Operation Clark County affected the election. Don't be so modest, Ian.'

I always liked Katz. If this was one of his capers (and I later found out it was), then I wanted in. I just had to figure out a way to do it.

After a couple of hours, it occurred to me that the assignment need not be as complicated or chaotic as I had first assumed. A banknote is used to seal a transaction. The trick, then, was to get in the middle of each one before it happened and to take control of it. This, in turn, would require skill, energy, tact, patience, bonhomie and enthusiasm.

Not really my strong points.

But I did it. With photographer Richard Baker, I whizzed around a succession of bars in London, a dinner party in Islington where the note was used to sniff cocaine, onward to the Derby in Epsom, a golf club in West Sussex, through petrol stations in East Sussex, pubs in Hampshire and on to a market in Thame, Oxfordshire, where, on the seventh day, our ten-pound note – serial number BE66 393677 – was banked.

I was surprised not only by how interesting the exercise was, but also by how keen people were to co-operate with it – and by how much fun it turned out to be, even when Baker insisted on telling each recipient of the note about his excruciating haemorrhoids.

'There are only two types of person in this world,' he would say. 'Those who have piles and those who are going to get them.'

During moments when we were trying to persuade someone to let us follow them, this actually served as a bafflingly effective ice-breaker, and I suspect Baker – nobody's fool – knew it. At one point, we had been becalmed at a golf club for twenty-four hours; all the members had credit accounts and so nobody paid with cash. When, finally, the ten-pound note fell into the hands of some cash-paying day golfers, reluctant to help us, Baker won their confidence by coming over misty-eyed and declaring, 'I've been dreaming of a long-distance lorry driver who'll take it up the A1.'

The ten-pound note project made me want to try something more ambitious. And once the seed was sown there was one idea I could not get out of my head: I would follow a ten-dollar bill around the United States of America for thirty days and thirty nights. Everyone I discussed it with agreed it was a terrific idea, but was it possible? Twice I set aside enough time to try, and just before starting out, I found excuses to cancel. This went on for almost half a decade. Finally, the excuses ran out and one late September morning I boarded a BA flight to New York. The following day I flew to Kansas City and on 1 October struck out for Lebanon, Kansas, to begin following the money.

Lebanon what?

Lebanon, Kansas. It was the obvious place to start.

Part I

Lebanon, Kansas
(39° 49.698' N, 098° 34.769' W)

In 1918 a group of scientists decided to find out exactly where the centre of the United States of America was. Locating the 'Center' was something that Americans had, perhaps understandably, obsessed about for some time. The Founding Fathers had toyed with the idea of having the seat of government centrally located, while travellers thought it might be useful simply to know where they were in relation to the heart of their nation. Maps were not as accurate as they are today, but the group, employed by the US Coast and Geodetic Survey, had just produced one using the latest methods and they were confident that they could find an answer.

They didn't have to worry about Alaska way up to the west of Canada in the north or Hawaii 2,200 miles to the south-west in the Pacific Ocean; these states didn't join the Union until 1959. The cartographers and mathematicians had only to consider the Lower Forty-eight states, known variously as the contiguous, conterminous or continental USA.

Still, it was a tricky puzzle and one they decided to solve with a piece of cardboard, a sheet of tracing paper and a pin.

The scientists traced over their map, put the paper on to the cardboard, cut around the shape they had outlined and stuck the pin into the underside of the card until it balanced. When they replaced the map on top of the cardboard and pushed the pin through, they found their Center: Lebanon, Kansas, a tiny farming community located south of the Nebraskan border, about 220 miles west of Kansas City.

When I read about this piece of low-tech genius, Lebanon became, for a short time, the centre of my world too. As it happened, the Coast and Geodetic Survey regretted the exercise almost as soon as its scientists had carried it out because what they had found was the centre of gravity of the cardboard, and even the kindest observers pointed out that this could have been tens of miles off target in the real world. It was enough, however, for the people of Lebanon to establish the 'Hub Club' to exploit and celebrate their new central status and, in June 1941, to unveil a monument and a motel one mile outside town at what visitors are still told is the geographical dead centre of the contiguous USA.

In fact, so few visitors have ever been there that the motel, at the end of Kansas Highway 191, closed long ago. And as for being at the centre, the monument is actually in the wrong place. It should have been built about three-quarters of a mile away on land owned by Mr Johnny Grib, a hog farmer of such miserable disposition that he declared he would tolerate no pesky sightseers traipsing over his fields.

None of this was enough to topple Lebanon as my own personal Center. Nor was the discovery that there were at least four more Centers dotted around the Midwest, all vying for the title like children arguing over a toy.

Forty-two miles south of Lebanon is a sign announcing the 'Geodetic Center of North America'. This sign, demonstrating a remarkable level of consistency on the part of Centerists, refers not to the spot on which it stands, but to one more accurately marked by a bronze plaque eight miles away on Meade's Ranch, twelve miles north of Lucas, Kansas. In case you're wondering, an exhibition at the monument in Lebanon explains that 'The Geodetic Center lies at a point where a reference ellipsoid (a mathematical approximation of the earth's shape) and a geoid (a standardized model of the earth's surface) coincide.'

But you probably knew that.

There is also the Geographical Center of North America, situated in the town of Rugby, North Dakota. This is determined as 'the point on which the surface area of the continent would balance if it were a plane of uniform thickness'. Which, of course, it isn't.

Add to these the Geographic Center of the Nation, which changed twice in 1959, first when Alaska became the forty-ninth state in January and again when Hawaii became the fiftieth in August. If anything about pinpointing the Center could ever be called simple, then the Geographic Center was described simply as 'The point at which an arc connecting the geographic center of the [48/49] states and the geographic center of [Alaska/Hawaii] would balance.'

When Alaska was taken into account, this method took the Center 439 miles from Lebanon and plonked it on Twin Tops Mountain, eleven miles west of Castle Rock, Butte County, South Dakota. With the inclusion of Hawaii, the Center moved again – six miles to its current location, twenty-one miles north of Belle Fourche, still in South Dakota, on a dusty piece of farmland.

This toing and froing has confused Americans for almost a century and blown fuses in the minds of legions of schoolchildren who thought they knew where the Center was, only to find that it had moved (and, as we shall see, is still moving). In a young country of migrants searching for an identity, perhaps the Center came to represent a beating heart, something tangible that suggested togetherness. Whatever the truth, some within the US Coast and Geodetic Survey found the obsession with it an unscientific distraction.

In an early essay entitled 'Geographical Centers', Oscar S. Adams, the Survey's senior mathematician, wrote:

> The conclusion is forced upon us that there is no such thing as the geographical center of any state, country or continent. The point determined will depend entirely upon the definition given by the one making the computation . . . If there were some rational definition so that all computations would necessarily lead to the same result, then some meaning might be attached to such a result. However, in most cases it is nothing but idle curiosity that leads to an interest in such a point, or some man may want it definitely located in his front yard.
>
> To all such, the warning should be given that the point is much like the proverbial flea: when you think you have it you have not . . . Since there is no definite way to locate such a point, it would be best to ignore it entirely.

Unfortunately for a mathematician, Mr Adams ruined the certainty of his argument by concluding: 'This is a case in which all may differ but all be right.'

Thank goodness, then, for the Global Positioning System and orbital mapping from outer space. That, surely, has put an end to all the confusion? Well, no. Even Google Earth, which allows users to home in on any point on the planet, suggests no fewer than three midpoints for the United States of America.

If you type 'USA' into the Google Earth search field and hit zoom, you end up at the edge of a pond on Fricke Farm, two miles north of Dearing, Kansas. But, rather spookily, if you are an American user of Google Earth and simply hit zoom without naming a search location when the program loads, it will home in on two different middle points depending on whether you use a Mac or a PC. If you use a PC, you are taken to the Meadowbrook Apartments in St Lawrence, Kansas. If you have a Mac, you arrive at the corner of Main Street and Lincoln Avenue in Chanute, also Kansas.

Could this have anything to do with the fact that Brian McClendon, vice-president of engineering at Google, lived in the Meadowbrook Apartments as a boy? Or that Dan Webb, senior software engineer at Google, grew up in Chanute, Kansas? Surely not.

It is probably just a huge coincidence.

I left US Route 36 at its junction with the 281 as the sun slipped beneath a glowing blanket of corn, flat as a piece of cardboard. It was 6.50 on the evening of 1 October. I had been driving due west from Kansas City for five hours and the turn north came as a relief. For a few moments, in the absence of glare, the road seemed darker until ahead and to the right I began to make out industrial shapes above the flatness. Great steel towers appeared to emerge from the crops, angular and jarringly out of place in an otherwise agricultural landscape. A town was coming and it looked drab and grim. I took my foot off the accelerator and coasted almost to a halt. There were no other vehicles to break the silence. To the east, through my open window, I could hear a soft breeze whistle through silks of corn. To the west, lit by the sunset's second wind, I could see clouds rising from a field of soya, but it was not smoke; it was dust from crushed bean pods. It had been a good year in Kansas and farmers were harvesting even as darkness fell. I edged forward, turning right, and through the gloom a water tower came into view, the kind you see in small towns all over America.

This one had the word LEBANON painted across its girth.

This was where I would begin to follow the money. I would launch a ten-dollar bill from here, from the real centre of the USA – forget Alaska and Hawaii – and follow it for thirty days and thirty nights to see where it went. I would travel alone and unpaid in the finest Corinthian tradition, propelled only by curiosity and itchy feet.

At least, that was the idea. More than once I had questioned my decision to take on this task. It was neither smart nor funny. It was just crazy. I was arriving at the heart of a vast land mass, a country in which I was an alien, with a ten-dollar bill, one night's accommodation, no Plan A and absolutely no Plan B. And I had no idea where I would be going next.

For months I had lain awake at night imagining all the things that could go wrong. Usually, I would be stranded, trouserless, in a bleak landscape as gunmen sped off in my car and with my ten dollars. Or I would wake up in a ditch with a sore head (if I was lucky). I would watch as the bill spontaneously burst into flames. Or drop to my knees as, on day 15, it was deposited at a bank, destined for the shredder at the Federal Reserve. Nothing about this strange and empty place seemed to brighten my prospects.

I turned off 281 and drove into Lebanon proper. The towers I had noticed through the dusk were grain silos. I had been wrong to see them as part of some industrial complex; this was a farming community and they belonged here. The town was laid out on a grid of a dozen streets and one by one I traversed them.

Along Main, through Chicago, up Walnut, down Chestnut and over Kansas. It took no longer than ten minutes. I was struck by the number of abandoned houses. There were clipped and clean properties with well-tended lawns and fancy garden ornaments one moment, then bedraggled and grey heaps of wood with peeling paint, overgrown yards and broken windows the next. There seemed to be no logic to the ruin, no bad micro-neighbourhoods or wrong sides of the track. In fact, all of Lebanon was on one side of the railroad; it meandered past the grain silos on the southern edge of town.

I was looking for Pine Street. At number 401 were Kay and Rick Chapin. Several weeks earlier, I had experienced mild panic when I discovered that there were no hotels, motels, hostels or guest houses for miles around Lebanon, but I did find mention of a hunting lodge on the Internet and emailed the owners, Kay and Rick, to ask whether I might reserve a room there. I thought an itinerant Englishman sleeping in his car might attract unwanted attention in a town of 200 souls. The Chapins usually rented out the whole lodge for eight or ten people at a time but they found me vaguely ridiculous and promised me a bed for the night.

The lodge was next door to their main home and Kay bounded up to me as I waited outside, convinced I had the wrong address. Kay and Rick's house was mock-Georgian, brick-built over three storeys with Palladian flourishes and a broad veranda out front. It was surrounded by tidy lawns and flower beds. Orange pumpkins lined the steps leading to the front door, a reminder that it would soon be Halloween, the arrival of which would mark the end of my adventure. If I made it that far.

Kay was a young-looking fifty-two-year-old with a broad white smile, an expensively tousled haircut and designer spectacles. After several email exchanges, I felt as if we knew each other and yet we didn't. I was so relieved to see her that I wanted to embrace her, but we just shook hands and giggled self-consciously. Kay turned out to be a prodigious giggler.

'How was the journey?' she asked.

'Wonderful,' I replied. And it had been. I was expecting a flat and dusty ride, recalling the western pictures of my childhood which nodded towards events in Kansas but which were actually filmed in the deserts of California. Rather stupidly, I had also anticipated something like the dust bowl of John Steinbeck's *The Grapes of Wrath*. The novel, about the desperate lives of drought-hit farmers and their heartbreaking migration to the cities (where they found they were not welcome), was based on people from 1930s Oklahoma, the next state south. But farmers in Kansas had suffered too as crops failed and the parched soil that should have nourished them blew away. Instead, the road had taken me past prosperous homesteads, ripe pastures and bursting fields heavy with corn, sunflower and soya. It had been a sunny day and by 2 p.m. the temperature had reached 82 degrees. It was autumn but few leaves had fallen and the wild prairie grasses still swayed thick and green on the breeze.

I grabbed my rucksack and Kay showed me to the lodge. It was an impressive wooden house with an L-shaped veranda wrapped around two sides. It had a steep pitched roof with four gables at right angles to one another. Seven round porch posts supported a skirt at the roof's edge, and this sheltered the veranda and the two-seater swing that hung on chains from its rafters.

Inside were five double bedrooms, a large lounge and a dining room with a long and beautifully polished blonde oak table. All the beds had sumptuous hand-sewn bedspreads and the floors were thickly carpeted. Some of the walls were lined in wood laminate, others were painted powder blue or covered in lemon wallpaper. Pictures of animals and hunting scenes hung on most of them: a buck at bay, ducks in flight, a pack of wolves in winter. There was an organ in the living room and on it a music book entitled *The Wonderful World of Popular Music* was open at 'Sunrise, Sunset' from *Fiddler on the Roof.*

I had expected nothing so grand or so comfortable. In the kitchen, with its lumbering ceiling fan, Kay had left out a coffee percolator and a plate of cookies she had baked herself. I took one, realising I had not eaten since morning. It tasted of butter and brown sugar.

I thanked Kay and asked, naively, where the nearest restaurant was. I might as well have arrived at the South Pole and asked for directions to the town beach. Kay just laughed.

'At Smith Center, about fifteen miles west,' she said. 'But clean up. You're eating with us tonight. Do you like venison?'

I smiled and nodded gratefully.

Kay left and I freshened up. There wasn't much point unpacking. I had only two pairs of jeans, some hiking trousers, a jumper, four shirts and four pairs of socks and underwear. I was wearing a pair of boots and there were some trainers in my rucksack. I reckoned I might need to be light on my feet if I was to keep up with the ten-dollar bill.

Its serial number was IA74407937A and it was burning a hole in my pocket.

I had marked it with little red squares in the top right-hand corner of each side so I could identify it easily, and this had been a private source of amusement since I landed two days earlier. In the US there is a long-running debate over whether marking money is illegal. Sticklers say that writing anything on a bill for whatever reason breaches Title 18 of the US Code, section

333, which deals with 'Mutilation of national bank obligations'. Under this:

> Whoever mutilates, cuts, defaces, disfigures, or perforates, or unites or cements together, or does any other thing to any bank bill, draft, note, or other evidence of debt issued by any national banking association, or Federal Reserve Bank, or the Federal Reserve System, with intent to render such bank bill, draft, note, or other evidence of debt unfit to be reissued, shall be fined under this title or imprisoned not more than six months, or both.

I didn't fancy six months in prison, but I needed to be able to identify the bill quickly if it was moving fast. I envisaged dark exchanges in bars and nightclubs, swift hand-overs in gas stations, shady deals for bags of crack under damp railway arches, ostentatious showers of notes from winners at the roulette table. I couldn't stop the world at each exchange while I put on my reading glasses and checked that this note *was indeed* IA74407937A.

People might think I was odd.

The whole issue of marking money is policed, rather quaintly, by the US Secret Service. When Secret Service agents aren't taking a bullet for the president, they sit around in their Foster Grants checking banknotes for defacement.

A general consensus seems to have been reached that it is all right to mark money so long as that marking is neither fraudulent, e.g. a lame attempt to change a ten-dollar bill into a hundred with an extra zero, nor likely to make a bill unusable by, say, scrawling all over it with a thick felt pen.

My marking was neither of these but, just in case, I had carried it out three hours into my flight from London to New

York, over the Atlantic Ocean and in international airspace. I reckoned that with a good lawyer the question of jurisdiction just might get me off.

Rick Chapin knew nothing of this. I figured he would be more comfortable with me in his lodge if he did not know I was a potential felon. He was a lean and quiet man, a handsome construction worker in a checked shirt and baseball cap. He was fifty-five but looked ten years younger, probably due to the physical nature of his work. We had known each other fewer than ten minutes before I thrust the ten dollars at him in the living room of the lodge, where he had come to say hello. It was exactly 7.30 p.m.

'You sure you're up for this?' I asked.

Rick frowned and looked at the red markings on the bill.

'Of course,' he answered. 'What do I have to do?'

I had chosen Rick to begin the bill's journey for a reason. I had discovered by accident that he was a good man, the sort of chap you would want beside you if you were in a scrape. During my research into Lebanon, I learned that there used to be a tiny wooden chapel, measuring about six feet by ten, next to the Center monument but that in 2008 someone had crashed their car into it, demolishing it completely. I had found the idea of a ten-foot-long chapel in an isolated field slightly surreal; it had only eight seats and was hardly ever used. In my mind's eye I saw Father Ted standing at its lectern, shaking his head at the size of his congregation.

When I heard of its fate, I laughed and immediately felt terribly guilty. In common with the monument, the chapel is in the middle of absolutely nowhere opposite a T-junction at the end of 191, the shortest highway in Kansas. Crashing into it would be like hitting the only rosebush in the Atacama Desert. The next day, to salve my conscience, I had emailed Kay expressing concern over the fate of the chapel. But she replied that I need not worry – Rick had built another. If I was looking for someone to kick-start the bill's journey, Rick had to be a pretty good candidate.

'You don't have to do anything,' I told him. 'Well, you don't have to do anything *special*. Just treat it like any other ten-dollar bill and spend it whenever you're ready.'

I wanted to say *within reason* but I stopped myself. Privately, I had two rules about the movement of the bill: I would not deliberately interfere or influence where it went and I would not tell people how to spend it. Of course, I might threaten physical violence against anyone who put it in a baby's piggy bank with instructions that it not be removed before the child's eighteenth birthday. I would also prefer the bill not to be dropped into an automatic deposit chute at a bank. That would not end its journey, though it would probably end mine. But I couldn't say as much.

So, telling Rick to do something, anything, *within reason* would be seen as applying pressure.

I shrugged. 'Spend it how you normally would. The only difference is that I'd like to be there when you do. So please let me know.'

It was a spiel I would have to repeat again and again if this thing was to work. I had to be there when the transaction took place, grab the situation by the scruff of the neck and smile insanely if I was to make it to the next leg of the journey.

We went next door to Kay and Rick's house. It was rather grand inside, though Kay kept apologising for being in the middle of building work; Rick was installing a downstairs bathroom. The property, the most beautiful in town, had once been owned by a banking family whose fortunes had declined with the Wall Street crash of 1929. (The bank itself had closed during the Great Depression and remained empty on Main Street until it became dangerous and was demolished in 2009.) It had cost the couple just 42,500 dollars in 2007, when the average family home in Kansas was selling for 125,000 dollars.

Kay was an intensive-care nurse at Salina Hospital, Kansas. That was a round trip of about 220 miles, so she worked in short bursts of long hours and stayed in Salina a couple of nights a week. When she wasn't working, one of her hobbies was making wine from elderberries – but she had nobody to drink it with. Lebanon was an ageing farming town at the buckle of the Bible Belt. Publicly, few people drank (privately, I was later to hear, it was a different story) and there was nowhere in town to buy alcohol. You had to make a thirty-mile round journey to Smith Center, the capital of Smith County, if you felt suddenly thirsty, and those who did take a drink generally favoured beer. Wine was considered an exotic thing for a woman to sip and was an altogether unsuitable beverage for a man.

So Kay had gallons of the stuff and, sensing that she had an English drinker in her kitchen, she offered me some. I was sure it would be awful, but she pointed out that it was red, had alcohol in it and we were, after all, having venison. So I said yes. She brought out two bottles and I held my breath while I took the first swig, resisting the temptation to pinch my nose with thumb and forefinger. And . . . it was wonderful. I'm not sure I can exactly bring to mind the flavour of elderberries, but this didn't taste like them. It reminded me of ripe merlot grapes from Bordeaux. It was deep, rich, elegant and very dry. Kay's face brightened as she saw the surprise on mine. This was good stuff. I held out my glass for more and, smiling, she began to pour.

Rick had a Budweiser.

It was dark now and colder. Through the shutters the crickets had begun to scrape and there was the occasional sound of a dog barking on one of Lebanon's empty streets. We sat at a round table in front of a broad window at one end of the kitchen and Kay served up tender venison stew with potatoes and more red wine. The Chapins were wonderful hosts.

'Rick shot it,' said Kay. 'The deer. With a bow and arrow.'

I was so hungry I wouldn't have cared if he'd strangled it. But I was surprised. I hadn't heard of anyone hunting animals with bows and arrows since the days of Robin Hood. Much later in my journey, I would find out that I was hopelessly out of touch when it came to deer hunting.

'There's a lot of game in these parts,' said Rick. He spoke in a low voice and with authority. 'Hunting deer with a bow is quite skilful. You have to be quiet and patient and you should try to shoot it behind the shoulder, mid-body, so the arrow goes through the lungs and heart. It's quick if you do it right. We also have duck and geese, rabbit, pheasant, wild turkey and some good fishing. We're very lucky.'

Rick and Kay were both out of unsuccessful marriages and had met over the Internet four years earlier. Within twelve months they were married. Kay had four grown-up children, Rick had three. They were very much in love. He had been born and raised in Lebanon, she had forsaken the bright lights of Lincoln, Kansas (pop. 1,163), and moved here to be with him. What quickly became clear as the wine and beer flowed was that they loved their town but were afraid for its future.

'We have big problems and we have to overcome them if we're going to survive,' said Rick. He was a member of the local council and spent much of his spare time trying to find ways to improve the town and its prospects. 'I reckon the population in Lebanon has fallen by about 25 per cent in the past ten years. Once kids go off to college, there's nothing for them to come back for. There are hardly any jobs outside farming, and because of mechanisation, there aren't even many farm jobs these days. Over the years you see schools and businesses close and families move away or die, and because nobody wants their homes they just rot and fall down. As a town, we're trying to bring in more industry so we're not so dependent on farming. But it isn't easy.'

In 2000, the US Census put the official population of Lebanon at 303. The 2010 Census had it at 218. It was slowly dying. As farmers aged and their children decided not to carry on the family tradition, huge tracts of land were being sold to big farming conglomerates. I wanted to ask some teenage boys what it was like to live in Lebanon and whether they wanted to be farmers when they grew up, but during my stay I didn't see any.

In 2006, the *New York Times* published an article on rural flight, as the phenomenon is called, by Charlie LeDuff. LeDuff interviewed farmer Randall Warner and his eighteen-year-old son, Travis, on their farm outside Lebanon. Warner senior worked long hours on his 3,000-acre spread. Is that what Travis wanted to do? He was about to go to college, but would he come back? His brother Dustin hadn't.

In the article, his response was telling:

'I like to work with people, I guess,' Travis says. 'Be around people. And we come out here every day. It's Dad and myself; that's not working with people.' He says this while sitting in the cab of his blue pick-up, a dirty older model, eating the sandwich his mother made him. His father is far off in the field, unable to hear the gloomy truth of the matter. 'I told my dad he could retire and cash-rent the land to the big farmer, but then what's he going to do with his time? This is all he knows. Come out here and work daylight to dark.'

Later, the article concludes:

Father and son have moved on to spraying fly repellent on the cattle. The sun is going low, the sky is growing golden. The father's gotten to thinking. The boy will soon go away to college. His voice shows no trace of his natural confidence.

'Do you think you'll come back to rural America? And farm? Raise cattle? Raise pigs?'

He talks obliquely, toward his son. The son mumbles, 'Depends if I find something better in the next couple years.'

'What could be better?' the father asks. 'What could be better than life on the Great Plains where the wind blows and you catch fresh air every day?'

'That's what I'm going to look for,' the boy says.

The boy turns his back. He returns to his work. The father watches after him.

Travis completed his degree at Kansas State University and he did return to run the farm in the spring of 2010, following an accident in which his father was killed.

The slow death of Lebanon has been reflected in the prices of its unwanted homes. The lodge, with which I was so impressed, cost Kay and Rick just 13,500 dollars in 2008 and it needed no major restoration work.

'Some houses have been sold over the Internet to people who haven't even seen them,' said Kay. 'There was one guy, a doctor from California, who bought a place on eBay for a few thousand dollars. But then he came here, took one look at what he'd bought and drove off without getting out of his car. That house is in really bad shape. Seems the doctor just wrote it off and now there's nobody to care for the place.'

I wanted to see more of Lebanon, learn more about why, with all its problems, the Chapins loved it so much, but it was too dark and I was too tired. I would do it tomorrow, if I didn't have to chase off after the bill. I thanked Rick and Kay for dinner, went back to the lodge and tried reading before falling into a deep sleep.

In Lebanon, at this time of night, there was nowhere for Rick to spend the money.

LaDow's
(39° 48.021' N, 098° 33.736' W)

I watched 2 October break bright and cold with a cup of tea and one of Kay's cookies on the porch swing. Rick was coming to fetch me for breakfast at eight and that gave me time to have a look at my neighbours' houses on Pine Street. At first, their layout seemed random, until I realised that the plots of land they occupied were relatively uniform. It was their location on those plots and the lack of fences – anywhere – that gave them an air of individuality. I liked the fact that people didn't build barriers between one another. Instead, they planted hydrangea, meadowsweet and American cranberry in their gardens and maple, oak and ash along the wide streets. Lebanon had probably been quite grand before the Great Depression.

The town is reputed to have been given its name in the early 1870s by a Bible student and man of letters called Jackson 'Jack' Allen. Settlers had established a village with a post office alongside a stream called Middle Oak Creek but they didn't have a name for it. They asked Allen to come up with one and he went to the Bible for inspiration. After reading about the cedars of Lebanon, which were used to build the temple in Jerusalem, he put that name forward as his choice. Whether he was influenced by the presence of cedar trees near Middle Oak Creek, no one could tell me, but the eastern red cedar, a hardy evergreen, is indigenous to northern Kansas, so perhaps he was. Either way, nobody opposed his suggestion and Lebanon was born and entered into official records in 1873.

However, just like the Center in modern times, old Lebanon just couldn't keep still. When news reached the town of the impending arrival of the Rock Island Railroad, the residents dug deep, as was common practice at the time, and offered money to the railway company to ensure its tracks passed close by. With the railroad would come more settlers, trade and prosperity, and that was worth paying for. Whether Lebanon's contribution was too paltry or whether the company's engineers simply made a navigational error is a moot point, but the tracks missed the town by about two miles to the north-east. Unbowed but probably very miffed, the people of Lebanon picked up their town, building by building, and, in October 1887, transported it on rollers to where it is today.

My plan that morning was to see the Center monument before the ten-dollar bill went into circulation, but first Kay served up a breakfast of bacon and eggs, potatoes, coffee and toast. We would go shortly, she said, but before that she had a request. She had been a little bashful all morning and had exchanged more than one amused look with Rick.

'A reporter from the *Lebanon Times* is coming to interview you,' she said suddenly. 'You don't mind, do you? It's Phyllis, Phyllis Bell. Actually, she's the only reporter. And the editor. And she takes the pictures. Well, she *is* the *Lebanon Times*. When she heard about you starting from Lebanon, she said she wanted to write the story. Is that OK?'

The *Lebanon Times* was a small pull-out section of the *Smith*

County Pioneer. Lebanon was obviously Phyllis's district and it was her job to find the words to go in the gaps between the advertising. But just who would be placing ads was a mystery to me. As far as I could tell, apart from Midway, the agricultural cooperative whose silos I had seen last night, there were only three businesses in town – LaDow's General Store, the Higby Brothers gun shop, which hardly ever opened, and Betty's Beauty Bar.

I wasn't enthusiastic about being interviewed, but I had been a cub reporter myself a long time ago and finding stories in a small and underpopulated patch is one of the toughest parts of a young journalist's training. Of course I would co-operate. It was the least I could do.

Phyllis arrived at precisely 9 a.m. She wore a petrol-blue trouser suit with a khaki-coloured jacket, over which was draped a small camera on a strap. She had round gold-rimmed glasses and it was my guess that she had come straight from Betty's Beauty Bar. Her hair, thickly lacquered and silvery grey, was fussed up into a precise parcel on her head like a little silk crash helmet. Phyllis, it happened, was eighty-one. Far from being a cub reporter, she had been the heartbeat of the *Lebanon Times* for forty-nine years. She was a local legend and I would later come to think of her as a heroine of the Fourth Estate. I shook her hand and struggled for something to say.

I had the impression that Rick and Kay had been looking forward to this. They effected some brief introductions and we all sat down at the kitchen table. Phyllis took out her pen and notebook and I waited for her to ask a question. She put her hands in her lap, looked at me . . . and said nothing. I glanced across the table at Rick and Kay but they were looking at the floor. I switched my gaze back to Phyllis. She stared back at me. This went on for some time. I began to think that perhaps this was an interviewing technique taught to American journalists before I was born. Embarrass your subject into telling you everything. Bombard them with silence until they can take no more.

It worked. Without being asked a single question I told Phyllis why I was there, what I was hoping to achieve, my deepest fears, professional background and inside leg measurement. Then I interviewed her. Her ancestors were called Bloomer and came from Birmingham (in the West Midlands, not Alabama). And as well as bringing out the *Lebanon Times*, Phyllis farmed 320 acres of land. She was something of a wonder woman and she had seen a lot of changes.

'It has sometimes been hard to keep the newspaper alive,' she said diffidently. 'Over the past fifty years, the town has lost a lot of businesses, and when you lose business you lose advertising.'

I asked Phyllis what were the biggest stories she could remember covering, but she didn't refer to any specifically. Instead, she spoke generally of bad fires and, tellingly, of things closing: the shops, the school, the banks.

But at a time, post-recession, when newspapers all over America were filing for bankruptcy – including companies behind such titles as the *Chicago Tribune*, *Los Angeles Times*, *Baltimore Sun* and *Philadelphia Inquirer* – and while others, like the *New York Times*, *Wall Street Journal* and *San Francisco Chronicle*, were announcing drastic job cuts, it had to be a cause for celebration that here, in the middle of the Great Plains of the United States of America, octogenarian Phyllis Bell and the *Lebanon Times* were still standing.

When Rick drove out of town and along Highway 191, all my questions about the mystery of the Center chapel car crash were answered. The road was little more than a series of hillocks between fields of crops. It went in a straight line but was so uneven, pitching wildly up and down, that sufferers of seasickness might have had a problem driving along its short length. My initial assumption was that alcohol must have had something to do with the chapel's demolition, but Rick corrected me.

'No, the driver hadn't been drinking,' he said. 'Turns out the guy used to live in these parts, but he'd moved away a long time ago. When they asked him what happened, he said, "Damn, it was dark and I thought I knew exactly how many hills there were on that road. I was counting them and I guess I must have thought there was one more to go. Well, there wasn't." Instead of stopping at the junction, he just kept right on until he hit the chapel. There wasn't much left of it but me and my partner, Gene Casteel, built another. It took us about a month.'

The chapel was made from wood and painted white with a pale grey pitched roof and grey-painted door and window frames. A sign above the door said simply: 'US Center Chapel'. It was non-denominational. Inside, there were eight seats and a lectern on top of which was a Bible. It felt distinctly odd because of its size, but also strangely spiritual given that it was hardly more substantial than a garden shed. About a hundred yards behind the chapel was the ill-fated motel that had closed down. It had since been bought for a pittance by a group of hunters from Texas and they continued to use it during the deer season. There were benches either side of the chapel and a covered picnic area behind it. And to the right of that was the monument, a stone flat-topped pyramid standing about seven feet tall. The Stars and Stripes were flying above it and there was an inscription that read:

THE GEOGRAPHIC CENTER OF THE UNITED STATES. LAT. 39 DEGREES, 50 MINUTES, LONG. 98 DEGREES, 35 MINUTES.

LOCATED BY L.T. HAGADORN OF PAULETTE & WILSON –
ENGINEERS, AND L.A. BEARDSLEE – COUNTY ENGINEER, FROM
DATA FURNISHED BY THE U.S. COAST AND GEODETIC SURVEY.
SPONSORED BY LEBANON HUB CLUB.

The date was given as 25 April 1940 but by all accounts the unveiling was not until 1941. The coordinates on the plaque did not exactly match those I had recorded on a GPS locator I was carrying. This might have been because of some simple rounding up or because they related to Johnny Grib's hog farm three-quarters of a mile away. I asked the US Coast and Geodetic Survey (now called the US National Geodetic Survey) if any detailed reports on how the location was identified had survived, but none had.

In *Geographical Centers*, our friend Oscar S. Adams described a number of complex ways in which some kind of centre (and he alluded to Lebanon) might be identified, but he believed different results would be achieved depending on the methods used and measurements taken. The one that pinpointed Lebanon was known as the centre-of-gravity method and was regarded as the simplest. But others, estimating the weights of land masses, accounting for the curvature of the earth and so on, were much more complex.

'If the fact is recognized that no method of determination of a geographical center of a country is entirely satisfactory, and if it is admitted that such a point can not be uniquely determined, then it is true that almost any one of the methods . . . will give a point that is accurate enough for all practical purposes,' he wrote, with the cynicism of a pedant who knows he is right. 'As a matter of fact, it is hardly conceivable that such a point should meet any "practical purpose" in any case. It is a conception that depends almost entirely for its existence upon the curiosity of mankind.'

I didn't care whether or not this was the centre of anything. It felt like the right place to be. There was an immense silence and a vast openness which reminded me that in London I could go for weeks without seeing the horizon. The air was cold but the temperature was rising. Trails of thin white cloud skittered across the sky. I heard the faint cry of a turkey buzzard carried on the breeze, but nothing else. Kay had brought along Christina, her smart and pretty eighteen-year-old daughter, and they were holding hands by the monument. Rick was off checking the chapel, fussing over a broken window. I turned through 360 degrees and tried to take in the enormity of the landscape, but I found it impossible.

Rick sauntered back and put his arm round Kay.

'Come on,' he said. 'Let's go get something to eat.'

We drove back into town and I had my first sight of LaDow's Market, the general store that doubled (or sextupled) as butcher, greengrocer, video rental library, hardware store and café. It was situated on Main Street next door to the American Legion and was the place you went to if you needed anything at all, up to and including the latest town gossip over a cup of coffee. Beneath exquisite but fading cornices, the creaking shelves were piled high. Pepsi and Mountain Dew vied for space with Advil, Zantac and shoelaces. There were plumbing wrenches and pork loin chops, milk and washing powder, nails, cheese, ice cream, potatoes, tooth picks and cigarettes. There was very definitely, though, no alcohol of any kind.

Chopping beef behind the butcher's counter was the proprietor Randall LaDow. He and his wife, Lori, took over the store from his mother, Margaret, and late father, Orville, in 1984, but Margaret, diminutive and friendly, still worked there.

'When we came to town in '58 there were at least four grocery stores,' Margaret told me. 'Now there's just us. As all the other stores closed we had to provide more and more services for the townsfolk. We do most everything here now, but it gave us no pleasure to see the competition die off.'

Rick, Kay and Christina had gone into the café on the other side of the shop for an early lunch while I had a look around. The cost of living in Lebanon reflected the disposable income of its population. Phyllis Bell had told me that a hired farm labourer could expect to be paid just ten to twelve dollars an hour and that the minimum wage was seven dollars twenty-five cents an hour. Neither working people nor pensioners had money to burn and the prices in LaDow's seemed to take that into account. You could have a meal of ham, beans and cornbread for two dollars or a hamburger for a dollar fifty. The food on the menu was the cheapest I was to see anywhere during my travels.

Just before noon I spotted Rick walking towards the cash register and my heart missed a beat. He was holding the ten-dollar bill and he gave it to Margaret LaDow as payment for lunch. He turned to me and shook my hand.

'If that's the last we see of you, I'd like to wish you luck,' he said.

I had known the Chapins for less than twenty-four hours, but I felt we had grown close. They had taken me into their home, fed me well and plied me with good wine. They had taken me to the monument and put up with all my annoying questions. I gave Kay and Christina a hug while Rick waited for his change. Outside, my rucksack was packed and stowed in the boot of the car and I was ready to go wherever the bill went next.

Which, as it happened, was Lebanon, Kansas.

Paul Coleman

I felt strangely naked once the Chapins had gone. Word had spread around town about the Englishman and his ten-dollar bill and it quickly became clear that pointing at someone and laughing was not considered rude in these parts. I would have preferred a much lower profile, but I couldn't help feeling that the attention was well meant. More than one stranger in dungarees and checked shirt, baseball cap and sunburnt neck walked up and wished me luck. But I was restless. If I paced the aisles inside LaDow's, people in the café would stop and stare. If I went outside, I looked anxious and out of place. If I hovered near the cash register, I made Randall and Margaret nervous. At one point I found myself hopping from foot to foot like a schoolboy waiting to be caned.

At 1.03 p.m. Paul Coleman, a bespectacled Englishman who had been living in America for twenty-one years, was given IA74407937A as part of his change for a twenty-dollar bill which he had used to buy a bag of bread rolls. He shook my hand and laughed when I told him that, unfortunately, I came with the bill. We were an item. Paul was over six feet tall and had a slim build, though the pot belly hanging over his khaki trousers suggested a fondness for beer. His face, brown and lined, sported a grey and reddish goatee and creased pleasantly when he smiled. He was fifty-two and he had moved to Lebanon from Denver, Colorado, nine years earlier with his wife, Susan, a nurse who had family in the county. Denver, said Paul, had become too busy. He loved the peace and quiet of Lebanon. He was originally from the horse-racing town of Towcester in Northamptonshire and when he spoke you could tell he was English. But more than anything, he had something of a southern drawl. His accent was very odd. Not only that, his language was colourful and he had a tendency to speak his mind.

'Good thing for you I came along,' he said. 'LaDow's shuts at four and doesn't open again till Monday morning. They's so tight in there your ten dollars might never have gotten out of the cash register!'

Then, without warning, he took a pager out of his pocket, read it and ran away with the ten dollars flapping in his hand.

I made to run after him, then froze. From the corner of my eye I saw more movement on Main Street and turned to see Rick Chapin also running. Paul jumped into Rick's four-wheel drive and they sped off. Farther down Main Street I saw Kay Chapin stranded at the side of the road. I ran up to her.

'What's going on?' I asked.

'They're volunteer First Responders – there must have been a call for help,' she said. 'The nearest hospital is about fifteen miles away, so when there's an emergency the First Responders provide basic care until an ambulance arrives. Rick and Paul both wear bleepers. They're also volunteer fire fighters.'

It had never occurred to me that people living in such isolation had to take control of their own crises. In big cities with large populations, the carefree – perhaps careless – assumption is that someone else will deal with emergencies. Tragedy is something that happens to other people. Here, the community has to be largely self-sufficient. I was to find out that everyone in Lebanon relied on everyone else to some degree and would accept help in times of need. *There but for the grace of God* was the mantra. In turn, the trust that this reliance fostered made the town and its people greater than the sum of their parts.

Kay and I jumped into my car and she directed me to the fire station, where the First Responders vehicle, a GMC 4x4 packed with medical equipment, was housed. It was no more than a few hundred yards away and we saw the GMC drive off as we arrived. We followed it to Willow Street and parked some way off. I didn't want to gawp and wanted even less to get in the way of Paul and Rick. The Responders' pagers had gone off at 1.10 p.m. and the pair had arrived at the emergency at 1.16. Not bad for a couple of volunteers. The ambulance, from Smith County Memorial Hospital at Smith Center, took about twenty minutes to arrive.

The emergency call had been from a man who had been at LaDow's earlier in the day and had gone home to find that his sister, who was in her early eighties, had suffered a stroke. Rick and Paul gave her oxygen and tried to make her comfortable until the ambulance arrived, then they took the GMC back to the fire station. Kay and I followed, a little breathless.

Rick was a certified responder, with training over and above first-aider level as taught by institutions such as the Red Cross. This meant he could apply splints to broken limbs, administer oxygen and use advanced equipment such as defibrillators in the event of a heart attack. Paul was working up to that but mostly just helped out where he could. We found them back at the station, stowing away equipment and drinking bottles of cold water. 'Hello again,' I said. Rick smiled and threw me a bottle.

I was to find out that Rick not only fixed up chapels, sat on the town council, volunteered as a fire fighter and a First Responder, but was also a weather watcher, looking out for tornadoes and other meteorological threats.

On the other side of the station was Lebanon's only fire tender, a red brute of a vehicle that had been bought second-hand from an airport fire service in Alaska for 55,000 dollars. I resisted an urge to climb on board and begin ringing the bell, but only just. There were thirteen volunteer fire fighters in Lebanon providing cover for an area that spanned seven miles to the north and ten to the south. For answering a medical call-out, First Responders were paid ten dollars. For attending a fire, they were paid nothing. These were duties they performed out of a simple sense of civic responsibility.

'It can be very costly if you put out a fire where arson is suspected, because someone has to stay at the scene until a full-time fire marshal arrives to investigate,' said Paul. 'And that can sometimes take days. When that happens, people in the community have a collection to make up for lost wages.'

The men were covered by Good Samaritan legislation that protected them from being sued should they – as dedicated amateurs – do something that resulted in accidental harm or loss. Among them were farmers, mail men, truck drivers, carpenters and mechanics. As we chatted, an elderly man shuffled into the station. Everyone nodded at him and he nodded back.

'Here's another of the volunteers,' said Paul, smiling.

I tried to keep the look of astonishment from my face but I'm not sure I was entirely successful.

'This is my dad,' said Rick. 'His name is Gene.'

Gene nodded and shook my hand but didn't say anything in particular to me. He asked what the emergency was about and Rick told him. Gene was eighty-two and still went on call-outs. How often he made it to the fire station before the other volunteers had driven off, I didn't like to ask. But he was still doing his best, helping out, asking for nothing in return.

While I was talking to the men about volunteering, Rick mentioned an accident in the spring in which a man had died. I knew nothing of Randall Warner at that time; I only learned of his existence after returning to London and finding the *New York Times* article about him and Travis. The connection between Randall's death and Rick's volunteering was explained to me by Kay. I wrote to her for details, and she replied that Travis had been visiting from college, helping his father, when the accident happened:

In the spring of this year Randall, aka 'Randy' Warner and his son Travis were out burning grassland. It was on a weekend and the conditions weren't the best; very windy. Rick, as you know, is a First Responder and a 911 call resulted in a page to the Lebanon First Responders. The only other Responder was out of town and so being an intensive care unit nurse, I went with Rick to assist him on the call. The page was for a 4-wheeler [quad bike] accident with fire in the vicinity.

We went to the general area and found Travis on his 4-wheeler. He led us to the exact location of his father. The fire had gotten away from them. Travis had heard a series of quick popping sounds and had gone to look for his father. Travis found him pinned by the 4-wheeler in a ravine and the fire had engulfed him and the 4-wheeler. The popping noise was the tires exploding from the heat. I immediately saw the burning legs of the victim. Rick did not recognize that Randy was under the 4-wheeler and asked Travis where he was. Travis stated, with tears in his eyes, 'He is burned alive, Sir.'

Rick turned his gaze as I pointed and then at that point saw the victim was beyond help. Rick, with understanding of the situation, turned his attention to the comfort of Travis and his girlfriend, who was also on the scene. I was so very impressed with my husband's wisdom in that moment and then also realized there was nothing we could do.

'The fire departments from Smith Center and Lebanon were on their way to the scene, as well as the ambulance and emergency medical service. As we stood and waited with Travis and his girlfriend, Travis's next statement, his eyes reddened with tears and his face covered with ash, was, 'I don't know how to tell my mom. I need help to tell her.'

Very soon the other emergency personnel arrived. Fire was still burning in and around the victim. His flesh was burning. A picture I won't soon forget.

Rick, being the considerate person he is, kept the other firemen from viewing the body and took the hose down to put out the burning corpse. In his wisdom, he knew it wasn't necessary to expose his fellow volunteer fire fighters and friends to this vision.

According to the autopsy, death occurred prior to consumption by fire. I'm sure this was a great comfort to the family. I do not know who or how Linda Warner was informed of her husband's death, though it was on my mind as Travis had asked so desperately for help.

As an afterthought, I asked about the elderly woman who had suffered the stroke. Kay told me that she had died too.

The front page splash of the *Lebanon Times* that week read 'Fall Festival at UM Church', with UM standing for United Methodist, and it was clear there was excitement in the air. The fall festival in America is similar to the harvest festival celebrated by Christians in the UK. The one in Lebanon was due to begin at 4 p.m. It would feature prayers and singing on the lawn outside the church in the shadow of the town's water tower. Children would be given horse and buggy rides and there would be drinks and cakes for all. I suspected Paul might go for the cakes but would not be joining in any hymn-singing.

'I don't hold with all that religion shit,' he said. 'I don't need an imaginary friend telling me how to live my life.'

Which was fair enough. I was worried, however, that he might accidentally spend the ten dollars on a raffle or tombola or some fruit juice. I doubted he would put it on the collection plate.

And so I began to shadow him. Paul, Rick and Kay were good friends (of course, here everybody knew everybody else) and after the earlier excitement Paul and Kay were strolling along Main Street and watching the local children enjoying the event. Rick had gone off to attend to some work.

Eventually, after bumping into Paul for the third or fourth time, he said to me, 'If you're worried about this bill, you're wasting your time. There's nothing to buy in this goddamn town and I sure as hell ain't giving it to the church. I'm driving a load to Hays at seven o'clock Monday morning and I won't be spending it until then. Now you can have dinner with me tonight, but you better stop following me or you'll get my boot up your ass.'

The load he was talking about referred to a consignment of

soya beans. Paul was a truck driver and just then the price farmers could realise for their soya was higher in Hays, Kansas, than in Lebanon. So he would be busy driving the 220-mile round trip twice a day until the price fell. I told him I would be delighted to dine with him that evening. He said he would barbecue some bratwurst and bring them over to the Chapins' house.

We stood for a while and watched the celebrations in hot sunshine. A series of benches had been constructed from planks on bales of hay and in front of them was a small stage on which a visiting preacher was directing hymns. There were two guitarists and an organist. Pumpkins and flowers were scattered about in the sunshine. Suddenly the preacher called for silence and everyone on the lawn stopped chatting and eating their cake.

'My momma taught me this song and I want you all to join in the chorus,' he yelled through broad white teeth. 'It's very easy. Do you hear these?' He held up two or three bells on a ribbon and shook them until they tinkled.

'She gave me these to help remember the song. Come on now!'

And to the blind astonishment of everyone present who had ever experienced even a fleeting exposure to rock 'n' roll, he began to sing Chuck Berry's 'My Ding-a-Ling'. Which, of course, is about penis obsession and masturbation.

He sang of being a little biddy boy and playing with his ding-a-ling. At school, he told us, he liked nothing better than to play with his ding-a-ling. At every opportunity, it seemed, he gave his ding-a-ling his fullest attention. Nothing, it seemed, could stop him.

Mouths opened and heads fell into hands and I wondered whether the meaning of the song could possibly have been twisted by the British with their lavatorial sense of humour. It was an American song by an American icon and here was a preacher singing it with evangelical gusto at an American celebration of fall. It must surely be suitable for a hymn service . . . ?

But I looked to my left and saw Kay with her hand over her mouth and Paul bent double with laughter. 'God damn it!' choked Paul. 'He doesn't know. He really doesn't know. Oh, my God, this is good.'

The adults froze one by one and the preacher beamed, delighted that he finally had everyone's attention, before describing how he once fell from a wall on to his ding-a-ling.

By now, Paul was crying and his face was the colour of Kay's wine. Kay had turned her back to the preacher so that all he could see was the barely disguised bouncing of her shoulders. I didn't know where to look.

Several couples stood up to leave, taking children with them, but still the onslaught outside the church continued.

Now the preacher was swimming from snapping turtles, ding-a-ling cupped protectively in both hands. Then I remembered what was coming next and the juxtaposition was excruciating. Nobody was singing along, of course, and the song's last verse allowed for this in a way that was surely never intended.

Taking on a look of frustration and realisation that *something, somehow* was wrong, the verse had him admonishing the conregation – if you ain't singin' along it must be because you're playin' with your own ding-a-ling! he wailed.

The preacher eventually finished to no applause and an opaque silence. His look of puzzled disappointment will stay with me forever.

The Centre of the Universe

Paul wasn't strictly correct when he said there was nowhere to spend the money once LaDow's had closed. On the edge of town, on the main highway, was a gas station, but he said he had a full tank and wouldn't be going there. Instead, he headed off to barbecue the bratwurst. Kay spared my embarrassment and didn't wait for me to ask if I could stay at the lodge again; she offered as soon as I told her what had happened to the bill. Then she went into the house to uncork some wine and let it breathe. Paul had a sideline roasting pigs for special occasions and word on the street was that he knew a thing or two about barbecuing meat. I was famished. I had enough time to go and freshen up, aware that half my clothes were already in need of washing.

At its height, the day was warm and the children had enjoyed their buggy rides. The visiting preacher left and there was some talk over whether he would visit again. The stars were clear and spun as dense as candyfloss.

Paul brought the sausages over at about 7.30 and we ate them with salad and potatoes prepared by Kay. Rick made sure that Paul was never without a cold beer and my glass was never empty.

Paul had moved to the US following four years with the Coldstream Guards in the mid- to late 1970s. He had served as a reservist guardsman for several years after that, but he wasn't keen to talk about his army career. He was, however, quite happy to talk about anything or anybody else. In certain parts of America, I would bite my tongue when the subjects of religion, abortion, homosexuality, capital punishment, evolution or guns came up. Paul had no such reservations.

'I'll tell you straight up, I believe in abortion,' he told us after dinner.

So he was pro-choice?

'No, I just think the world would be a better place if some of the sons-o-bitches out there had been aborted.'

I wasn't sure whether Paul did this for effect or whether he really believed it. But I thought he was about to reveal a soft underbelly when he said, 'There's something wrong with the death penalty, though.'

Ah. What?

'It takes too goddamn long to fry those bastards.'

Kay and Rick struck me as quiet liberals, thoughtful in their responses and generous of spirit, but they couldn't help shaking their heads and chuckling each time Paul pushed the boundaries of good taste. He badmouthed the neighbours, his wife, God and every politician who ever wore a suit, but he wasn't convincing. It was as if he was daring you not to like him, and failing. He pretended to be grumpy and unkind, yet during the two days I spent with him I saw a warmth that he did his best to hide. He would curse the old people of Lebanon and their non-drinking religious ways, then jump out of his pickup to help one struggling with a ladder. He would insult farmers who paid him poorly and didn't feed him while he was loading crops in the field, then be the first to offer help if he heard they needed it. And, of course, I already knew that he was a volunteer fire fighter and First Responder. When he forgot himself, Paul would ask after my welfare and make sure I had everything I needed. He would slag off goddamn journalists – and English motherfuckers at that – and then drive me round town explaining how the grain business worked, who had lived and died in each house and where one man's land finished and another's began. At one point, he took me to the town's abandoned jail and led me into its only cell in complete darkness.

'That'll give you something to write about,' he said.

On the morning of 3 October, a Sunday, Paul picked me up from the lodge to show me the farming countryside around Lebanon. As there was still nothing for him to spend the ten-dollar bill on, I left my possessions behind. It was bright and warm again and the fields were empty. All the farmers would attend church in the morning and not come out until the afternoon. But they would come out; there was too much harvesting to be done to take a day off at this time of year.

We were on a dirt track heading north out of town when another pickup came towards us. Both drivers slowed to a halt and wound down their windows. Paul nodded. The other man, Chuck Warner – brother of the late Randall, I later found out – was one of the farmers for whom he drove loads to Hays. Chuck nodded back. It seemed to be customary in these situations to say as little as possible and if you had nothing to say then to shut up altogether. Throwing insults was also acceptable, even encouraged.

'Saw you fishin'. (Chuck)

'No, you didn't.' (Paul)

'I did. I know where your spot is.'

'No, you don't. You'd have to hang me upside down and tie a

cinder block to my chicken sack to get it out of me. I ain't been fishin'.'

'Darn, I was bluffing.'

Silence. Then they talked about wheat and corn prices, hauling grain, who's selling up, who's buying land. Then silence again.

'What we gotta pay you for hauling this year? I thought the second year was free.' (Chuck)

'In your dreams.' (Paul)

'So long.'

'So long.'

I could hardly keep up.

In spite of the grumpiness aimed at farmers who did not pay him enough, it became clear that Paul had a deep respect for them. He told me there were two harvests a year, the wheat harvest, lasting around three weeks in June to July, and the fall harvest, which lasted from September into November. That was for corn, soya beans, sunflowers and milo, which is called sorghum in Europe and is used for animal feed.

'Farming is a risky business,' Paul said. 'Can you imagine at the start of every year taking all your money and investing it in something that can be ruined by the sun, the rain and the temperature? You have to have sunshine and rain at the right time. If you don't have enough of one or too much of the other your crops will fail. The international price of oil or seed affects how much it costs to produce your crop. If you have rain at harvest time, then you can't get your crops in. And if you do get them in, the price you're paid for them is fixed by how well other farmers have done in other states or even other countries. I tell you, it's goddamn gambling.

'You can even gamble with how you're gonna get paid. You

can go to the Midway Cooperative at the start of the year and say you'll give them so many bushels of corn or wheat or whatever at a fixed price. You don't get the highest price for that, but at least you get a precise income that you can work with. But if you don't manage to grow all those bushels for the cooperative, you gotta make up the difference at the market rate after the harvest. And even if you do manage to grow what you said you would, you could watch the price go high and see your neighbours getting paid more than you for the same crop.

'You could ignore fixed-price contracts altogether and just go with the market price when you harvest. And that's a goddamn gamble too, because the price could fall. Might as well go to the casino and put your money on the roulette wheel. I tell you, you gotta have balls to be a farmer.'

Two or three miles outside town I spotted an overgrown homestead and what looked like a derelict farmhouse and asked Paul if we could take a look at it. He agreed, saying that he had driven past this one many times without pulling over. We turned off the dirt track, stopped the pickup and climbed out. The farmhouse was on the brow of a small hill surrounded by dry brown grasses. Its wooden boards, those that had not fallen from the sides of the house, were almost black with age, but the chimney stack was still standing. Next to the farmhouse was a rusting, corrugated-iron barn and down the hillside, a short distance away, an antiquated plough had sunk deep into the soil and been inundated by weeds. Closer to the farmhouse, in front of what was left of the porch, was a wild marijuana plant.

We stepped carefully through the front door, testing each floorboard before investing our trust in it. Inside was depressing confirmation of what Paul had been arguing only minutes earlier. Farming was a risky business. There were winners and losers and we had strayed into the home of somebody who had lost in apparently desperate fashion. Just inside the doorway, to the right, was a hook and on it was a man's jacket and mildewed dungarees. Whoever used to live here had left in a hurry.

In a room to the left, past heaps of rubbish, boots and old pans, were two mattresses, abandoned on the floor and rotted with age. Over to the right was another room, strewn with pots, wood and tiles from the collapsing roof. In this, a substantial old stove had fallen over backwards and was leaning against an upright piano, its lid open to expose black and yellowing keys. Finally, in what must have served as the kitchen, was a tall refrigerator with a fresh mouse's nest in its icebox. I glanced over at Paul. His expression was dark and grave. What disaster could possibly have befallen these people to make them leave so suddenly, without their jackets, their boots, their piano? I shivered and felt like a stranger at a funeral. I turned to walk out and saw an old magazine on the floor. I bent down and picked it up. It was a supplement of the *Washington Post* dated 1969.

Earlier in our drive, we had come upon a combine harvester that had become stuck in the mud of a drainage channel. Paul had heard about this; it was the talk of the town. The combine was Ernie Schlatter's Case IH 2588 Axial Flow and its front left-hand wheel was half buried. Ernie was Paul's favourite farmer, a man he described as generous and kind, and he had been concerned for him.

'Usually, everyone in the community helps everyone else,' he said. 'You don't do it for personal gain. You give your help because you know sure as hell that some day you'll need help too. You give it without a fuss and you'll get it without a fuss. It's the way people function in these parts. If you have spare vegetables, you take them down to LaDow's and leave them in a box there, and people help themselves. They'll leave anything they have to spare without any show-boatin'. There isn't really need to advertise who left what or to say a big thank-you. Everybody does it.

'But there's a sort of unspoken understanding that during harvest time you're on your own. Everyone's too busy bringing in their own crops to stop for anyone else and nobody expects help. I want to make sure Ernie's OK. He's seventy.'

When we went back to Ernie's field, he was there working on the problem with his sixty-seven-year-old wife, Barbara. She was in a four-wheel drive being as supportive as she could and, for reasons I chose not to enquire about, she was hooked up to an oxygen tank. Ernie had run a chain from a tractor to the combine and he was about to pull as we arrived. He gunned the engine and I imagined what might happen if the chain broke or the tractor became stuck in the same drainage channel in which the combine had foundered. But Ernie had done this before and knew exactly how much purchase he could get from the tyres. It was enough to pull all fourteen tons free at the first attempt with a satisfying slurp of mud and suction. Paul, Barbara and I cheered.

While Paul helped Ernie to disconnect and stow away the chain, I chatted to Barbara. She was very proud of Ernie and of her son, Walter. Walter had a degree in agronomy and had worked with Ernie for twelve years before giving up farming and moving to Missouri with his wife to study for a second degree, this time in nursing. He was forty-five years old and, to me, that seemed late to begin a new career. It was certainly a source of great sadness for Ernie and Barbara. They missed him.

'The problem is that Lebanon has been going downhill for years,' said Barbara, looking into her lap. 'Farming has been good to Ernie and me, but for the young ones, well, it's very hard. There are fewer farms and fewer jobs, and there's no other industry to keep them here or bring them back once they go away. I truly don't know where the next generation of farmers will come from.'

I realised I had nothing to say, so I said nothing.

It was warmer now and there was a light breeze. We were in a field of soya beans, some of which had already been cut, but it was so big I could not see how much was left.

'Hey, son,' came a voice from behind.

I looked over my left shoulder. It was Ernie. I trudged over the dried welts left by the combine before it had become trapped and stretched out my hand to the farmer. He was about five foot eight and was wearing pale jeans and a blue fleece. Under his baseball cap were a pair of sunglasses and a cherubic face with few lines. He looked nowhere near seventy.

'How'd you like to cut some soya beans?'

I said I would like that very much. The boy in me was hopping from foot to foot again. I was going to cut soya in Ernie Schlatter's combine harvester! Yesterday it was a big red fire engine. What would tomorrow bring? John Wayne's chuck wagon?

Ernie told me where to put my feet and I climbed up and sat beside him in the combine's cab. Paul had told Ernie why I was in Lebanon and I think this tickled him.

'Welcome to the centre of the universe,' he said.

Below us the rotating flex header, the rotor that actually cut the crops, began to spin when Ernie started the engine and put it into gear. The machine roared into life in a riot of smoke and vibration. To Ernie's right was a flashing control panel which told us the rotor speed was 460 revolutions per minute (though it could go much faster) and the speed of the cleaning fan, which separated the beans from their pods, was 1,200 RPM. We began moving forward at about ten miles an hour, with sensors moving the rotor up and down over the uneven ground as we went. The header was eleven feet wide and, at this speed, we quickly covered large tracts of Ernie's field. The combine had cost Ernie a quarter of a million dollars. It was easy to see how labour-intensive farming had become a thing of the past.

'In one hour this can do the same work as it used to take ten men one whole day to do,' Ernie shouted over the engine. 'That's where all the jobs went.'

Ernie had been in farming since he was sixteen and had just been honoured with the title of Master Farmer in a Kansas agricultural ceremony. He had a quiet dignity that appealed to me and I could see why he was Paul's favourite. This year's harvest, Ernie said, had been fabulous, but he wouldn't be celebrating.

'The smart farmer doesn't make too much of the good years, because he knows there's bad years down the line. You put some money aside, upgrade your equipment and carry on with your work. You heard of the Dust Bowl?'

I said I had.

'Well, after the 1929 Wall Street crash, the banks wouldn't guarantee money to the farmers to see them through. A lot of folks remember that, put money away just in case of need. So it's been a good year but you won't see people crowing about it.'

We sat in silence for a while, Ernie steering the combine in broad, straight sweeps before periodically unloading the beans into a long white truck parked at the side of the field. The sun was casting long shadows now and, judging by the stock-still soya stalks, the wind had settled to almost nothing.

Suddenly, Ernie leaned forward and looked at me conspiratorially. 'How you getting' on with them Germans?' he asked.

I was slightly taken aback but I tried to keep my composure.

'Fine, thank you, Ernie,' I replied. 'We're getting on pretty well with the Germans.'

'You sure?'

'Yes,' I said.

'They were planning to bomb the hell out of you and invade, huh?'

'Well, yes, but that's quite a while ago. We're getting on much better now.'

'You definitely sure?'

'Yes. Really.'

'Well, OK then,' and he pressed his jaw forward and carried on cutting soya.

Ernie told me he had been reading a book on European military history and was shocked by accounts of the London Blitz. If we had still needed help against the Boche, then I had the firm impression that Ernie would have been on the first boat across the Atlantic. And he wouldn't have been the first Schlatter to do so. Ernie lost his uncle, another Walter Schlatter, in France during the Second World War. Walter had survived a landing on Utah Beach on D-Day but had been killed by a shell shortly afterwards.

'He lived for about thirty minutes after they got off the beach,' said Ernie. 'He left behind a letter saying he had thought the war would be over quickly, but that after a time he realised it wouldn't be. He wrote: "If I ever get back to the good old USA, just about anywhere would be good enough for me to settle." But he never made it back.'

Walter was one of 2,499 Americans who died that day.

It was touching to know that Ernie was still concerned about the fate of Europe even after the loss of a family member to its cause. It didn't matter to me that the concern was misplaced or wildly out of time. It was there and his loyalty was strangely comforting. He really cared.

I asked Ernie whether he ever intended to retire and he said he did, one day. 'I think I'd like to do some travelling, but I'm not sure where I'd go.'

'Well, if ever you come to London, I'd be honoured to be your guide.'

He smiled and chewed on the invitation for a while. 'That's nice,' he said. 'Will you take me to see the Eiffel Tower?'

I did my best not to falter, and replied, 'Yes, of course.'

There was no way I was going to hold a tiny geographical slip against such a man. I mean, what are 211 miles between London and Paris when you live at the centre of the universe?

Golden Ox Truck Stop, Hays, Kansas
(38° 53.765' N, 099° 19.026' W)

My mobile phone had not had a signal for days but I found a use for it on the morning of 4 October. I had set its alarm the night before with a warning from Paul ringing in my ears.

'I'm leaving at 7 a.m. I'm not knocking on your door and I'm not wiping your nose. And if you're not there I'll take off anyway and I'll spend your goddamn ten-dollar bill when and where I please.' Then he cackled. 'Hell, I could get used to this. I really got your balls in a vice.'

We had both had a little bit to drink. After leaving Ernie we had rushed back to the Chapins so that I could keep a promise: to cook a traditional English Sunday roast as my way of saying thank you. Apart from Paul, neither Kay nor Rick, nor two neighbours they had invited to eat, had ever tasted roast potatoes. This seemed implausible in a country used to feasting on turkey with all the trimmings not once a year, but twice. I was going to knock 'em dead.

Kay and Christina had insisted on driving into Smith Center to buy the ingredients for the meal while Paul and I were hanging out with Ernie. A thirty-mile round trip seemed an awfully long way to go for a couple of chickens and some veg, but they didn't appear to mind. When they returned, I was quickly installed in the kitchen and Kay wasted no time in finding an apron for me on which was printed the image of a woman in a see-through nightie. She had had the wine breathing for quite some time.

I began making the meal, reducing Kay's orderly kitchen to chaos. Paul and Rick were enjoying their beers while Kay entertained her other guests with tales of wine-making punctuated with liberal tastings. I had given an estimated time for dinner, but I got it hopelessly wrong. I didn't have the oven hot enough to cook the chickens, let alone crisp up the roast potatoes. I forgot to make stuffing and I overcooked the carrots. Meanwhile, we were drinking more and more on empty stomachs.

Almost two hours late and rather drunk, I served up overcooked chicken with soft roast potatoes, lumpy gravy, mushy veg and stuffing that had almost caught fire when I tried to rush it into production at the last minute. Everybody said it tasted good but they were merely being kind. One of Kay's guests wouldn't go near the gravy, choosing instead to moisten the roast potatoes with fresh tomato. It was a strange combination and it looked something like a sawmill accident.

For some reason, one of the neighbours began talking about God and I felt a tightening in my stomach. I looked over the table and saw Paul smiling, his eyes grown large like a wolf's.

'So,' he began, 'tell me about your imaginary friend . . .'

At the end of the evening I found myself saying goodbye to the Chapins once again. I would be gone when they went to the lodge in the morning. This time was even more difficult, and not just because of the wine. We had become firm friends. In particular, I thanked Rick and said I wanted to apologise for something that had been on my mind.

'What?' he asked. He looked surprised.

I explained that I had driven past hundreds of small towns like Lebanon during visits to America and had always felt sorry for their inhabitants. From the interstate highways they had seemed sad, grey, boring.

'I actually pitied the people who lived there,' I said. 'I couldn't understand why anyone would choose such a life. And I'm embarrassed now, because that smacks of arrogance. I finally think I get it.'

Rick didn't say anything as I shook his hand. He just smiled and gave me the smallest of nods.

It was still dark when I pulled up outside Paul's house at the end of Main Street at 6.55 a.m. We would be heading broadly south-west in a series of dog-legs; all the roads ran either north–south or east–west, so there would be no more direct route to Hays.

'You set?'

I said I was and sat while Paul fired up his long white truck and let the engine warm for a few minutes. It was very cold. He started moving and I followed, taking as many last glances at Lebanon as I could. I doubted I would ever find my way back there. I had arrived with a sense of trepidation and was leaving with fond memories and lasting friendships. A wave of sadness rolled over me.

We headed south along Highway 181 to Downs, where we kicked west again through Osborne and on to the 24 to Stockton for the final leg south to Hays on the 183. Paul said it was a journey of 106 miles. The sun was coming up fast now and each time we slew west it shone red and blinding in my rear-view mirror.

Either side of us, almost all the way, were fields that had

50

already been harvested, looking bare like shorn sheep, or that were full and pregnant and would soon be cut. The terrain was flat for mile after mile until we entered Ellis County on the 183. The road rose steeply over the Saline River and climbed higher, eventually slicing across a broad, bleak plateau. I was taken by surprise at the appearance of a nodding pumpjack. Then another flew past, and still more. There was oil below us.

At 9.05 a.m., we arrived outside Hays and Paul asked me to park beside farmland next to Interstate 70 while he delivered his load of soya. We were still on high ground and when I climbed out of the car to wait for him I felt a bitterly cold wind. It was stark and uninviting; I did not envy Paul his daily journey here. I had thought about bringing more substantial cold-weather clothing but it was too bulky. I was beginning to wonder whether I had made a mistake. I had only a jumper and a thin Gore-Tex jacket for warmth; what if the bill went north? It was too late to worry about that now.

Signs at the junction of the 183 and the I-70 pointed west to Colorado, south to Oklahoma and north to Nebraska. I wondered where I would be going next.

At 9.30 Paul's rig emerged from the compound and he honked me to follow him. After a few minutes we entered Hays and he pulled over at the Golden Ox Truck Stop, an unremarkable gas station and pit stop on the 183. I parked the car, followed him inside and watched while he chose something to drink for his journey back to Lebanon. He took a bottle of Pepsi from the refrigerator, reached into his pocket, pulled out a ten-dollar bill which bore red markings and headed to the cash register. This was the point where I was supposed to take control of the situation. But I failed. Before I could explain what was happening, Paul had already paid.

'Excuse me!' I shouted lamely to the cashier. 'I'm, ahh, I'm following that bill. I'm erm . . . If you don't mind could we have a chat? You see . . .'

'Sorry, buddy,' said the cashier. 'I'm busy. She's getting it.'

He pointed over my shoulder. I turned around and there was a smiling woman holding a hundred-dollar bill in front of her chest. Paul, the cashier (whose badge said his name was Chuck Patel) and I were all looking at her.

'What?' she said, taking a step back. '*What?*'

'Sheee-it, you in trouble,' Paul whispered to me.

Chuck told her how much he wanted for the gas. She handed over the hundred and got IA74407937A in her change. I introduced myself and carefully took her to one side so Chuck could carry on selling gasoline. She looked at me with wide eyes.

'I'm a journalist from England and I'm, ah, following that ten-dollar bill,' I explained, and put my index finger against the one with the red markings. 'I've already followed it 106 miles from Lebanon and I'd really rather like to see where it goes next.'

Her name was Nicole Kilgore, she was twenty-nine years old and she was travelling with her four-year-old son, Kadden, in a Toyota Land Cruiser. She told me she was heading 260 miles east to Harrisonville, Missouri.

There is no word other than 'creepy' to describe the act of asking a lone woman, travelling hundreds of miles with her four-year-old son, if you can follow her. But, suffocating on my embarrassment, I did. Her reply came instantly.

'Sure,' she beamed. 'Sounds like fun!'

I barely had time to thank Paul and promise to call him before jumping into my car and screeching off in hot pursuit.

Nicole handled her Land Cruiser like a racing car, weaving her impatient way past slower vehicles and speed-limit sticklers. I began to understand why she was so relaxed about letting me follow the ten-dollar bill. Judging by her driving, she wasn't afraid of anything.

When she told me she was heading east, my heart had sunk. Although the bill's journey officially began in Lebanon, we had already travelled together from the airport at Kansas City and Nicole's route would take us back almost to where we had started. For a fleeting moment I wondered whether I could give her a substitute ten-dollar bill and apologise for troubling her. I would be able to hand over IA74407937A to Chuck, make a better fist of explaining to him what exactly I was trying to achieve and relax a little. Chuck would join in the spirit of the thing and hang on to the bill until he found a cowboy heading to Montana, a professional gambler en route to Nevada or an actress bound for Hollywood.

But that would be cheating.

I consoled myself with the thought that we were at least taking a different route. I had dawdled into Lebanon on rural Highway 36 and was now whizzing away from Hays on Interstate 70. It was still cold but weak sunshine crept between thin clouds as we rolled across deforested plains on the northern and southern borders of Ellsworth and Lincoln counties.

Farther back the ride had been memorable for anti-abortion hoardings at the side of the road: THANK MOM FOR CHOOSING LIFE, ABORTION STOPS A BEAT IN MY ❤ and JESUS IS REAL. I wondered what Paul would have made of it.

As we rolled on, the landscape – craggy fells and sudden deep troughs – was taken over by scores of wind turbines that appeared to grow low and dangerous out of the road itself. It was an illusion, of course. They were rooted and hidden farther down the hillside, but as they grew closer I fully expected their blades to scrape along the highway, casting off showers of sparks.

At length, the rocky terrain around us flattened and the road below opened up, revealing vast, rolling plains as we crossed the Saline County line. And as we headed down, small pines like Christmas trees began sprouting. Over to the north was Culver and a field of dust devils dancing like dervishes. It seemed the landscape changed every fifteen minutes.

At times I struggled to keep up with Nicole even though she appeared to be almost constantly on her phone, driving one-handed and with ease.

Salina flew past to the south and on we went towards Junction City and the US Cavalry Museum at Fort Riley before passing a section of the military base itself. Parked on a broad forecourt were rows and rows of armoured vehicles painted, ominously, in desert camouflage.

The countryside was becoming more contoured and greener. At the side of the road was a billboard that read: 'One Kansas farmer feeds 128 people – and you!' And I could think of no reason to argue with that.

We passed Topeka – which means 'to dig good potatoes' in the language of the Kansa and Ioway native Americans – and then instead of hitting Kansas City we swung south on the I-435 and made a pit stop in Lenexa. Here, Nicole wanted to do some shopping, but first she knocked several years off my life. She pulled into a supermarket parking lot and I rolled in neatly beside her. She climbed out of the Land Cruiser with a comforting smile – she had a lovely smile – and I noticed that Kadden was flapping about inside the vehicle, squeezing between the seats and forcing his head under them as if looking for a misplaced toy.

Nicole turned to me and said, 'I'm sure it's in here somewhere.'

'What?' I asked.

'The ten-dollar bill,' she said breezily. I froze and tried not to appear at all alarmed. 'I had it tucked up between the sun visor and the windshield, but the windows were open and, well, it blew away. But I'm pretty sure it didn't go out the window.'

She was cool as ice. Inside, I was panicking. Day 4 and already finished. I nodded and smiled through gritted teeth. I had made a promise to myself that if anyone lost the bill, then that would just be hard luck and I wouldn't apportion any blame. There would be no recriminations; all of my ten-dollar carriers would be doing me a favour. But if she really had lost it I would, I would . . . well, I would go home.

Until this journey, I had no idea that hopping from foot to foot was a trait of mine. I was sure I remembered that one of my childhood heroes, Jennings, the schoolboy creation of the late novelist Anthony Buckeridge, had a foot-hopping habit whenever he was in trouble. Had it rubbed off? Had I grown up at all? I was doing it again.

Kadden was squeezing between the seats and cup holders. I couldn't decide whether he resembled a greased racing snake or a chimney sweep. One moment he was on top of the upholstery, the next he would disappear altogether. I had no idea there was so much empty space in a car. I stood my ground beside the Land Cruiser and wondered how forced my smile appeared. To anyone else, this would just be a ten-dollar bill and losing it would not be the end of the world. But, already, I had endowed it with such importance as to render it priceless. My situation was as hopeless as it was preposterous. From the beginning, my fate had been tied to an object I was unlikely even to touch as it passed from one stranger to another – and there were another twenty-six days to go. Not for the last time, I wondered what on earth I was doing.

'Here it is, Mommy,' Kadden said suddenly.

His grinning face and mop of hair emerged from behind the passenger seat and he was holding a ten-dollar bill. I asked if I could check it for markings and there they were. I waved my hand nonchalantly and smiled at Nicole as if to say, 'Heck, I'm almost sorry we found it . . .'

And, as usual, she smiled right back.

Harrisonville

(38° 39.1' N, 094° 20.93' W)

We crawled into Harrisonville at around 4 p.m., Nicole driving slowly for the first time and me marvelling at the colonial beauty of the architecture. We skirted round the centre of town and headed towards the home of Nicole's sister-in-law, Krystal, past one- and two-storey wooden houses with gently pitched gables, clapboard sidings and broad porches. The streets were wide and tree-lined, which lent a dappled coolness to the torpid Missouri heat.

Outside one of these houses in Arnold Avenue were two women, arms folded across their chests, stern looks on their faces. Nicole pulled up in front of them. She jumped out of her car, smiling, shouted, 'Hi!' and gave each one a hug. In turn, they kissed and fussed Kadden before focusing their attention on me.

'This is Steve,' Nicole said.

'This the guy been following you?' This was Candice, Nicole's sister.

'Yeah, isn't it exciting?'

Candice's expression suggested she was excited, but not in the way Nicole meant. It was the kind of excitement you saw on Muhammad Ali's face before he floored an opponent. She was sizing me up for a haymaker and I remember thinking that I probably deserved it.

'Do you normally follow women around?' Candice asked.

Ba-boom.

Before I embarked on this journey, I had hoped it might turn into a voyage of self-discovery. It would require patience and stamina; would I have enough of both? I would need to shake off a deep-rooted sense of bored cynicism with the world; could I free myself from it? I would have to overcome exhaustion and exasperation in turn; could I face them with stoicism and kindness?

These were big themes, but all I had found out so far was that I had a tendency to hop from foot to foot when the going got tough. Now, faced with Nicole's uncompromising relatives, I had another flash of self-awareness: I had an awful Hugh Grantesque way of explaining things under pressure.

'Aha, yes! I mean no! Harrumph,' I meandered. 'You see, I thought you might, ah . . . quite unusual . . . not your everyday encounter!'

'So who the hell are you?'

Before I could answer, Candice turned to Nicole and said, 'Do you know we nearly called the police when you didn't check in?'

Nicole turned to me and smiled. 'Don't you worry about them. They just asked me to call every ten minutes to make sure you hadn't kidnapped me and, well, we went through a cellphone blind spot for a while back there. Turns out they were worried. Can you believe that?'

Actually, I said, yes, I could. So this was why Nicole was constantly on her cellphone. Oh, God. How could I have been so thoughtless? They must have been worried sick. I stopped hopping and stammering and introduced myself properly to Candice and to Krystal, who was married to the sisters' brother, Colby. I pulled out my press credentials, passport and a copy of my original ten-pound-note article and handed them over, hoping they would not add forgery to kidnapping on my list of suspected crimes. They checked the passport, pointing out that the picture looked nothing like me, but the original ten-pound story seemed to tickle them. They pored over it, giggling, and a noticeable thaw set in. They took me inside their pretty wooden home and gave me coffee, asking dozens of questions while a small but indeterminate number of children whizzed and bumped around my shins.

'How long you been doin' this?'

'Four days.'

'How long you goin' on?'

'Thirty.'

'Why you doin' it?'

'I'm not sure, really.'

'Who's payin' for it?'

'I am.'

'Where you goin' next?'

'I have no idea.'

'Are you crazy?'

'. . .'

Nicole and I went out to the back porch and sat down while the sun sank behind oak and sycamore trees. Shining gadflies were weaving gold into the fading light.

Nicole described herself as an erstwhile stay-at-home mom. She lived in Fort Collins, Colorado, with her husband, Jeramie, and their other child, eight-year-old Vivian, and they were very happy there. 'It's a big university city, very artsy, open-minded and pretty,' she said. Indeed, so pleasant is Fort Collins that *Money* magazine named it the best place to live in America in 2006. But recently something had changed.

'I've been helping Jeramie with his work,' said Nicole. 'He used to work as a handyman but now we have a new business – clearing out repossessed properties. So many small companies have gone out of business and when that happens the owners usually have their homes repossessed. As if that isn't bad enough, the bank expects them to clean up before they hand over the keys. If you just walk away, the bank will charge as much as 10,000 dollars for cleaning.'

Nicole was not only talking about lost homes here. The cleaning was for retail or industrial premises too, often where they were attached to a family home. It was an ugly business.

'Well, we thought it must be bad enough to be repossessed without having to pay all that money to the bank too, so we came up with a new way of doing things,' she said. 'We go in and clear everything out and in return we just ask for a few antiques or something of value that the family no longer needs. But it can be heartbreaking.'

Did she feel comfortable with the work?

'Well, I don't think you ever feel comfortable, but it is possible to feel OK about the way you're doing it. Our last job, for example. It was with an asphalt business, so you can imagine the mess. We found lots of things the family had forgotten and we put them aside. Often they just can't face going through their stuff. It's too painful.

'In this case, there were pictures that the couple's children had painted and things that the wife's father had worn – his cap from the navy, some of his shoes and medals from the Second World

War. She had forgotten she had them. There were some personal documents and even a land grant for the original property signed by President Taft.'

William Howard Taft, one of America's less-remembered presidents, was in office from 1909 to 1913.

'We gave her the things and she just sat down and cried. It was sad, but I think we made it more bearable, less impersonal. It was a job I was happy to see done. In return, we asked if we could take an old safe, some antiques and a trailer, and the family said we could.'

We sat quietly for a while, contemplating our own good fortune. In 2010, more than a million Americans had their homes repossessed, the effect of a credit-crunch hangover that refused to abate.

We didn't stay long at Krystal's. Candice wanted to visit her future father-in-law, Ray Holman, not least because Nicole had to pay him for fetching some pork ribs for her and she was going to use the ten-dollar bill to pay for them. Ray lived a five-minute drive away on a small farm with his wife, Patti, seven horses, a mule, a pot-bellied pig called Priscilla (which slept in Ray's garage), twenty-one cats and five dogs that took an unhealthy interest in my groin the instant I set foot out of my car. The short drive had been unerringly lovely in the golden glow of sunset and I wondered whether Harrisonville might not just be the prettiest American town I had ever visited. I would find out later that not everything about it was attractive.

Ray shooed away the dogs and held out his hand to me. I shook it and said hello.

'Strangers are always welcome on this farm,' he said. 'You'll stay with us tonight.'

These were the first words Ray said to me. There was no

preamble; he went straight to hospitality while the sisters and their children said hello to Patti. My car door was still open – for some reason I felt it would be impolite to assume I would be staying for any length of time – and my rucksack lay untouched inside the boot. None of the niceties of arriving unknown and unannounced had been observed. Ray didn't do niceties and I came to suspect later that this was because he found them insincere. So he cut through all that, leading me to a paddock and introducing me to Dudley, a Missouri foxtrotter mule, and a striking, if scrawny, Arabian mare that had cancer and seemed most comfortable with us at a distance. Dudley nuzzled Ray's armpit and sniffed at me curiously.

'I love this boy,' said Ray, and kissed the mule's muzzle.

Ray was sixty-three years old and stood about five foot nine. He almost always had a cigarette hanging from the left side of his mouth, next to a pronounced gap in his teeth, and sometimes it would burn so low you felt it would set fire to his grey beard. The days I knew him, he wore jeans with braces, striped open-necked T-shirts and a baseball cap, and in common with the few people I met in Harrisonville, he spoke with an accent that I felt belonged somewhere farther south. More than anything else, what characterised Ray was his concern for others, whether animals or strangers. He didn't care where they were from or how many legs they had.

'Is he bothering you?' came a voice from behind us.

I spun round to see Patti marching over. She was in her fifties with an attractive shock of greying hair and a no-nonsense attitude that recommended her as the person you went to when you needed something done. Ray had been a truck driver and met Patti at a trucking company in Illinois. Patti was white and Ray was black and I later found out that in Cass, the county in which Harrisonville was situated, mixed marriages could be difficult. The fact that they had stuck at theirs for twenty-four years said something about them that doesn't need spelling out here. It was clear Ray adored her.

'She's tough,' he later told me. 'And she can sometimes be a bit sensitive if she thinks people have a problem with us. There was this time we were in some redneck bar shooting pool and my quarters were on the table ready for the next game. This drunk guy came up and announced he was gonna play before me. That was his first mistake. His second was to lay his hands on Patti. Well, she hit him with her pool cue. First she hit him in the balls, then she got him on the jaw. Everyone in the bar apologised and we just picked up the quarters, cool as anything, and we went home. On the whole it was a good night.

'There's a lotta stuff we don't agree on. We always tell the truth and we don't always like what we hear. But it works for us because we have no secrets and we understand each other completely. All things considered, we're best friends.'

The couple had owned their forty-one-acre farm on the south side of Harrisonville for fourteen years but lived in it – and farmed it in a small way, mainly for hay – for only nine.

When Patti had called out, she was talking to me but nodding at Ray, laughing.

'No, he's not bothering me.' I grinned. 'He's just introducing me to Dudley and the gang. They're an impressive bunch.'

'Oh, hell,' she came back, 'I sometimes think he'd rather spend time with Dudley than me. Has he shown you where you'll be sleeping. You don't mind a trailer?'

I said I didn't. I had brought a sleeping bag because I expected there to be nights when I couldn't find a bed and would have to hunker down in the car.

'Well, this one ain't so bad,' said Ray.

The couple led me away from the paddock and towards an enormous silver vehicle parked in an open-sided Dutch barn. I had seen longer caravans, but this was what the English call a motor home and the Americans an RV, or recreational vehicle, and it was the biggest I had ever seen. Ray took me inside. There was thick-pile carpet on the floor, spotlights in the ceiling and cabinets fashioned from what looked like beech. Here and there were wallpapered panels and flowered cornices. At one end was a bathroom with a large shower, in the middle a kitchen and diner, and at the driver's end a raised platform with a large double bed like a padded catafalque slung just below the ceiling. It smelled of wood and plastic, cotton and a fresh newness.

'It's forty-six feet long,' said Ray, chuckling. 'And it's got room for six horses in the back. You like it?'

Did I like it? I jumped out and went to the rear of the vehicle and, as Ray had said, there was a horse box built into it. It was clean and pristine and waiting to be inhabited by the most pampered horses in Cass County. I ran back to the front and jumped inside again. This time I noticed a microwave oven, a stereo system and a flat-screen TV. Ray was laughing at my enthusiasm.

'If it gets too cold you can heat it up.' He flicked an air-conditioning unit into life. 'Anyway, it's yours for the night.'

I didn't know what to say. It seemed like an age since the sun had come up outside Paul's house that morning when I had been filled with a sense of doom. After a weekend in the bubble of Lebanon, among friends who couldn't have spent the ten-dollar bill even if they had wanted to, I had headed out into the unknown and what I feared might be a terminal lack of co-operation. The night before – just last night – I had sat on the porch of the lodge, slightly drunk, and stared at the stars with the truck driver.

'You know,' I had slurred, 'it'll all be downhill from here.'

'Whaddaya mean, you crazy sonofabitch?' Paul had answered.

'Well, I might have fun, it might get interesting, but I doubt I'll meet anyone who's as good to me as you guys have been.'

'I'll give it two days before someone shoots your ass off.'

And it had not gone downhill.

Ray took me outside, closed the RV's door and led me to his long, single-storey farmhouse. He put his arm round my shoulders and said, 'How 'bout some soup? You like some soup?'

It was dark now and the sky was clear, stars as bright as any I had seen in Lebanon. There was the merest hint of a frost and I could see my breath as I said, 'Thank you. I'd like that very much.'

Ray smiled broadly and turned his head as if looking at something beyond the farmhouse. 'Well, all right,' he said.

The Circle D Ranch

After we ate, Candice and Nicole went to bed and Patti, Ray and I moved to the back porch with the dogs. It was cold and I was pleased that the couple's boxer had taken a shine to me. He curled up at my feet, warming my legs and demanding to be petted whenever my hands went to sleep.

We chatted about the farm but I wanted to know more about life as an interracial couple in Cass County. Ray seemed keen to brush this aside; he didn't like to make a fuss, but it clearly rankled with Patti that he was often treated with a lack of respect. They had experienced open disgust from complete strangers, dirty looks, sly comments made in restaurants behind flat palms and a reluctance to provide service. One story made the hairs on the back of my neck stand up. Ray had had a business cutting lawns and the vast majority of his clients were white (there were very few black faces in Harrisonville). One day he reversed his vehicle on to a driveway to turn around and the householder had taken umbrage and run out, shouting at him to get off his drive. The man was younger than Ray but called him 'boy'. I could think of only one other word that might have been more offensive. I thought such open prejudice was a thing of the past, but clearly I was naive.

When I raised the driveway incident, Patti was mad as hell, telling me that such open disrespect was not unusual. Ray played it down.

'Now, honey,' he said, 'it isn't so bad.'

But Patti felt it was. It was racism, plain and simple. She saw how people looked at Ray in ways that he did not notice. Or in ways he chose not to. Ray was a Vietnam veteran and he said the things he had witnessed and experienced in South-East Asia allowed him to prioritise the daily difficulties he faced without complaining.

'It's a game and if you're smart you can play the game to your advantage,' he said. 'I've had some successful businesses over the years and I've taken advantage of programmes to help minorities. You can do that if you play the system. I've played the system and I've won. All the other stuff I can let roll off of me. The only side of it I won't stand for is when it affects my family. I won't tolerate that. But when it's me, I can look after myself. The farther south you go, it's worse. People will talk about it in your face. Here, it's in the closet. It goes unspoken and it's mostly behind your back. Well, that don't hurt me.'

But it hurt Patti and where Ray was not sensitive to the subtleties of prejudice, her antennae detected them on his behalf.

'There's lots of white folks I won't have anything to do with that he calls "friends",' she said. 'They're friends to his face, but I've seen the looks behind his back.'

Ray rolled his eyes. 'They *are* my friends, Patti.' He looked at me. 'She's protective of me because she doesn't want me to be hurt, but she gets herself hurt in the process.'

They must have been at this for twenty-four years. Him trying to ignore prejudice, her being wounded by it because she loved him. They looked exhausted.

Ray changed the subject, telling me to expect an early wake-up call in the morning and a long drive during the day if I wanted to follow the bill. Nicole had left IA74407937A in the kitchen as part of her payment for the ribs before taking Kadden to bed, and Ray was planning to take it to Hot Springs, Arkansas, some 380 miles away. The name sounded familiar but it wasn't until the next day that I realised why.

At the age of sixty-three, when most people are looking forward to retirement, Ray had woken up one morning with an idea he could not get out of his head. He told me more than once how fortunate he felt and how life had been good to him. Well, he said, it was time for a little payback.

'Have you ever seen the look on a kid's face when you put him on a horse for the first time?' he asked.

I was thinking 'terror', but Ray was on a roll and I didn't want to stop him.

'Or how a kid from the projects feels when he sees real wild country for the first time?'

He wants to know where the mall is?

'Well, I'm gonna give it to them. I have a plan for a 9,000-acre ranch for kids from poor backgrounds. There will be sixty cabins with four kids to a cabin, there'll be trail riding, a 120,000-square-foot activity barn for rodeos and steer riding, and fishing and hiking. And it'll be a not-for-profit business with an RV park, a restaurant and grocery store. The kids'll love it.'

The site Ray had identified was in Thomasville, Missouri, and he showed me maps and business plans that had been given the approval of business organisations, senators and congressmen. It was the real deal. He wasn't kidding.

'There'll be shower-houses and blacksmiths from an Amish community and we'll employ twenty-one people to start with, rising to eighty when we get going,' he enthused. 'We'll get kids in from St Louis, Kansas City, Memphis. It'll be real good for them, the outdoors, the fresh air and exercise – and the horses. When they get on a horse for the first time . . .'

There was just one flaw in Ray's plan and that was the small matter of the start-up costs. He had done all his sums and come up with a figure of 15 million dollars just to get the project off the ground.

'I need to attract investors and I've worked it out so that they could get a guaranteed return over five years, then they get their money out and the operation can support itself. And because it doesn't have to run at a profit, prices can be kept low. So all I have to do now is find those investors.'

The whole operation was to be called the Circle D Ranch Complex, with the 'D' standing for Dudley the mule. And, Ray informed me, we were heading to Hot Springs on a mission to see a man who could help him raise that 15 million.

I went to bed and had an awful dream about IA74407937A being mixed up in a suitcase containing 15 million dollars in ten-dollar bills. Dudley galloped past, one hoof landed in the case and a bill stuck to it. The dilemma I wrestled with all night was whether I should rummage in the suitcase or chase after Dudley.

I was woken at 6 a.m. by a tapping on the door and I banged my head on the ceiling as I sat bolt upright. At first I thought I had been kicked by a mule. 'Rise 'n' shine,' came a voice from outside. I tried to rise but I couldn't shine. I felt tired. Where was I? Kansas. No, Missouri. Somewhere-ville. Dogs were barking. It was pitch black outside. Cold. My bones ached.

'We got a long way to go,' said the voice. 'We goin' for breakfast first.'

Who the hell was that?

I felt like a computer booting up in the Arctic. Cold drains batteries, slows impulses, puts the whole thing into hibernation. I was falling asleep again.

Then I remembered Ray and Patti and the journey so far and woke with a jolt, banging my head again.

'Coming, Ray,' I said, and crawled out of my sleeping bag.

I went into the main house and was handed a towel by Patti so I could take a shower. They were both better morning people than me and seemed to have been bouncing around for some time. I showered in seconds and was handed a cup of coffee as soon as I stepped out of the bathroom. The dogs sniffed at me disapprovingly.

It was then that I saw Ray's gun locker. It was a five-foot-high black steel and concrete cabinet, and it was a thing of menacing beauty. It was in the living room and the sight of it made me feel diminished as a hunter-gatherer; the most dangerous thing in my living room was the wiring on my stereo. I am not into guns and would go so far as to say I disapprove of them, especially on the occasions when they have been pointed at me: once in Northern Ireland, twice in Macedonia and Albania while covering the exodus of refugees from the war in Kosovo and several times in Iraq. But there is something about the sight of guns that fascinates me, and here I was being drawn to the open safe. Inside was a 12-gauge Magnum shotgun and a .44 Magnum carbine.

'The shotgun's for shooting coyotes and the carbine's for general hunting,' said Ray.

I knew that he was using the word 'general' loosely. There would not be much point shooting a rabbit with this rifle as the rabbit would, generally speaking, explode. This was a gun that would bring down an elk. A long time ago, during days of spectacular ignorance and stupidity, .44 rifles were used successfully – depending on your definition of success – in elephant hunts. The thought made me recoil as surely as if I had fired the gun myself.

Ray told me to hurry up for breakfast. The night before he had mentioned his breakfast club – the place where he met his friends and caught up on gossip – and that was where we were headed. He said so long to Patti; he would be back in a few days. I said thank you and goodbye. I had the impression that Patti was not a fan of this breakfast club, but she said nothing. She squeezed my arm and smiled. She had been kind to me.

Ray put the ten dollars into his wallet, jumped into his black Ford Escape and I followed in the darkness. After ten minutes we pulled off the road and on to the parking lot of the Halfway Restaurant and Tire Shop. Inside, it was warm and almost full, even at 6.45. Rows of strip lights cast an unsympathetic glare across white Formica tables and on to the brown plastic seats of seven or eight banquettes. There were windows at the front of the restaurant, bricks at either end and wood panelling behind the service counter. On this was a sign that read:

TRY OUR SHOW ME CHALLENGE TODAY!!! $13.99
3 X 10OZ PATTIES, 5 STRIPS BACON, 3 SLICES CHEESE + FULL
BRICK SQS. IF YOU CAN EAT IT <u>ALL</u> IN 45 MINS OR LESS
IT'S FREE!

Ray asked me what I wanted for breakfast and I asked for coffee and toast. He ordered and introduced me to his friends, a group of men spread across two tables. They appeared to be in their fifties and sixties, in jeans, baseball caps and T-shirts. One wore a windcheater, another a leather waistcoat. I wondered whether these were the friends of whom Patti disapproved, but they seemed welcoming enough. There were nods and weak smiles as they began to size me up. They appeared unimpressed by what they saw. Slowly I began to imagine that Ray was working harder at this than they were, but that was probably because he had brought me into the company and I had not been invited. They asked what I was doing and said I was crazy when I told them. I was growing used to that. For some reason I felt more like a city slicker among these men than I had among the farmers in Kansas. And I couldn't understand much of what they said. I imagined them having the same difficulty in Liverpool or Newcastle or Glasgow.

Against my better judgement – given that we were about to drive almost 400 miles – I drank four cups of coffee and left most of the toast. I had only been there for twenty minutes before I began to feel uncomfortable. I noticed that only one of the men was being overtly friendly to Ray. The others seemed either uninterested or, in the case of one who bore a disturbing resemblance to Boss Hogg from *The Dukes of Hazzard*, overtly sneering. But was I wearing Patti's antennae? I couldn't be sure and, anyway, was it any of my business? Ray seemed perfectly happy. Hell, I was probably looking for signs and misinterpreting them. Too much coffee.

When it was time to leave, Ray insisted on paying. I watched him go to the cash register and strained my eyes to see what he was using. They were dollar bills. That meant the ten would be travelling with him and I wouldn't have to stay here, and that was fine by me. I picked up my jacket, took some pictures and said goodbye, moving to intercept Ray at the exit.

Then Boss Hogg spoke up.

'Hey,' he said. 'It true you driving to Arkansas with Ray?'

'Yes,' I replied.

'Well, it's a long way. It could be dark by the time you get there. If it is and you can't find Ray, just shout for him to smile. That'll give you a helluva clue.'

He laughed at his own joke and one or two others sniggered. Only one gave the impression of being annoyed but even he said nothing.

I made the shape of a pistol with my hands, pointing my index finger at Boss Hogg, and winked as I pulled the imaginary trigger. He wasn't sure how to take that, but he wasn't laughing when we left.

Out on the lot I wondered whether to say something to Ray about the incident but he was smiling and whistling and urged me to get a move on, so I said nothing. It was light now and the sun had risen with an amber glow that changed the colour of everything. There were cornfields at the side of the road that looked as if they had been drenched in dark honey.

I began to follow Ray and put on my sunglasses to guard against the low glare from my left-hand side. We would be heading due south for hours and hours on Route 71. I opened my window, sucked in the cold morning air and wished I hadn't had all that coffee, before reaching forward and switching on the radio to search for some music. I had been frustrated more than once by the radio, finding myself bombarded with either Christian preachers or country singers with a right-wing bent. Unfortunately, I was to have no more luck than usual. I flipped from white noise to Bible to country and then stopped at 98.5FM, where someone calling himself the Mancow was educating the people of Missouri on the subject of Muslims (though he pronounced it Moslems). And my jaw literally dropped. This is not verbatim, because I was driving with one hand, trying to keep up with Ray, and taking notes with the other, but it is a fair representation of what the Mancow was saying.

'They will kill you,' he said. 'It is the duty of every Moslem to kill you. The Koran says that the hands of infidels – that's us – have to be separated from our bodies. They must kill us. It is their duty.'

The Mancow then went on to claim that Rima Fakih, the first Muslim Miss America, was 'proud of her relatives who killed innocent people'. It was seamless and breathless hatred peddled in the name of free speech.

'I was in Italy recently,' he went on, his voice deep and filled with wise authority, 'and I was sitting with some of my Moslem friends in a café . . .' – Would such a man really have Muslim friends? – 'and those beautiful little Italian girls in their short skirts were going past on their scooters and I asked my Moslem friends what would happen to those beautiful little girls if Islam got its way.

'"Well," said my friends, "we would stone them or make them wear the veil." "And what about that beautiful church over there?" I asked them. "Well," they replied, "we would pull that down."

'What a delightful religion of peace.'

The Mancow continued by saying that Muslims intended to 'kill every Jew and Christian on planet earth' and that 'our President sides with Hamas'. This seemingly endless torrent of rabble-rousing detritus stopped only briefly, for a commercial advertising a gun and knife show.

Tragically, Erich 'Mancow' Muller's rants were not limited to Missouri. He was actually based in Chicago with the Talk Radio Network and, according to his website biography, his morning show was syndicated to more than fifty 'markets' across America. Again according to the site, he was 'perennially listed in the top ten of the most influential radio personalities in the nation', which was depressing. In common with most shock-jocks, he would do anything for publicity, wading hungrily through Howard Stern's wake, clutching at whatever scraps fell overboard from the good ship *Narcissus.*

In 1993, after an incident in which Bill Clinton had held up flights at Los Angeles International Airport for more than an hour so he could have a haircut aboard Air Force One, the Mancow decided to do something similar on the San Francisco–Oakland Bay Bridge during rush hour. Broadcasting live, he and his chums used vans to block the westbound lanes – those heading into San Francisco, used by people who needed to get to work – while one of his team had a haircut. He described this as a parody, but it was more a case of simply repeating something particularly stupid and inconsiderate in the name of satire.

For that, the Mancow became hero to a generation of Neanderthal frat boys and was given three years on probation, fined 500 dollars and ordered to carry out a hundred hours of community service. The radio station for whom he worked, KYLD-FM in California, subsequently paid 1.5 million dollars to settle a lawsuit brought by an angry commuter. How we laughed – and how his career took off, with the Evergreen Media group offering to double his salary if he would move to Chicago to work for them. For years his show, 'Mancow's Morning Madhouse', was the most popular slot among males aged between eighteen and thirty-four. In spite of myriad complaints to the Federal Communications Commission about obscenity and inappropriate behaviour, in 2008 the Mancow landed a prestigious 9 a.m. to 11 a.m. slot on Chicago's news and conservative chat station WLS-AM radio with veteran American broadcaster Pat Cassidy. He lasted just sixteen months, but this period was to produce his finest hour.

During one show in the spring of 2009, Mancow declared that

it was wrong to describe waterboarding as torture. So convinced was he that simulated drowning amounted to little more than gentle persuasion with added refreshment that he invited a US Marine, Sergeant Klay South, to waterboard him live during a broadcast. According to Sergeant South, the average person lasted fourteen seconds before panic set in and they began pleading for the waterboarding to stop. The Mancow lasted six seconds, after which he declared he had changed his mind on the subject.

Hot Springs

It was unseasonably warm and the temperature rose fast the farther south we travelled. Down through Bates, Vernon and Barton counties we sped, gradually leaving open farmland behind as we skirted Carthage and Joplin, just east of the Oklahoma state line. Once we crossed the I-44 at Fidelity and pushed on through Newton County there was a marked difference in the terrain. The road rose and fell precipitously, slicing through thickly wooded forests and wide valleys, deciduous and lush. I stuck my head out of the window like an excited puppy, squinting as the trees whizzed by: white oak and black cherry, hickory and maple, sycamore, elm and pawpaw. And where the forest thinned there was flowering dogwood, redbud and walnut. As we neared Anderson the sky seemed to open up and give way to forest before meeting again on a blue and lazy horizon. The landscape was as green as a rainforest and it was not until Pineville that I saw my first turning leaves; I counted seven shades of gold. The Huckleberry Ridge State Forest was off to the east. It was tantalising and I wanted to stop and walk in the woods, paddle in the cool streams and creeks at the side of the road. But I had to follow Ray and on he went, up and over stubborn hills and past rocky outcrops carpeted in wild chokeberry and leatherwood.

At 10.10 a.m. we crossed into Arkansas at its north-western corner. We were still on the 71.

Signs flew by for Bella Vista, Bentonville, Springdale, Fayetteville and Fort Smith, the second-largest city in Arkansas (after Little Rock), but I was too consumed by the beauty of my surroundings to take much notice. We were entering a part of America called the Interior Highlands, a range of mountains and crushed plateaux of limestone, sandstone and shale that extends magnificently from the Boston Mountains – through which we had been driving – down through the Ozarks (of which the Bostons form a part) and on to the Ouachita Mountains just north-west of Hot Springs, with our final destination about 150 miles away. The route took us over dizzying canyons and through small towns that nestled in prairies or on plateaux that felt like alpine villages but which were probably no more than 1,000 feet in elevation – much lower, even, than Lebanon up on the Great Plains. Everywhere, and puzzlingly, there were yellow flowers that looked like buttercups and which gave the day a spring-like feel. The sky was as blue as the Aegean and I had to keep reminding myself that it was really autumn. I had felt a little subdued before we set off, but now I found myself singing, light as a feather and curious. Ray led me down through Sebastian County before finally turning east on Route 270, through Montgomery County and into mile after mile of sweet-smelling pine trees.

With the sun still high in the sky, we drove through the city of Mount Ida, 'Quartz Capital of the World' (Pop. 981), and skirted big, beautiful and frustratingly inviting Lake Ouachita before finally arriving at Hot Springs (Pop. 39,467), which advertised itself – immediately – as the Boyhood Home of Bill Clinton.

The journey had been 381 miles long and, by my reckoning, the ten-dollar bill had travelled 1,168½ miles so far. We had made two pit stops but Ray hadn't spent the money. I would snack on nuts and dried fruit, but Ray hardly ever ate. He had diabetes and never seemed to be hungry. I wouldn't have minded at all if he had bought something up in the Ozarks with IA74407937A. It was heartbreakingly beautiful country. Who knows, I might have gone mining for quartz. Or hiking with lean, bearded outdoor types. Camping with a Scout troop. The more I thought about it, the more attractive Hot Springs became.

Ray slowed down as we edged around the southern outskirts of town. It was clean with manicured lawns. Lake Hamilton, wide and blue and serene, floated out to the west, radiating shards of evening light like motes of ground glass on the breeze. Ray had been here before but it took him a while to find his bearings. We were skirting the town centre proper and were still surrounded by trees and water. There was a sign at the side of the road that read 'Boss Hogg's Club' and I thought back to the darkness of morning.

We were looking for a man named Clarence Hicks, a former petroleum economist with Exxon. He lived somewhere called Vanadium Point. Ray had told me he was eighty-four years old, didn't suffer fools gladly and had no idea I was coming.

We turned off a main road and on to what seemed to be a cross between a retirement community and an upmarket trailer park. Ray would stop periodically, shake his head and turn round. I would wave and follow, signalling him to take his time and not to worry on my account. I had all the time in the world.

We finally pulled up outside a small purple bungalow with a grassed yard which the long summer had reduced to dust. The house had a concrete veranda with a pitched roof from which hung bamboo and steel wind chimes. There was a garden table in front of a window that looked into the living room and another to the left of the entrance. To the right of the door was a plastic sign that read:

NO TRESPASSING

VIOLATORS WILL BE SHOT

SURVIVORS WILL BE SHOT AGAIN

I climbed out of the car and looked at Ray. There was a long pause filled only with birdsong.

'When you said you hadn't told him I was coming, you were joking, right?' I asked.

Ray stood with his belly hanging over his pants, a cigarette balanced precariously from the left side of his mouth. He took off his baseball cap and scratched the back of his head.

'Well, no,' he said. 'But he won't mind. Clarence is a gen'leman. He ain't gonna shoot you. At least, not if you're with me.' He chuckled and took a drag on his cigarette.

When Clarence emerged through the creaking screen door, he was unarmed and underwhelmed.

'Took your time,' he said to Ray. He looked me up and down but said nothing.

'This is Steve,' said Ray, waving a hand in my direction. 'I'll tell you about him later.'

Clarence and I shook hands. He moved very slowly and deliberately and I had to remind myself of his age. He wore a blue checked shirt and black cardigan, a green baseball cap and jeans. His face was not without wrinkles but the overall impression was of it being taut and freckled. He had keen blue eyes and a way of looking at you that made your knees tremble. During the Second World War, he had served as a US Navy pilot, flying missions over the Atlantic and Pacific oceans and across North Africa and South America. He flew anti-submarine aircraft and conducted air-sea rescues of downed pilots. He was a widower who lived alone, and he had four children, seven grandchildren and a great-grandchild.

Ray told me Clarence owned several properties and that one of his granddaughters was staying in an A-frame of his next door. 'He's a clever man. He made his money when he was younger,' Ray whispered. 'One of the things I like about Clarence is that everything he does is low-key, including the way he chooses to live.'

Inside, the bungalow was comfortably furnished but it was obvious a man lived there alone. You could see which chair Clarence favoured from the proliferation of books, newspapers and magazines. The kitchen was utilitarian and clean. It was a pleasant home, peaceful and quiet except for the sound of birds and crickets. Clarence led us through the living room and kitchen, along a narrow corridor, past a bathroom and through a back door which opened on to a wooden deck surrounded by trees. We sat at a wide wooden table and he offered us drinks. Ray accepted but I declined. It was clear that Ray looked up to Clarence. Their meeting reminded me of a boy seeking the approval of his father and there was something masculine and touching about that. I stood up.

'You have things to talk about,' I said. 'I'm going for a look around.'

Clarence smiled and for the first time since I had begun following Nicole, I had the feeling that I had done something right.

Hot Springs is named for the thermal waters that flow from forty-seven bubbling fountains on the western slope of Hot Springs Mountain at a toe-scorching 143 degrees Fahrenheit (62 degrees centigrade). Carbon-dating by scientists has established that the 1 million gallons or so that come to the surface every day are actually in the region of 4,000 years old. Rainwater fell all those years ago, filtered slowly down to superheated sections of the earth's crust, gathering curative minerals on the way, and is now shooting to the surface imbued with the dual properties of healing and heating. There is evidence that native Americans gathered at the springs more than 10,000 years before Europeans arrived, Europeans who would later, of course, claim the waters for themselves. The first of these to do so, for France in 1673, was Father Jacques Marquette. Marquette epitomised the sheer ambition of expansionists in the New World. They explored it, learned the languages and ways of the indigenous tribes and then appropriated as much as they could. First, though, it was crucial to map the continent's waterways, the arteries that would allow trade and growth – for better or for worse. A Jesuit priest, Marquette had been assigned as a missionary to Quebec in 1666 at the age of twenty-nine, at just about the same time as the Great Fire was consuming London. He demonstrated skill at learning tribal languages and because of his fluency in Huron, he was sent farther up the St Lawrence River to the western edges of the Great Lakes. He founded missions that would later become cities in Michigan and Wisconsin.

At La Pointe on Lake Superior, near to Ashland, Wisconsin, local tribespeople told Marquette about a waterway that could take him all the way to a great ocean. They were talking about the Mississippi River and if they were telling the truth, the discovery could have crucial importance for the swift movement of goods and people, and the colonisation of vast tracts of land. Since the arrival of Christopher Columbus in 1492, large parts of North, South and Central America had been claimed and colonised but there was still much to play for. The state of Louisiana, for example, had yet to be established but it would be in 1682, largely thanks to Marquette. It was not the first time that rumours had emerged of the length and power of this magical river, and a few early arrivals had sailed sections of it. The first European to encounter the Mississippi, where it flows through what we now call the state of Mississippi proper, was the Spanish explorer Hernando de Soto in 1541. But nobody had tried to explore and map it. Running north to south for 2,320 miles, the Mississippi is the longest river in North America and the fourth longest in the world.

Marquette teamed up with Louis Joliet, an ambitious explorer and fur trader, and on 18 May 1673 they set off across Lake Michigan to what is today Green Bay, Wisconsin, with five companions of French-Native extraction. They paddled up the Fox River to a spot where local guides told them they could carry their two canoes to another waterway. The route is known today as the Chicago Portage. They hauled their canoes a couple of miles to the Wisconsin River and paddled for a month until they came upon the mighty Mississippi. They joined it at present-day Prairie du Chien, Wisconsin, and kept going until, at its confluence with the Arkansas River, they befriended a tribe of natives who, they were alarmed to see, were in possession of European goods and, according to some accounts, guns. The natives had acquired them from white explorers some ten days' journey (about 450 miles) to the south. They assumed correctly that these were Spaniards and so, after exploring the region and claiming it for France (Hot Springs included), the Marquette–Joliet expedition turned round and, on the advice of the local Illini tribe, returned to Canada via the Illinois River, a shorter route to the Great Lakes, passing what is now Chicago on their way. By the time they returned to Green Bay in late September, they had travelled 2,500 miles, proved that the Mississippi flowed into the Gulf of Mexico and become the first white men to travel through Illinois.

They had not, however, achieved what they had set out to do. Marquette and Joliet had hoped that the great river would take them west and on to the Pacific Ocean, the fabled Northwest Passage. They must have been crushed by the realisation that the Mississippi flowed south and emptied into the Gulf of Mexico; travelling its full length would simply lead them into the hands of the Spanish, with whom they were almost constantly at war.

I followed signs for downtown and found myself disappointed by block after block of ubiquitous modern Americana. Fast-food joints on every corner. Denny's, Arby's, Burger King, McDonald's. Tyre and lube shops. Walgreen's, WalMart and Best Buy. In much the same way as British towns have become depressingly homogeneous – Boots, Tesco, Next, Superdrug – it all looked awfully similar and terribly dull. I knew nothing about the town itself and I was to find this a constant, and often embarrassing, problem. Usually when preparing for a foreign assignment, I would conduct extensive research and learn a little of the local language if I didn't already know some. But now I was just following randomly, going wherever the bill went, and I would often arrive as the most stupid individual on the block. There were times I had to ask strangers not only where I was, but also, confused by time and travel, what day it was. It might have been easier to say I had just been freed by aliens.

My ignorance today was no exception and I almost turned round and went back to Clarence's house. Fortunately, I didn't. I had been looking for a motel and thought I had seen just the place about halfway down Central Avenue. I would come back and check in later. Then I saw a sign for Oakland Park racetrack and the historic district. I followed north and the road narrowed, block by block, from eight lanes to two, until I felt the unfamiliar urge to get out of the car and walk. I found myself surrounded by picturesque shops and restaurants, magnolia-lined avenues, bars advertising live music, magnificent hotels built in Spanish colonial and art-deco styles, grand bathhouses dripping with history and ahead, high, imposing and darkly magnetic, a seven-storey brick building that dominated the skyline and lent the rest of the town a sense of confident gravitas. This was the Hot Springs Rehabilitation Center, a former army and navy hospital that was opened in 1887 and had treated hundreds of thousands of military personnel, making use of the restorative properties of the local waters. After the Second World War, thousand upon thousand of returning servicemen were brought here, given treatment, both physical and psychological, and encouraged to enjoy everything the town had to offer. When the hospital became full, the government bought the Eastman Hotel opposite and then requisitioned the rather splendid Arlington and Majestic hotels to handle the overflow. I was to think of this place several times later in my journey when I spoke to Vietnam veterans about the contrasting reception they had received when they came home from war.

My mobile rang.

'Where are you?' It was Ray. 'We're gonna have some dinner. Do you like Chinese food? Well, get back here, because we're hungry. I might just spend that ten dollars of yours.'

Ray's call reminded me that I was forgetting to eat and had not been hungry at all. I was too busy taking in the sights and sounds and smells. I hoped I would have a chance to see more of Hot Springs, but if Ray was dining out he might spend the money and I would never have the opportunity.

I found my way back to Clarence's, turned off the ignition and stepped out of the car. The oil man was waiting for me.

'You really following a ten-dollar bill?' he asked.

I said I was. He shook his head. We were standing in the front garden.

'You can stay in there tonight.' He shrugged and pointed to a small RV. 'Might be a bit cold, but you should be all right.'

He opened the door. It was untidy and the bed was covered in junk. It was a far cry from the luxury I had enjoyed the previous night, but it was still like a palace to me. We cleared a space on the bed and Clarence showed me the fridge, which contained cold beer. 'Help yourself,' he said.

We went for the meal and I insisted on paying as my way of saying thank you. That meant the ten dollars stayed in Ray's wallet. Back at Clarence's, I left the old friends to talk about the Circle D Ranch and went out to the trailer, where I cracked open a beer. I sat on the steps of the RV and looked up at the stars. A couple of dogs came over and sniffed at my trousers and the rich mix of Ray's animals. One of them lay down, chewing on my shoelaces.

I took a long pull on the beer and wondered where I would be this time tomorrow.

Lucky's Bar & Grill
(34° 30.359' N, 93° 03.225' W)

Several years ago I bought a British Army sleeping bag which I was promised would keep me warm at temperatures of minus 5 degrees centigrade and fold up into a bundle only slightly larger than a grapefruit. For decades the British military had had radios that didn't work, ships that would melt, planes that couldn't fly and armoured vehicles that failed to protect the men and women inside them, so I found myself asking more than once what on earth I was thinking of when I put my faith in this piece of military equipment. I asked the question at 2 a.m., then again at 4.30, 5.20 and 6.40, when Ray pulled me from the brink of hypothermia with a bang on the door. I swear that before he called my name, I could see the light and was travelling, blissfully, into it.

'Mornin',' said Ray. 'Sleep well?'

'Like a log,' I said. In my experience, nobody likes anyone who complains about lack of sleep, blisters, constipation or credit card bills.

The windows inside the RV were dripping with condensation and my sleeping bag was wet. So was everything in my rucksack, and as I scrabbled to find clean clothes, the moisture accentuated the smell of damp dog that they had inexplicably taken on. I had expected some problems with washing, but smelling like a mongrel wasn't one of them. I wanted to ask Clarence if I could use his washing machine but I daren't until I knew exactly what Ray was planning to do next.

'I'll be heading off later this morning,' he told me. 'But I want to go into town first to buy a present for Patti.'

That wouldn't give me enough time to get my things washed and dried, so I pulled some socks inside out and put them on before turning a pair of underpants back to front and slipping into them. I threw talcum powder over everything and left the RV smelling like the perfume counter at a department store.

Inside the house, Clarence was cooking breakfast. Pork patties, scrambled eggs, potatoes, toast and coffee flavoured with vanilla. My near-death experience in the RV had left me feeling hungry and I ate everything with deep gratitude. Outside, the chill of night was being burned off by hot sunshine and a light mist covered everything. It was going to be another hot day. I wanted to ask Clarence what he thought of Ray's business plans but I figured it was a private matter and that Ray would tell me if he felt the need. Instead, I moved to the kitchen and washed the dishes.

'You wouldn't believe his age,' Ray said to me, pointing at Clarence. 'He's a sly old dog – still dating women, still taking road trips. You know, he just took a lady down to San Antonio, Texas, for a square-dancing convention.' Then he turned to Clarence. 'Go on, tell him about the German!'

Clarence had to be pressed hard for information. I stood still with my hands in the washing-up water and cocked my head to one side.

'Well,' he said after some time. 'We were having a helluva time and we met this German feller, and I asked him how he was enjoying it there. And he said, "Much better than the last time I was here. Back then I was a prisoner of war.'"

Ray slapped his knee and laughed out loud. 'P-O-W!' he wailed, pointing at Clarence, who took a breath and howled at his own story.

I had absolutely no idea why this was funny and considered asking Ray and Clarence whether the joke invoked in them a sense of Schadenfreude regarding the German's unhappy status as a POW. How often do you get the chance to use the word Schadenfreude in the context of a pitiable German?

I began to dry the dishes when suddenly, and without warning, the men were saying goodbye and Ray was asking whether I was ready or not. I wasn't, but I scrambled. I had laid out some damp clothes to dry in the RV. It turned out to be a pointless exercise but I had hoped the smell of dog might dissipate if I took the items out of my rucksack. I had a small computer and a camera charging in Clarence's front room and I hastily swept them up. And so, damp, dirty, dishevelled but with good company and a full stomach, I thanked Clarence for his hospitality and jumped into my car.

Ray moved off in his four-wheel drive and I followed. Even though he had been to Hot Springs more than once, he had never explored the old town. Along Central Avenue we swept, past the racetrack, Burger King, Arby's and the big white First Baptist Church, motel after motel and, finally, into the funnel of the old town, with its antiques shops beyond Grand Avenue. We parked near the Ray Lynn Theater, which was hosting a run of Neil Simon's *The Sunshine Boys* starring Jerry Van Dyke, Dick's brother. He must get that a lot, I thought.

Ray was impressed with the wide streets and promenades, the avenues of trees and the imposing architecture. He was annoyed he had not visited previously. 'Heck,' he said. 'It's beautiful. Patti would love it.' That made me feel less craven for almost missing it. We strolled for a while and climbed the steps of the rehabilitation hospital with its sweeping art-deco foyer and magnificent tiled floors.

'Those boys got a real welcome home, huh?' Ray said. I nodded and he shook his head. 'I gotta get that present.'

We turned around. I wondered whether he planned to use the ten-dollar bill and felt the weight of his leaving settle on us both. Again I realised how close to a person one could become in only forty-eight hours. I had grown to admire Ray, his resilience and ambition, and I wanted so badly for him to succeed.

I caved in.

'What did Clarence say about the Circle D?' I asked.

'He didn't say anything,' Ray said, but he didn't look disappointed. 'He's going to study my plans and weigh them up before giving me his opinion. I wouldn't expect anything less of Clarence.'

Over to our left was the Golden Leaves Bookstore and Ray steered me towards it. He wanted to look for that gift. We walked through the door and my spirits sank. Ray had told me that Patti was a keen reader but neither of us thought she would want to read the books here. It was a spiritual, religious, self-help and metaphysical bookshop and as I scanned the shelves I felt a rising panic. There were healing stones and tarot cards, statuettes of Buddha and Ganesh, bottles of Thai crystal deodorant and – randomly – T-shirts of Bill Clinton.

Book and DVD titles swam before my eyes: *Seven Spiritual Centers, Deciphering the Signs of God, A Dictionary of Gnosticism. Fifty Ways to See Through People, The Reptilian Agenda – Amazing Confirmation That a Reptilian Extraterrestrial Race Has Controlled the World for Thousands of Years.*

I searched for Ray across the store and each time I found him he was shaking his head. If he spent the money here, the next person to receive it would be a hippie with a cat-infested home that smelled of nut cutlets and patchouli oil. It would be a heavily bangled woman with henna tattoos, toe rings and wild hair trussed up in tie-dyed silks, a flying yogi who would refuse to spend the money until I had mastered Sanskrit and the tittibhasana. Or perhaps it would be a man, a refugee from the 1960s with a bandanna and flares, his expression oscillating between vacant and puzzled, his brain shrunk from the chemical destruction, a billion at a time, of what few brain cells he had been born with. I considered breaking the rules and pleading with Ray to buy Patti a nice hat from the shop across the street.

Instead, I watched as he chose a packet of vanilla-scented joss sticks and walked towards the checkout.

'We love the smell of vanilla,' he said apologetically.

Ray's eyes were fixed on the floor as he edged closer to the till. He was holding a ten-dollar bill and it bore the red markings.

He looked up. 'Man,' he said, nodding towards a section on yoga, 'I hate to do this to you.'

At 12.01 p.m., he handed IA74407937A to the sales clerk and wished me luck. He said goodbye with a handshake and walked to the door.

'Ray!' I called. He turned to look at me.

'What?'

'Thanks for everything.'

'No problem.' He smiled and left without looking back.

The sales clerk was called Byron France and looked as if he had washed up from the west coast. He must have been a very patient man. I explained what I was doing and asked if he would call me when he was handing out the ten-dollar bill in change. I wanted to get some air but I would be just outside the door. Byron agreed and there was no hint of surprise or curiosity in his voice. He must see weirder people than me every day.

The sun was high in the sky now and it was touching 80 degrees. The traffic on Central Avenue was light and the streets were quiet. The height of the tourist season had passed and the speed of life had slowed down. Hot Springs felt . . . relaxed. It was a few minutes past noon and I cheered myself with the thought that the town's hippies would barely be out of bed. They would have to eat some muesli and feed their plants before even thinking about buying new crystals. I figured I had until about 2 p.m. until the mood took them.

Time was playing tricks on me and I was finding it more and more difficult to remember what day it was. Travelling in darkness and light, meeting people briefly and then for days on end had thrown my internal chronometer out of sync. Was this day 5? A newspaper had been discarded on the floor and I picked it up. It said 6 October. Assuming this was today's paper, then I was almost a week into my journey. I could feel I had lost weight from the looseness of my jeans, my clothes smelled bad and I was about to be abducted by the Children of God. But aside from that, things were going well. I was surprised at how nostalgic I already felt about the people I had met. Kay and Rick, Margaret and Randall LaDow, Paul, Chuck Patel, Nicole, Ray and Patti, Clarence, Byron France . . .

I was chewing on the ridiculousness of feeling nostalgic for someone you had just met when Byron called out my name. I ran back inside the shop to find him handing out the ten-dollar bill to a wonderfully normal-looking woman. I glanced down and when I saw that she wasn't wearing sandals I broke into a smile.

Byron pointed at me and the woman turned around.

'What's going on?' she asked.

Without resorting to stammering or hopping from foot to foot I explained, simply and without fuss, that she was not losing a twenty-dollar bill; she was gaining ten dollars and an Englishman. She took it surprisingly well.

'Well, you'll have to follow us to the bar,' she said. 'We're going for a drink.'

Her name was Elisabeth Fox and she was a special constable from Harrow in Ontario, Canada. She was on holiday with her husband, Elmer, the proprietor of a boat and fishing-tackle store, and their friends the Stevensons, Lin, an operating-theatre nurse, and Grant, a retired car worker.

Lin had been in the bookstore with Elisabeth when the money changed hands and they had bought the only two sane volumes in the shop: cookbooks that even contained recipes for meat.

'You're following this wherever it goes?' asked Lin.

'Yes.'

'Well, we're going home tomorrow, so you might have a long journey.'

That worried me. They would drive 1,500 miles or so and Elisabeth would screw up her American dollars and put them in her sock drawer ready for the next trip to the States. I didn't want to spend months in Elisabeth's sock drawer.

The women led me outside and down the street to their car, where Elmer and Grant were waiting.

'We're going for a drink,' Elisabeth informed Elmer. He looked at me and then back to Elisabeth. 'Don't ask,' she said.

I smiled at Elmer and Grant.

Elisabeth led us across the street and into Lucky's Bar & Grill.

It was dark and cool inside. When my eyes became accustomed to the gloom, I saw two men sitting at a long wooden bar to the right. To my immediate left was a low stage, while farther along was a raised dance floor with a Wurlitzer juke box and a DJ booth. The walls were brick, there was a pool table at the far end of the bar and dotted about were encouraging numbers of neon signs advertising beer. The ceiling was painted black to camouflage racks of speakers and lights. It was a good bar. I liked it immediately.

'What would you like to drink?' asked Elisabeth.

I ordered a beer and sat down with the others, the men looking slightly bemused. Our drinks came and Elisabeth studied me with the eyes of a trained interrogator.

'OK,' she said, 'what's the scam? What's going on? Is this ten-dollar bill a forgery?'

Up until now, I had been welcomed into the homes of strangers, suspected of being a kidnapper and treated with pity by some who thought I was a bit *special*. Forger was a new role and I must say I quite liked it.

'Yes,' I replied furtively. 'You got me. What gave it away? Was it the red marks?'

Reluctant as I was to divest myself of the kudos that went with international counterfeiting, I explained to Elmer and Grant what my journey was about, but they wouldn't believe me.

'Oh, come on,' said Elmer. 'You're up to something.'

Strangely, none of this felt awkward, not even the fact that three of the party had lined up on one side of the table with just Elisabeth next to me. It felt a little like a job interview with nice people who actually wanted to give you the job.

Grant wagged his finger and insisted to the others that I was *definitely* a con artist. I held up my hands.

'OK, OK. I give in,' I said. 'What I do is this: I take off six weeks without pay, I get flights from Britain to America armed only with a forged ten-dollar bill, I spend money on motels, cars, gas and food and eventually find four saps like you who buy me a beer and pay for it with the forged bill. And you fell for it!'

They narrowed their eyes and shook their heads.

'Nah, you've got an angle,' said Grant.

We spent a pleasant, if slightly suspicious, hour together before Elisabeth called for the check. I'm not sure whether she paid with IA74407937A because that was the only ten dollars she had, or because she wanted to be rid of it, and me. After all, it could have been a forgery. The four left still wondering exactly how they had been scammed.

I moseyed on over to the bar to introduce myself to the barmaid and explain what I was trying to do. She had put the money into the cash register and I asked her to take it out again so I could show her the markings.

Her name was K.K. Snyder. She was a young-looking fifty-six-year-old and had been in her job at Lucky's for just one week. She was from Battle Creek, Michigan, but had lived in Hot Springs for eight years.

'I love it here,' she told me. 'The people are friendly, the scenery is lovely and you don't get so much snow and cold weather as in Michigan. That's the main reason I moved south; the cold.'

K.K. told me that June to August were the busiest months in Hot Springs and that now was the best time, still warm but not so busy. I wanted to say that I had planned my visit for that very reason but I hadn't planned anything at all. I didn't even have a place to stay.

I asked for another beer.

The two men at the bar were Patrick Bennett and the

magnificently named Willard Cupples. I decided that if Charles Dickens had been American, he definitely would have created a character called Willard Cupples. Willard was a fifty-year-old dishwasher and Patrick a twenty-six-year-old pianist, both at the Belle Arti Italian restaurant next door. I wondered if either would get the ten-dollar bill in their change, but they paid with dollar bills and coins and went on their way, leaving the bar completely empty except for K.K. and me. I took advantage of the lull to run outside and feed the parking meter. Then I ordered a hamburger with which to feed myself. Before setting out on my journey, I had resolved to avoid eating junk food. I had been on too many assignments in the US where I was working to deadlines and covering punishing distances, and that meant grabbing food on the go, which was invariably junk. After several days I would feel sick, hate myself and begin reading bulimia websites for tips. Fortunately, I have always been too mean to spend good money on food before immediately throwing it away, or up.

On this trip I was eating well, but only occasionally, and I couldn't go on like this for a month if I was to have the energy to follow the money. I decided that I would force myself to eat whenever I had the chance, even if I wasn't hungry, because I never knew where or when the next opportunity might present itself. In these circumstances, a lovingly griddled pure-beef burger in a bar like Lucky's is anything but junk. It is a thing of beauty and after eating one I felt ready for anything.

This, however, might have been a tad premature. It would have been better if I had been ready for nothing, because that is exactly what happened. Business was slow, one or two people came and went. If they ate, they paid by card. If they had a beer they paid in ones or fives or tens. It was about 5 p.m. now, the lunch service had long since passed and it was unlikely to grow busier until after 7 p.m. I had been there almost five hours.

'How busy do you get between now and 7?' I asked K.K.

'This time of year? My guess would be dead,' she replied.

K.K.'s shift was almost ending and she was being replaced by the manager, Connie Bisett, who would be here until closing time. We said hello and I told Connie about the bill and my mission.

'U-huh,' she said, wiping down the bar. 'Don't get in my way.'

I had some housekeeping problems that needed to be addressed. One, I had no knowledge of the local parking restrictions and was worried my car would be towed away if I did not keep feeding the meter. Two, I had nowhere to sleep. Three, I desperately needed some clean clothes. Four, if I was to spend hour after hour in a bar, I might as well enjoy it. The last thing I needed was a car outside. I remembered the motel I had sized up yesterday and wondered whether I dare risk checking into it and scrubbing some socks, a shirt and some underwear while the ten-dollar bill lay unattended. It was quiet, yes, but there was no guarantee that a customer wouldn't come in at any moment; a customer with twenties or fifties in his pocket and a need for change once his thirst had been slaked.

I would have to risk it. I reckoned I could be back within an hour. I told Connie and K.K. what I was doing and said that I would be back soon, then I sprinted to the car. Was this madness? Did I have a choice? Subconsciously, I was hoping the staff would understand and wouldn't give out the bill even in the unlikely event that they needed to. But that was not incumbent upon them. They were not obliged to smooth the way for me and, anyway, they had their own jobs to do.

I drove like a madman up Central Avenue to the All Seasons Motel. I parked the car outside reception and ran in. There was a girl at the desk and if she secretly believed that check-ins ought to be conducted swiftly, then her actions did nothing to give her away.

'What brings you to Hot Springs?' she asked.

I was tempted to tell her I was an international forger, but I thought better of it and told the truth.

'You gonna write a book about that? Well, *I've* written a book and I'm hoping to get it published. It's called *Bring Your Own U-Haul* – you know, like the trailers you can rent? It's about lesbians and how they just want to move in with each other as soon as they meet. It's about the difference between straight girls and lesbians. Straight girls want to keep their own place as long as they can, but lesbians, they can't wait to start living together. Don't get me wrong, I got nothing against lesbians, and just because you go with a girl doesn't mean you are one. I have a real pretty friend and she gets so tired of being hit on by men in bars that she sometimes just comes up to me and French-kisses the ass off me.'

Her name was Stacey and we had known each other for thirty seconds when she told me this.

I got my key, went to my room, washed some clothes . . . and fell into a deep sleep.

Dean Agus

I woke in darkness and something told me I was late. If only I could reach the door of the RV and breathe some fresh air, I might even be able to remember what I was late for. I jumped up and sprinted towards the spot where the door should have been. It was when I ran into a wall that I remembered I had left the RV behind earlier that morning. Slightly dazed, I sat on the floor and gathered my thoughts. Clarence . . . Ray . . . Bookstore . . . Hippies . . . Lucky's . . . Lesbians . . . Oh shit, what time was it? I groped around for a light switch and found a lamp. It was almost 8 p.m. I had left the ten- dollar bill alone, in a bar, for three hours.

Lucky's was about half a mile away, a distance I covered in five minutes. I figured that if the bill was gone, at least I would have somewhere to get a drink. I opened the door and found the bar almost as empty as I had left it. Trying not to draw attention to myself, I stopped running and affected a quick-step that possibly made me look something like an Olympic walker. K.K. had gone and Connie was restocking the bar. She turned around.

'What can I get you?' she asked.

'Well, you wouldn't happen to have that ten-dollar bill in the cash register, would you?' I asked timidly, pointing.

Connie narrowed her eyes and I thought she was going to ask me what the scam was. It was only a matter of time before someone from the Sheriff's department nabbed me for doing something strange but unspecific. There was probably a law against that in Arkansas.

Connie rummaged in the till while I swallowed hard. My heart was in the back of my throat. Seconds seemed stretched like time in a black hole. And then, with the kind of flourish that might normally be associated with a magician, a rabbit and a hat, she smiled and pulled out IA74407937A. I examined its markings and heard myself whoop.

'Connie!' I yelled. 'I love you!' She smiled and shook her head. 'Now, please may I have a very, very cold beer?'

Lucky's Bar & Grill was a well-known music venue and late-night watering hole, which explained why it was still almost empty. I sat on a stool at the bar and felt relieved. My journey had nearly come to a premature end and I scolded myself for putting it in jeopardy. After fetching my key from the loquacious Stacey, I had taken my rucksack from the car, pulled out my clothes and decided to have a shower. I had put all my dirty washing on the floor of the cubicle and lathered myself down while stamping on the wet clothes in much the same way as a French peasant might tread grapes. The water that poured down the plug was a reddish brown and I thought back to Kansas and Ernie Schlatter's farm.

I threw everything into cold water in the bathroom sink, soaked the floor, got mud on the shower curtain and wrung everything out as much as I could – which wasn't much at all – before realising there was nowhere to dry anything. I threw it all in the bath and lay down to ponder this unfortunate state of affairs before sliding further and further into sleep.

It had been a stifling day outside but I hadn't noticed it in the air-conditioned cool of my car and the bar. When I had run out from my motel room into the evening heat, I was taken by surprise and now found myself sweating. The beer cooled me and I ordered another. I would have clean clothes tomorrow, I thought, one way or another.

People came and went in ones and twos. Nobody said much and the ordering of drinks was done with nods and smiles. I watched every transaction and was ready to leap into action, but the ten-dollar bill was not given in change. Most people who spent more than twenty dollars paid by credit card. Those who spent less used tens or smaller. And each time that happened, IA74407937A went further and further down the pile. I needed someone to spend less than ten dollars and to pay with a twenty or a fifty. But that didn't happen.

Connie was a professional bartender, the kind that has as much presence behind a bar as a good actor has on stage. She knew when your glass was nearly empty and she remembered what you were drinking. As the bar filled up, she guessed who was next in line without being told. And she had that greatest of assets, one that few drinkers appreciate: good hearing. You never had to ask for anything twice.

At 8.30 p.m., two drunken couples came crashing in through a back entrance and headed for the bar. Connie was waiting for them, palms down, shoulders raised. 'Gonna behave?' she asked with rhetorical certainty. The four nodded and politely asked for their drinks. I must have smiled, because one of the men, in baggy jeans, white vest and black and white bandanna, came towards me.

'I'm a businessman,' he said, as if I had accused him of not being able to pay for his drinks.

'You must be very proud of yourself,' I replied.

He smiled. It wasn't the kind of smile that meant he was satisfied and on the verge of going away. It was the kind of smile that suggested he had found someone who appreciated his business acumen and wanted to hear more about it.

'It's beer,' he said. 'My business. My idea.'

'Beer is your idea? You invented beer?'

'No, I deliver beer.'

'You invented delivering beer?'

'No. I invented delivering beer when all the stores have closed.'

Where I live, taxi drivers perform this function illegally if you're lucky, but in Hot Springs, this skinny, glassy-eyed youth had cornered the market. I had run out of responses so I congratulated him, turned around and ordered another drink. After a few seconds, I felt a tap on my shoulder.

'Where you from?' He was slurring and unsteady on his feet.

'London.'

'Can you get beer in London?'

I felt that somehow he was getting the better of me. I enjoyed toying with drunks. There was something slightly dangerous about it. If you pushed the right buttons you could have hours of fun. If you pushed too hard you got a bottle over your head. Whichever way it went, it was much more interesting than darts. But there was nothing I could say that could match the sheer comic value of this question.

'Yes, and running water, and electricity,' I said.

He rocked back slightly on his heels. His hot breath was on my face and it smelled of stale booze and cigarettes.

'No, do you get it *delivered* in the middle of the night?'

'Officially, no. Unofficially, yes. By taxi drivers. But not everywhere. You have to live in a run-down part of town. I sometimes feel sorry for people who live in smart neighbourhoods.'

'And they deliver beer?'

I was beginning to see why he was a businessman. He had *focus*.

'Yes, and cigarettes and drugs and women, but I don't trust the quality of their drugs or women, so I pass on those.'

He seemed deflated and shook his head.

'I was going to sell you a franchise,' he said.

I took a swig of beer and thought about this until I realised what he meant.

'Hang on,' I said, with as straight a face as I could manage. 'You were going to sell me a franchise for delivering beer to people in the middle of the night? Using my car to shuttle beer from party to party . . . would require a franchise from you?'

His face became smug and he rocked back again.

I couldn't resist it. 'Tell me,' I asked, 'how much would that cost?'

He raised a finger but I never found out how much a night-time beer delivery franchise would have set me back because his girlfriend pulled him away and began kissing him violently. It was a moment that could have changed my life. I might have bought a beer franchise and become the night-time Beer King of the East End, bringing cheer to dried-out dipsomaniacs everywhere. Now we would never know. I looked away. A few minutes later I heard a commotion behind me and turned round to see all four leaving, Mr Beer arguing that he was perfectly fine to drive the car. I wondered whether any of them would remember where they had parked it.

Just after nine two men came in carrying guitar cases and put them on the stage. They went outside again and came back with black and silver boxes that I took to be amplifiers and other sound equipment. I didn't take much notice at first, but then I realised that the bar was filling up and wondered whether it was because of them. It was a Wednesday night off-season and I had figured business would be slower than this all evening. The background noise was rising and the air was filled with cigarette smoke. Smoking in bars was permitted in Arkansas and that was fine by me. I had always felt live music should be watched through a blue haze. And, anyway, I was fed up of smelling like damp dog. Now I could smell like an ashtray. Almost everyone else did.

The two men on stage began plucking at their guitars and blowing into microphones. I remembered that one of them had been setting up equipment while I was eating earlier in the day. That meant they didn't need a sound-check. Instead, they nodded to one another and got straight down to business. One was seated and picked at a black electric guitar. He was overweight, had short, greying hair and was wearing jeans and a black T-shirt. He had a glazed and expressionless face. The other, the singer, was standing with an acoustic guitar on a strap across his left shoulder. He was younger and stocky with short dark hair and olive skin. He wore jeans and a grey print T-shirt with crows and a guitar emblazoned on it. He had a remarkably powerful voice and a swagger when he sang; intense but honest. I shifted on my stool to get a better look.

They did covers – mainly rock, blues and soul – and they performed them with ease and grace. The lead guitarist was eerily perfect. He never missed a note but his face stayed blank as if he needed something more challenging to interest him. The singer had everyone's attention. Nobody spoke when he sang. He reminded me of Bruce Springsteen, but the similarity was not affected. It was American blue collar and it came to him naturally. They played songs by the Rolling Stones, Muddy Waters and Johnny Cash before stepping down for a break to enthusiastic applause from the audience. I couldn't remember when I had seen such accomplished musicianship in a small-town bar. Possibly never, and I had hung out in more bars than most.

The lead singer came to the bar through a sea of glad-hands. He stood next to me and ordered a beer, which he was given on the house, and swigged as if he needed it.

'I thought that was a great set,' I told him.

He smiled and held out his hand. He was naturally handsome, with brilliant teeth and an open, friendly face.

'Thanks,' he said. 'Dean. Dean Agus. Glad you enjoyed it.' He squeezed my hand and I felt my compliments roll off him. He was used to them. 'But if you like this, you should hear my band – there are four of us. Blow your mind. We're playing Friday. Be happy if you came. Will you be here?'

I wasn't going to start with explanations so I just said I hoped I would be.

'Man,' he said. 'I promise you won't be disappointed.'

Dean looked over my shoulder, waved at someone and excused himself, joining a group of people who had made camp at tables in front of the stage. One of them caught my eye. He was a skinny, short white man of about fifty with long grey hair and a Zapata moustache. I couldn't decide whether he looked more like a Grateful Dead roadie or a 1970s porn star. He had arrived a few minutes into the set with a tall and large-breasted black woman a foot taller than he was. Remembering Ray and Patti's experiences, I glanced around the bar to see if anyone had reacted to the sight of a mixed-race couple, but no one had.

During the break, two girls climbed on stage to fill in. One was a short tomboy wearing a jockey cap and ice-hockey shorts. She had a pretty face and a mischievous smile. The other was taller with long hair, more reserved and conventionally feminine.

I was expecting some embarrassing karaoke but was surprised again by fine singing and polished harmony. They sang a couple of songs peppered with expletives. The crowd joined in the swearing and Connie shook her head.

When they had finished, the women came to the bar and I complimented them too.

'Thanks,' said the tomboy. 'Where you from?'

I told her.

'You play pool over there?'

They were called Rachel and Sarah, they were in their early twenties and they were an item. They were also mean pool players. We played cut-throat, a three-way game which involved potting your opponent's balls until only yours remained. They played that to include me, but weren't so kind as to let me win. I played over and over again but never won at either cut-throat or regular pool while Rachel or Sarah were at the table. We drank more and they encouraged me to join them in shots. Before long the night grew hazy. Then Dean took the stage again and we stopped while he sang. The kitchen was in full swing and the aroma of barbecued food, alcohol and cigarette smoke mingled with the acrid street smell of day's end wafting through the open back door. I felt incredibly happy.

Every few minutes I would catch Connie's eye and she would shake her head. I was never sure whether she was annoyed or just busy, but she would frown occasionally and that was enough to shut me up. I wondered whether they ever had fights at Lucky's but I doubted it. At least, not on Connie's watch.

Dean finished his set to hoots and stamping of feet and he began unplugging his gear, carrying amps and equipment out through the front door with the help of the man with the Zapata moustache. Rachel, Sarah and I were swapping jokes over the pool table with several other players when Dean's guitarist walked over and stood among us, saying nothing. I finished telling a story and my audience laughed. I was never sure if people understood my jokes. The guitarist nodded but his face didn't move a muscle.

'Yes,' he said absently, 'I can see why that would be funny.'

His name was Wayne Scott and I began to wonder about the bored look he took on when he played. He wasn't trying to be cool. He was just extremely good at playing guitar but not so good at playing social situations. I later found out he was mildly autistic, which, in him, manifested itself in a form of genius with a guitar. Wayne's father had owned a pawn shop and given him an unredeemed guitar when he was three or four.

'Here son,' he had said. 'See if you can do something with that.' And, without any lessons, Wayne did.

He got bored with our jokes, walked over to the pool table and began looking at the balls.

I had drunk far too much and decided to rein in on the shots. A little late, I realised that I would have to be alert if the ten-dollar bill moved. I hoped it wouldn't go far; I couldn't drive and would have to leave my wet clothes behind. Perhaps I could find Mr Beer and get him to chauffeur me.

At 2 a.m. the lights came up and people began to leave. I was leaning against a wall wondering if I would ever see the ten-dollar bill again, when Dean approached me.

'Hey, man,' he said. 'I just got paid and they tell me I gotta see you about this.' He spoke with a rising inflection, like a question, and he was waving the ten dollars.

I explained my relationship to IA74407937A. His eyes widened and he began to laugh. We moved over to the bar and Dean took a last beer on the house. He explained that he and Wayne often played together but his real passion was the band he shared with his brother, Medo, who played lead guitar, and two other musicians, Daniel Keith on bass and Hampton Taliaferro on drums. They were called Crash Meadows, a play, apparently, on his brother's name, and they were a big deal in Hot Springs. They had released several records, were regularly on local TV and had opened for, among others, Joan Jett and the Blackhearts and the Spin Doctors. I took to Dean immediately. He wasn't smug, faux cool or rock-star dumb. He was easy-going and easy to talk to.

'Are we going on somewhere?' I asked, worrying that he might spend the money in some dive bar.

He shook his head, finishing off his beer. 'Nope, got a busy day tomorrow. I got some stuff to do at home in the morning and then I'll be setting up at Rolando's on Central Avenue. Wayne and I are playing there tomorrow night.'

We exchanged phone numbers and I asked him to call me if he was going to spend the money, then he left. The fact that he would be at home all morning appealed to me. I could sleep in and do something about my clothes.

The bar was empty and Connie was clearing up. I wondered why I was always the last person to leave. At least this time I had an excuse.

'You got your eye on that bill?' she asked, without waiting for an answer.

I thanked her and said a drunken and sentimental goodbye.

Majick

The Sun was high in the sky when I woke with a punishing headache and a dry mouth. The ten-dollar bill was somewhere in Hot Springs but so long as Dean stuck to his plans it would not be spent until 2 p.m., which was when I had arranged to meet him at Rolando's. I looked at my watch. It was 11.10 and I had just enjoyed the longest sleep since my journey began; it was the first time I had woken in daylight. I ate some leftover nuts and dried fruit and turned my attention to my wet clothes. In my zeal, I had washed everything except the clothes I was wearing yesterday, which meant I would have to wear them again today while the others dried.

I needed to pack and check out by noon; where would I dry my clothes? For a moment I considered calling Dean and asking whether he had some fabric conditioner and a tumble dryer, but I decided that was not the sort of thing you asked a rock star. No, I would wring out my clothes as best I could, drape them across the back seat of the car and leave them there, in direct sunlight, while I met Dean. By the end of the day, I would have clean dry clothes. Stacey waved through the office window while I carefully filled the car with my laundry. Passing pedestrians would soon be arrested by the sight of my steaming underpants. Men would covet the football-print Y-fronts that I had bought especially for the World Cup. I locked all the doors.

I had already paid for my room but I went into the office to say goodbye to Stacey. I had told Rachel and Sarah about her book and they had squealed in agreement. Apparently, lesbian lovers really do move in with each other remarkably swiftly. Stacey was delighted. As I walked back to the car and glanced at my glistening socks, creased shirts and broiling underwear, I wondered why straight women were not quite so anxious to move in with men.

The day was bright and the temperature had risen into the nineties. I had some time to kill, so I strolled into town in the midday sun and worried that my hangover was growing worse. What I really needed was a hot bath to draw the alcohol from my pores, and I was in the right place for that. Hot Springs plays host to Bathhouse Row, a strip of eight grandiose bathing establishments situated along – and in one or two cases, over – Hot Springs Creek.

The bathhouses that occupy the row today are actually third- or fourth-generation buildings; the originals were included in land acquired by the federal government for the nation in 1832 when Hot Springs Reservation became America's first national park. Collectively, the baths were designated a National Historic Landmark in 1987. They were truly grand in appearance, with neoclassical, Spanish colonial and Renaissance features, fountains and landscaped gardens that attracted more than half a million bathers a year at the height of the fashion for taking the waters. If you suffered from polio, paralysis, rheumatism or a thousand other ailments, the springs were said to do you good. A hundred years ago, Hot Springs rivalled anything Europe had to offer.

The early to mid-twentieth century would have been a

wonderful time to visit the town, walk along the promenade high above the creek, dine at the Arlington Hotel, place an illegal bet on the outcome of a race at Oaklawn Park or watch, mesmerised, as the Boston Red Sox, Chicago Cubs and Pittsburg Pirates limbered up with some off-season training. It all happened here. Showbiz stars rubbed shoulders with gangsters who laid questionable bets on their sporting – and transparently bribable – heroes, while politicians grew rich by looking the other way. If you had a time machine anchored in the foyer of the Arlington, you could pop back and forth for a Martini with Frank Sinatra, Babe Ruth or Al Capone. If I'd had one just then, I would have gone back to Lucky's last night and drunk a lot less beer.

A sign outside the Maurice bathhouse said it had been opened in 1912. In 1946, the height of the craze for bathing, the Maurice provided more than 67,000 baths and hydrotherapy treatments in seventy-nine rooms over three floors of luxury. By 1974, it gave just 6,500. According to a report commissioned by the US Department of the Interior on Hot Springs, the town reached its zenith in 1946. Just shy of 650,000 hot baths were taken along Bathhouse Row that year. By 1979, the figure had fallen to just 96,000. It seemed that the population of America, in common with the rest of the developed world, had been seduced by the wonders of modern medicine – medicine that actually worked. Not even the most nostalgic bather could have wished for the continuation of mercury baths to treat syphilis once penicillin had become widely available.

The Maurice closed long ago but the good news was that it was being renovated by the National Park Service as part of a wider rehabilitation plan for Bathhouse Row, and bathing numbers were once again on the increase. Of the others, the Buckstaff, the Fordyce, the Hale, the Lamar, the Quapaw, the Ozark and the

Superior, only the Buckstaff and Quapaw were operating while I was there. I decided to pop into the Quapaw.

Very recently renovated, it smelled of wood and carpet but not, as you might imagine, sulphur. The town's springs were devoid of anything foul-smelling. Behind the reception desk was a barrelled stained-glass ceiling and the sound of running water and I suddenly felt as if I were making the place look untidy. When cowboys and prospectors used to come here it was, literally, to have a bath, probably the first they had had in months. I had taken a shower last night, but right now I felt like John Wayne at the end of a long cattle drive.

'I have no bathing shorts – will that be a problem?' I asked the nice ladies at reception.

They looked me up and down. Of course it would. There were old people here. They might hurt their sides if they saw me in the nude. I was directed to a small shop where a garishly awful selection of men's swimwear was on display. I couldn't decide whether to opt for the purple paisley or the gay check.

'Is this all you have?' I asked the girl at the counter.

'Yes. They're terrible, aren't they?' she replied, looking at her nails. 'We get a lot of old people here and they think they're really cool.'

Resisting the temptation to argue that Mark Spitz was over sixty but wouldn't have been seen dead in these, I bought a strange pair of lime-green plaid shorts with a confidence-boosting gusset that was far too tight and headed for the baths.

Inside were comfortable robes and slippers, soft loungers and refreshments, parlour palms and mosaic tiles. On the walls were Indian motifs, a reminder that the springs were once frequented by the Quapaw tribe. Native Americans used to call the region of Hot Springs 'The Valley of the Vapours', which you might argue is a more romantic name than the one it has today. There were private spa rooms but I opted for the public area, which comprised four pools of varying temperature. My fellow bathers were all elderly and it quickly became clear that one's ability to withstand heat was important on some unspoken scale of social acceptability. One pool was on a higher level than the others with waters at temperatures of 85 degrees. It was the coolest and I made a beeline for it. Theoretically, it was not as hot as the air temperature outside, but with a hangover and rampant dehydration it felt hot to me. I dipped my toe in and winced. Then I noticed two of the older men below smirking at one another. I had seen this look before, among cool Italian sunbathers watching me negotiate hot sand on European beaches. After several minutes I moved down to the left-hand pool, which held water at 92 degrees. By now, I was even more dehydrated and I almost swooned. I was aware that I was becoming increasingly red, but I pretended to laze and emitted ostentatiously loud groans of satisfaction.

Nobody was buying it. An Eastern European woman wearing a rubber swimming cap looked at the men who were smirking at me and she smirked too. At length, I ventured, lobster-like, into the third pool, the one on the right. This was at 94 degrees and I began to think of Dante's Inferno. There was only one more circle of hell to endure but it would have to wait a while. It was a full ten degrees hotter: 104 degrees. This might not seem hot to you, but your woollens would shrink at that temperature.

I stayed where I was for a while and the oldies turned their attention away from me. There were subtle moves and practised eye contact. The men would saunter from hottest to coolest pools and back again, plunging in without so much as a raised eyebrow. The women would watch and feign impressed surprise. One, a septuagenarian Sophia Loren lookalike with large breasts and too much make-up, was casting admiring glances at a tattooed octogenarian male. I suddenly realised that this was a geriatric singles joint. Once I saw it, I saw it everywhere. Here a little glance, a muffled giggle; there a masculine wink and an offer of help up the steps. It was tasteful, elegant and gentle and I envied them the simplicity of their courtship rituals. My clumsy attempts at picking up women had involved thumping nightclubs and cheap cocktails.

There was nothing elegant about my entrance and swift exit from the centre pool, the hottest. I tried to sit down with a practised insouciance but the tears streaming down my cheeks gave me away. As I left the baths, I could hear laughter behind me.

Dean had texted to say he would be delayed until 4 and in capitals wrote HAVEN'T SPENT THE MONEY so I went for something to eat and found a shaded spot for a nap. It seemed to me that everything of importance in Hot Springs was either on, or just off, Central Avenue and that proved to be the case with Rolando's. It was a Tex-Mex bar and diner at the northern end past the Rehabilitation Center, but as I entered I could not work out where the boys would play. It was a large restaurant without a stage. All became clear when I was directed through a back door which opened underneath a solid rocky outcrop. I climbed a flight of stairs and found myself in a beautiful garden in the shade of another wall of rock with a shallow cave at its foot. I instantly realised that was where Dean and Wayne would play; it would offer excellent natural acoustics. There was a bar at the back of the garden, tables and chairs were scattered among shrubs and trees. Lights were draped through and across anything that would bear their weight. It wasn't a big venue but it was one of the prettiest I had ever seen.

Neither Dean nor Wayne had arrived and no equipment had been set up. I was alone and a waiter arrived to ask if I would like a drink. I ordered a mineral water. He frowned.

'You should really try a margarita,' he said. 'We're known for our margaritas. I've just mixed a bucket. It tastes fantastic.'

I looked at my watch. It was 4.10. I had set out my clothes to dry, taken a walk, endured a steam bath and lain down for a nap. That was a full day by anyone's standards. A drink mixed in a bucket didn't sound particularly appealing, but he was right. It was time for a margarita.

Dean arrived before Wayne, which didn't surprise me. I had the impression that Dean was particularly taken by what I was trying to do – and much later I found out why – whereas I didn't think Wayne knew I existed. The singer bounded up to me with his guitar, said hello to the waiter and took the seat opposite mine. He grinned and surveyed the venue.

'Some place, huh?' he said.

Dean was thirty-six and past his prime if he wanted to be in a boy band. Thankfully, he had no such ambition and so looked just about right for an earthy blues and rock singer who had lived a little. He and his brother Medo had been born in Skopje, the capital of Macedonia.

'I have one younger brother, Medo, and an older, Kazim, but I haven't seen Kazim since I was five,' he said.

His mother, Jula, a Gypsy, and father, Javid, had married at the age of twelve, which was not unusual in that community at that time, and they were struggling to make ends meet as their children arrived one by one. Then, as unlikely as winning the lottery, the family was identified as a worthy cause by members of an American church working in the region. They were adopted by the church and brought to the US via France and Belgium and to opportunities beyond their wildest dreams.

Macedonia today is a vibrant and increasingly prosperous part of Europe, but it was quite poor back then. I told Dean that I had spent some time there while covering the war in Kosovo from Albania and Macedonia. His eyes lit up when I told him that old Skopje was a beautiful town and that eating out there had reminded me of pleasant evenings in Greece. There was little to separate the two countries except, of course, for a powerful enmity stretching back before Alexander the Great. Macedonians believe themselves to be a race apart from Greeks (and point out that before Alexander, Greeks used to describe them as barbarians); the Greeks tend to argue that Macedonia is simply part of an older Greece and should be recognised as such.

When the family left in 1979, Kazim stayed behind to look after Javid's grandmother. 'After she died, he moved to Düsseldorf in Germany, but we haven't seen one another since we left,' said Dean. He looked sad. 'It's strange to think you have a brother out there and you wouldn't recognise him if you met in the street.'

Originally, Dean had been called Dejon, but he softened it to make it sound more American. At school he and Medo were taunted at first because of their accents (which are now pure Arkansas), but it just made them stronger. Dean became rebellious and, watching himself spiral out of control, he volunteered to spend a year at the Goodland Presbyterian Home for Boys in Oklahoma, which has a history of helping struggling kids from diverse ethnic backgrounds. He became a model student and achieved good grades.

'At Christmas the boys were allowed to write down ten things that they'd like as presents,' he told me. 'I just wrote down one word: Guitar. When I went home for Christmas break and went to church, the preacher told everyone about my grades and they all clapped. Then they gave me a Kramer Ferrington acoustic guitar, which even back then was worth about 2,000 dollars. I decided I wouldn't let them down and I practised every night for hours and hours in between curfews and chores. I wanted to be able to play it for them when I went home, and I did. But I got so into music that I quit school before graduating. And I've been singing and writing ever since.'

Wayne arrived and he and Dean began setting up for the show. It would be a low-key affair and Dean would perform some songs from his latest album, *Eleven Worlds Apart*. It helped to pay the rent, he said, but later he showed me his business diary. He was hardly struggling. Almost every night for the next three months either he and Wayne or he and the band were booked to play somewhere in and around Arkansas. That would be considered a success for most musicians, but I began to detect a sense of disappointment in Dean, a feeling that he didn't think that was anywhere near successful enough.

The boys began to play and I was joined at my table by the man I had seen the night before, the porn star/Grateful Dead roadie. He had a hang-dog look as if he fretted that you doubted everything he said. He held out his hand and told me his name was Magic. I thought this was a fantastically immodest name until he explained that it was spelled 'Majick' and had been given to him by Medo because of his interest in Native American medicine and shamanism. This would normally be enough to make me run screaming from the bar, but I remembered I had a bucket of margaritas to finish.

'People used to ask me to make medicine bags and herbal teas for them if they were ill and eventually they started calling me the Witch Doctor,' he said. 'After a while Medo changed it to

Majick and decided to spell it like that for the hell of it. It's stuck with me ever since.'

Changing the subject entirely, Majick suddenly said, 'You do know there's something special about Dean?'

He put the question as if this was the time to take sides, and he said it with such conviction that I wondered whether I should believe him. Until then, I had felt that Dean did have something that set him apart, but I also wondered whether my judgement was impaired – whether I was simply being seduced by the idea of hanging out with musicians.

'Have you seen the band yet?'

I told him I hadn't.

'Well, I've worked with some great musicians and I've seen 'em all, and these guys have got it. They should be much bigger. Their sound's amazing. Wait till you see 'em. Wait till you hear Medo play guitar.'

I bought Majick a beer and wondered whether I should explain that I might not be in Hot Springs tomorrow night. I might be at Disneyland or in Alaska. But I didn't bother. Majick had a fairly serious interest in alcohol and periodically he would vanish and come back smelling of marijuana. Dean sang some songs I didn't recognise and Majick would tell me which ones had been written by Dean, which he liked best and why. He began to grow on me. I had never met anyone who was able to say something such as 'I was baptised by the Reverend Al Green' – the legendary soul singer – without making it sound like a boast. Al Green happened to come from Arkansas and he just happened to get his hands wet over Majick's head. No big deal.

After I had drunk the bucket of margaritas I had a beer as the gig ended and the boys began packing up. I toddled over and asked if I could help.

'I never ask for help but I never turn it down,' said Dean.

There was a van parked below a fire escape at the side of the garden and I lugged guitars and amps and other bits of kit down and loaded them into the back with Majick. We climbed up again and sat for a while longer, drinking and talking under the garden lights, and I was surprised once more by how warm it was. I was introduced to Nacho, another band devotee, wiry, tattooed and always laughing, and I felt rather special. I kept my eye on Dean to see whether he spent the money, but rock stars don't spend money. Enamoured people buy them drinks and venues give them food. I shifted back in my chair with a contented sigh and wondered whether I might not be in for the long haul.

Eventually the lights were switched off and we made our way down to the van. We packed the last remaining items of gear into the back and slammed the doors. To my right, Dean and Majick were arguing.

'. . . I'm not saying it doesn't make you a better driver,' said Dean. 'I just wish you wouldn't do it on the van.'

'Aw, come on,' replied Majick. His head was lowered but his eyes looked up. He bore more than a passing resemblance to Droopy, the cartoon dog. 'I only did that once.'

'Yeah, but you've been getting closer and closer to the van and then you did it out the window.'

'Well, what if I do it over there?'

I felt a tug on my left sleeve. It was Wayne.

'You live in London?'

'Yes,' I said.

'You know Mick Jagger?'

'No.'

'Ever met anyone from the Rolling Stones?'

'No,' I said. And then I remembered . . . 'Actually, yes, I have.'
Dean and Majick were still arguing.

'It went inside. I just don't want it going inside, and if you do it down the door again, then it will.'

'I told you, I only did that once.'

'That's one time too many.'

Wayne was tugging at my sleeve again. 'Who?' he said. 'Who?'

'Charlie Watts,' I said.

Watts is the Stones' drummer, as hang-dog as Majick and as verbose as Wayne himself. I swear I almost detected a flicker of excitement.

'When? How?' Wayne asked.

'Not inside the van,' Dean was saying.

'Makes me a better driver,' replied Majick.

'But it doesn't make me a better passenger.'

'Where? Where?' asked Wayne.

'At Bill Wyman's wedding. In 1989, when he married Mandy Smith.'

'*You* were at Bill Wyman's wedding?'

'Well, sort of.'

'You know Bill Wyman and Charlie Watts?'

'I didn't say that.'

'Some of it went on my trousers,' said Dean.

'I don't believe you. You would have said 'fore now,' said Majick.

'I didn't want to hurt your feelings,' said Dean.

'Then why were you there?' Wayne asked.

'I was covering the reception for a newspaper.'

'You were sitting with Charlie Watts at Bill Wyman's wedding?'

'No, I didn't say that either. I was outside. Charlie Watts came over and some of us reporters asked him what he thought of the marriage. Mandy Smith was just a kid. We all thought it was a sham.'

'So what happened?'

'I told you, it went down my legs,' Dean interrupted.

Majick was walking away disconsolately.

'Whose legs?' I asked.

'No, not you. Him,' Wayne said, pointing at me.

'Who?' asked Dean.

'Me, I think,' I told him. The floor seemed to be moving under my feet.

'He's friends with Charlie Watts,' said Wayne.

'I am not friends with Charlie Watts.'

'You're friends with Charlie Watts? Wow,' said Dean, slapping me on the back.

'No, I am not friends with Charlie Watts.'

'Then he's friends with Bill Wyman.'

'I am NOT friends with ANY of the Rolling Stones.'

Wayne frowned.

'Then why did you say you were?'

Between burps that tasted of lime juice, I explained that as Charlie Watts left the reception, we had asked for his thoughts on the wedding day.

'Well,' he replied cooperatively in a rich cockney accent, 'it was all very nice. It was a lovely day but, come on, it won't *laaaast*. Not a fucking *chaaaance*. G'nite, boys.'

I explained that Wyman had been dating Smith since she was thirteen years old and how she later claimed they were having sex when she was just fourteen. The marriage lasted less than a year. Watts had been right.

'Wow,' said Wayne. 'That Charlie Watts, huh? Bang on the money.'

He was delighted. The Rolling Stones were his favourite band.

I felt my way around the van and asked Dean where Majick had gone.

'He's driving us home but he's just gone to throw up,' he said. 'Says it makes him a better driver. Get in.'

The Gangster Museum of America

Dean called the next morning to say he was about to spend the money. Or, more accurately, he was going to mail it to St Louis, Missouri, 406 miles away.

'Oh, God,' I, said under my breath. 'Please, not the mail.'

I had another hangover. The night before, we had gone our separate ways except for Nacho and I, who asked Majick to drop us off at Lucky's for a nightcap. I sensed Majick was thinking of joining us until Dean gave him a withering look. He wasn't in the mood to wash the van again.

Connie looked up from the bar and waved as we walked in.

'I thought I'd seen the last of you,' she said. 'You lost the money?'

'Nope,' I said, as if I had skilfully retained my grip on it in some magical way. I hadn't had it in my hands since Kansas.

The bar was half full and noisy. Rachel and Sarah were there and I joined them for a drink while Nacho worked the room.

'You here for the band tomorrow night?' asked Rachel.

I said I didn't know. There was a lot of excitement, she said. It was going to be a big night. After some small talk about my sky-rocketing motel bills, Sarah told me that she was house-sitting for her boss. I had noticed last night that she was also car-sitting. Huge Mercedes car-sitting. I half wondered whether her boss was at the bottom of Lake Hamilton.

'If you're still around on Saturday you can stay with us,' she said, and I said thank you.

For me, this was simply a kind offer, but some drinkers at the bar heard it and began exchanging lewd glances. It was depressingly predictable – the only thing a lesbian needed to become straight was a night with a real man like them. It was a view I had never subscribed to, particularly since the night, at the age of twenty-two, when I slept with a beautiful actress. She was way out of my league and looked, memorably, like a young Elizabeth Taylor. Sexually, it was probably the highlight of my life, at least until the next day, when she came out to her friends – and mine – as being gay. She wasn't kidding, either. From that day forth her interest in men ceased. Saying I had determined her sexuality would be almost as stupid as saying I could 'cure' it, but it was an advertisement for my sexual prowess that dogged me for years. My closest friends began to call me Bedspread, because I got turned down every night.

I thanked the girls, finished my drink, went back to the motel and checked in again. Stacey found my continued presence as funny as everyone else. When I opened the car everything inside was damp. I hadn't left any windows open, so the steam inside had been recycled back into my clothes. They were soaking wet. I sighed.

'Why are you mailing the bill?' I asked Dean, picking some fluff out of my belly button.

'Doos,' he said, which I mentally translated into 'dues'. 'Doos for a fantasy football league. I owe ten bucks and the guy who runs the league called me today and asked when I was going to pay him.'

'Can't you write him a cheque?' I asked, aware that this was verging on a breach of the rules: interference. I was tired. It wasn't easy hanging with musicians.

'Nope, I always send cash. Seems like you're going to St Louis.'

I was dehydrated again and in a state of mild exhaustion.

'What if it goes missing? What if someone steals it?' I asked.

I looked around my room. It was a mess and I began thinking how good it would feel to leave and go somewhere else. I really believed that cash would move faster than this.

'Nah,' he said. 'Be all right. I'll be mailing it at noon. You wanna be there to see it?'

I scratched my head and reached for my clean clothes. They were clammy and cold.

'You could always deliver it for me,' said Dean, but I said I wouldn't.

'I'm supposed to be *following* the money. It wouldn't feel right to carry it.'

I heard him laugh.

'Look,' I said. 'I'll do you a deal. What if you send it with FedEx or UPS and I'll pay for it to be tracked, recorded, signed for? Anything. I'll pay.'

I simply couldn't afford to lose it.

'OK,' he said. 'You're the boss. I'll pick you up and we'll take it to the UPS office. How's that sound?'

It sounded like a compromise. A scary one. And it felt like a long time since I had been the boss of anything.

I showered, packed again and put on my wet clothes. I went outside and stood in the sunshine, hoping they might dry. Stacey was supervising the cleaning of some rooms and she caught me with my arms open wide like the statue of Christ on Sugarloaf Mountain. She looked at the floor and I heard her giggle. I didn't care. I was wearing my underpants with the footballs on and felt strangely invincible. What could go wrong?

Dean came for me and I said goodbye to Stacey once more. She wished me luck and I said I hoped her book would be a success.

It was Majick's birthday the next day and he had told me that he had a fondness for dark rum. As we drove off the motel forecourt I asked Dean if we could stop to buy some. It was a wonderfully bright day again and we talked with the windows open as we drove through town and past Oakland Park. The magnolia-scented wind cleared my head and if it hadn't been for the anxious knot in my stomach the fresh air might have given me an appetite. I spent half a moment trying to remember the last time I had eaten. It was yesterday, after the baths. I should have been starving.

Dean took me to a liquor store and I cheered up immediately. It was a drive-thru bottle shop, the first I had ever seen. You drove your car up to a window, asked for your alcohol, paid and had it passed through a small serving hatch, all without getting out of the driver's seat. We bought a litre of dark rum and I resisted the temptation to ask if it came with fries. I thought this was a wonderful addition to the retail sector, a real boon for the discerning drinker. You could buy booze even if you were too drunk to walk into the store.

We drove off and I noticed that Dean was lively and fidgeting in the driver's seat. He seemed confident and upbeat and said he was looking forward to playing the gig. I could only imagine how that felt.

The UPS office was in a retail park at the edge of town in a nondescript brick building that suggested dull reliability. Once inside, I told the cashier that this was the most important item of mail she would ever handle. She looked at me earnestly. 'Of course it is, honey.' I took pictures of the envelope and of Dean handing it over. I thought it would be the last time I would ever see it. The cashier gave me a shipment receipt with a tracking number: 1Z2Y27X94481549012. It said the item would be delivered the next day, 9 October, at noon, to a Mr Ron Zoller in Caseyville (which is across the Mississippi River from St Louis and so actually just inside the state of Illinois), but the cashier said it was unlikely to arrive before 4.

It cost me forty-two dollars and twenty-seven cents to send a ten-dollar bill.

If the UPS cashier was right about the bill not arriving before 4 p.m., I would be able to watch the gig, get up early and drive to St Louis before it was signed for by Ron Zoller. That meant I had some time to kill and so I decided to visit one of the highlights of Hot Springs: the Gangster Museum of America. A gangster museum was the last thing I had expected when I rolled into town. A museum celebrating gangsters? In Arkansas?

It was ten dollars for a tour of the museum and I had to wait in the gift shop until the previous one finished. I was terribly excited. Through a door and above some unseen partition I could hear the sound of gunfire. I was the only person waiting and was relieved when a fat couple in shell suits came in. The husband smiled at me and said, 'Al Kapo'. He wore a baseball cap and T-shirt that had on it a picture of Barack Obama. The woman was wearing something with a sticker that intimated she had been to Kauai in Hawaii. Their accent was Eastern European but I was not able to place the country. 'Al Kapo,' I said back to them, and smiled.

They were odd, but at least their presence meant I wouldn't be alone with the guide. I had been on my own on obscure tours in the past – the Lawnmower Museum in Southport, the Pencil Museum in Keswick – and had had to feign a deep fascination for the Anzani Lawnrider or the Derwent Colour 19 Series.

A group of satisfied-looking customers emerged from behind a curtain and it was our turn. Our guide was a slim and pretty girl called Molly, who had apparently attended the Shirley Temple School of Acting. It wasn't so much a tour as a wide-eyed and hotly enunciated performance with an emphasis on shock and awe.

'Hello, everybody!' she projected, and surveyed the room as if she were talking to a much larger group of people.

I looked over my shoulder but there was nobody there. She asked us where we were from and it transpired that the increasingly excited Eastern European couple were Romanian.

'Welcome to the *worrrld*-famous Gangster Museum of America!' began Molly. 'Today, we will see how Hot Springs –'

The shrill sound of the Romanian man's mobile phone cut her dead.

'Allo, allo! Dotter, dotter!' he shouted, pointing at the phone.

It was his daughter. He had no intention of halting the conversation, so poor old Molly had to stand silently like a DVD on pause.

The man continued snorting and laughing into the phone while his wife tried to wrestle it from his grip. I glanced at Molly. She looked at the floor and put her hands behind her back. What patience. What a trouper. I decided I would be the most attentive person she had ever guided.

I frowned at the fat Romanian, as if to say, 'Come on, pal, let the lady do her job.'

He ignored me and shouted, 'Yahh, zbuggy, zbuggy, stjerzybog, al kapo!'

Then his wife grabbed hold of the handset and yelled, 'Yahzy berzy, stjerzybog, al kapo!'

I have a low tolerance threshold so I took a step towards to the couple and pointed at my watch. They yelled al kapo into the handset and got with the programme.

Molly told us that Hot Springs had been a thriving hotbed of criminality for half of the nineteenth and twentieth centuries. When gambling was illegal everywhere else, you could come here, lose all your money and not even get a fine. This was Las Vegas before Las Vegas had been thought of. During Prohibition, you could buy a drink and get fleeced at any number of illegal roulette tables in any combination of nightclubs or brothels. Tourists flocked to the town, the vast majority leaving much poorer than when they had arrived.

In the early days, the mid- to late 1880s, two criminal families, the Flynns and the Dorans, headed by Frank Flynn and Confederate Army Major Alexander Doran, vied for control of the town. Flynn already had seven illegal gambling joints by the time Doran arrived in 1884 to begin carving out some territory for himself. Foolishly, not taking into account the major's army training, Flynn challenged Doran to a duel and was shot in the chest. The injury was not fatal but it began a feud that lasted for four years; by the time Doran himself was killed in 1888, word in town was that he had murdered at least ten men.

Flynn continued to flourish because he bribed the Hot Springs Police Department and, to a lesser extent, the Garland County Sheriff's Department to look the other way. So powerful was Flynn that sheriffs and police officers actually collected unpaid debts for him. By the century's close, tension was building again

– not between Flynn and new criminal rivals, but between the town police and county sheriff's departments, over who was to get the biggest slice of the pie. Matters came to a head on 16 March 1899, when Sheriff Bob Williams took umbrage on hearing of a meeting at which the police chief, Thomas Toler, a new mayoral candidate, and several members of the Independent Party had discussed cutting Williams's share of the profits.

During the fight that ensued, Police Chief Toler, one of his sergeants, a detective, a bartender at Lemp's Beer Depot and Deputy John Williams, the Sheriff's nephew, were shot and killed. In subsequent trials, hung juries and self-defence pleas meant that nobody went to jail for the killings. Tourism suffered for a while and Frank Flynn was run out of town, but all that meant was that the middleman was gone and there was now more money for the police and sheriffs. Hardly anyone has heard of the Hot Springs Gunfight, yet it resulted in two more deaths than the Gunfight at the OK Corral, which was far less interesting and lasted – according to witnesses – a paltry thirty seconds. The Hot Springs shoot-out flared up twice during a long dog-day afternoon and actually gave onlookers much more bang for their buck.

In the twentieth century, gambling took on an air of respectability – not because it was legalised, but because elected politicians took a hand in running it. Successive mayors, judges and police chiefs took bribes, turned a blind eye and, in many ways, actively encouraged criminals in their illegal enterprises. I was delighted to find out that the greatest criminal in Hot Springs during this period was an Englishman called Owney Madden. Madden had been born in Leeds in 1891 before his parents took him to Wigan, which, when I was young, was where I learned about nightclubbing and drinking. If you exchanged moonshine for Merrydown cider, I imagine there wouldn't have been much difference between Wigan and Hot Springs on a Saturday night.

Madden sailed to New York with his brother and sister in 1902 and immediately embarked on a life of crime that included theft, racketeering and murder. After several decades terrorising the good people of Hell's Kitchen, Madden fled to Hot Springs in 1935 because of an argument involving booze, guns and Italians. He lived a long and happy life in the town, pulled the strings of the police and the political elite and was generally regarded as being a straight up and down crook. What I liked best about him, though, was the company he kept. As a one-time owner of the Cotton Club in New York (Bob Hoskins played Madden in the film of the same name), he had a partner called George Jean 'Big Frenchie' DeMange and was implicated in the murder of a man called Vincent 'Mad Dog' Coll. When did criminals stop giving themselves such colourful names? Was there once something akin to the Patent Office where a man could walk in as plain old Harry Ronson and walk out as Harry 'Psycho Razor' Ronson?

During the 1920s and 1930s – what you might call the golden age of gangsterism – organised criminals would vacation in Hot Springs. Here they could relax, drink, womanise and gamble without having to worry about being picked up by the FBI, with whom the local police had a deliberately obfuscated relationship. Arrest warrants seemed to evaporate as quickly as the steam from Bathhouse Row.

Not only did the reduced likelihood of incarceration help alleviate the workaday stress of running prostitution, bootlegging and protection rackets back in Chicago and New York, but also there was the comforting guarantee that in Hot Springs you were unlikely to get a bullet in the back. The St Valentine's Day Massacre might have been the culmination of a business disagreement between Al Capone and Bugs Moran, but that did not mean they pulled their guns on each other when they passed in Hot Springs. Here there was an unspoken truce and disputes were left at home. Capone was one of the town's most popular visitors. He had a regular suite, number 442, at the Arlington Hotel, while Bugs favoured the Majestic, just one block away. I am not suggesting they doffed their caps as they passed on the street, but neither did they try to shoot one another through the eye with a Derringer.

I wasn't enormously impressed with the Gangster Museum. I couldn't imagine an attraction with fewer exhibits except, perhaps, the Wall Street Museum of Corporate Governance. Molly, though, made it worth the money and there were some terrific videos explaining who was who and what was what in the Hot Springs underworld before Justice Department spoilsports brought it all to an end in 1967.

We were about to finish when Molly picked up a fake machine gun and led us to a life-sized model of Al Capone. He was seated and wearing a white three-piece suit, a white hat and grey boots. In his right hand was a fat cigar and either side of him were huge plastic dice on which we were expected to sit and have our photographs taken.

The Romanians went wild. The wife ran at me with her camera and thrust it into my hands while her husband took a seat next to Al.

'Al Kapo! Al Kapo!' she shouted, pointing at the gangster.

I had no idea what the word for 'cheese' was in Romanian, but I didn't need it.

Crash Meadows

I arrived at Lucky's early so I could meet the rest of the band. I was relieved that the money was finally moving but I felt strangely guilty that I was not. Should I be on the tail of a UPS delivery van or dogging the footsteps of some postal service executive? I didn't know. There was no international body that laid down rules for following cash. I knew where it was going, I would follow it and be there before it was next spent. I decided to stop worrying and have a drink.

I had been nervous at the prospect of meeting the rest of Crash Meadows. I suspected they would be much too cool to be seen in the same room as me, so I was relieved when they turned out to be regular guys whose egos had been left at the door. There was Medo, who was slimmer and younger than Dean. He was clean-cut with short cropped hair and an aura of confidence. If it could be said of any of them, it was Medo who checked me out. I could see he was suspicious of the Limey who had been following his big brother around, and I thought that was fair enough.

To his left was Hampton Taliaferro, the band's ridiculously handsome drummer. He had long blond hair held in place with a headband and he looked as if he belonged more to LA than to

Hot Springs. He had sharp cheekbones and a chiselled jaw and was the personification of cool. On the other side of Medo was the bass player Daniel Keith, a very tall, thick-set character with a bald head and reddish beard. He was the quiet and gentle one, steady and rock solid. I could tell that they were going to be tight. They were comfortable in each other's presence and no one was vying for dominance. They had the air of a group of people who felt they had nothing to prove.

We had a drink and, unexpectedly, I decided I wanted a cigarette. I had given up long ago but suddenly felt all kind of rock 'n' roll.

'Have any of you guys got a fag?' I asked.

There was silence.

I froze. I should have known better – I had made this mistake before. And, after spluttering an apology, I told them about it.

I had been to San Quentin Prison, on the outskirts of San Francisco, to conduct an interview for *The Times* with a man called Stanley 'Tookie' Williams on Death Row. Williams had been convicted of four murders which I doubted he had committed – all the witnesses who gave evidence against him were criminals who later went on to receive suspiciously light sentences for other seemingly serious crimes. Nobody cared too much about that, though, because, as founder of the Crips, America's most notorious gang, he had probably killed other people anyway. What was remarkable about Williams was that during the twenty-four years he had been on Death Row, he had undergone an incredible – and genuine – transformation, educating himself and writing numerous children's books which urged their readers to steer clear of a life of crime and of gangs in particular.

His work had earned him five nominations for the Nobel

Peace Prize and four for the Nobel Prize for Literature, but here he was just days away from being executed by lethal injection. Some Nobel nominations come cheap – each year, thousands of academics, politicians, former Nobel Laureates and certain research and reform bodies are asked for their suggestions, which are then kept secret for fifty years, so it is possible for campaigners to influence nominations for the publicity they generate. We cannot know for sure, then, just who nominated Williams, but nobody ever nominated me. Surely, I thought, he was more use alive than dead?

I was led to a small cell lined with bars and Perspex and Williams was pushed inside with shackles on his feet and wrists. He thrust his arms backwards through a flap in the wall and his cuffs were removed for our interview. It was just before Thanksgiving and earlier that day I had watched President George W. Bush pardon a turkey on TV, a tradition that comes before the annual feasting, yet my own enquiries had established that Arnold Schwarzenegger, the Governor of California, was unlikely to grant a reprieve for Williams. I suspected Tookie thought Arnie just might. He was calm. I was nervous. Interviewing someone who is effectively already dead is not an easy thing to do. He was facing death, but I could tell he was trying to make *me* feel more comfortable.

When I left he gave me a bear hug. He could have squeezed the life out of me with hardly any effort at all. And he thanked me for coming.

I went through all the layers of security involved in leaving one of America's most violent prisons and, a smoker at the time, reached for my last cigarette as I sat in the parking lot mulling over the events of the previous two hours before driving back towards San Francisco and pulling into a bar.

'Where you come from?' asked the barman, passing me a beer.

Without thinking, and looking down at my notes, I replied: 'San Quentin Prison. Hey, have you got any fags? I could murder a fag.'

Of all the places not to say this, San Francisco probably tops the list. Fortunately, the obviously gay bartender had been to London and he knew what a fag was. 'But you better watch your mouth, sugar,' he reproached me after I'd apologised.

When I told the band about this verbal clumsiness they seemed to warm to me, slapping their thighs and choking on beer. Self-deprecation usually does that. From that moment we became friends. They called cigarettes 'fags' and spoke to one another in truly awful English accents culled from Austin Powers movies.

As for Tookie Williams, he was executed at the age of fifty-two on 13 December 2005. I believe I conducted the last newspaper interview with him, but just before his execution he gave another to WBAI Pacific radio station in which he said:

[For] my lack of fear of this barbaric methodology of death, I rely upon my faith. It has nothing to do with machismo, with manhood, or with some pseudo former gang street code. This is pure faith, and predicated on my redemption. So, therefore, I just stand strong and continue to tell you, your audience, and the world that I am innocent and, yes, I have been a wretched person, but I have redeemed myself.

And I say to you and all those who can listen and will listen that redemption is tailor-made for the wretched, and that's what I used to be . . . That's what I would like the world to remember. That's how I would like my legacy to be remembered: as a redemptive transition, something that I believe is not exclusive just for the so-called sanctimonious, the elitists. And it is not predicated on colour or race or social stratum or one's religious background. It's accessible for everybody. That's the beauty of it. And whether others choose to believe that I have redeemed myself or not, I worry not, because I know and God knows, and you can believe that all of the youths that I continue to help, they know, too. So with that, I am grateful . . . I say to you and everyone else, God bless.

Witnesses said prison staff struggled for more than twenty minutes to find Tookie's veins and insert the needles that delivered the fatal doses of chemicals to his heart.

While the boys set up I took Majick for a pint of Guinness at McCardle's Irish bar a block away. I had become increasingly fascinated by Majick. He seemed to tell the most unlikely stories but when I checked them with members of the band they always turned out to be true. The Al Green episode was a case in point.

One I could not confirm but which I found easy to believe was a story about the day Majick was responsible for Andre Agassi's exit from the 1987 ATP tennis tournament in Memphis, Tennessee, just as Agassi was being recognised as a rising star on the international circuit.

'I was living in Memphis from 1985 to 1988 and used to get work at a Pizza Hut stall at the tennis tournament,' Majick told me. He took a swig of Guinness which left a white foam melting across his Zapata moustache. 'Well, Andre Agassi was just a kid then and he liked pizza, and one year I got to know him. I think he was bored, but, man, did he eat a lot of pizza. He was seventeen. One day he joined some of us for a game of basketball. Like I said, he was just a kid, but he liked to party and we partook of some really good stuff, you know, pot.

'Well, after a while I said, "Hey, Andre, you sure you should be doin' this shit?" And he said, "Don't you worry about me." But the next day he was knocked out of the tournament in the first round. I said to myself, "Majick, that was your fault." I felt guilty about it and I still do.'

Many years later, in his autobiography, *Open*, the tennis player admitted using recreational drugs and smoking marijuana as a young man. He also said there were times when he hated tennis. One can only imagine him the year after his first-round knockout, under enormous pressure and the weight of expectation, making his way to the Pizza Hut stall in the hope of finding the crazy hippie who had given him such a good time the previous year. Perhaps it was just as well for him and for tennis lovers everywhere that Majick had moved on; Agassi went on to win the tournament.

The other extraordinary thing about Majick was his apparent attractiveness to women. He was quite a scrawny individual but he had a certain burnt-out charm that was appealing and a quiet way of talking that had people in thrall to him. I had been amazed when I first saw him walk into Lucky's with the statuesque black woman but it emerged that she was not his steady girl. He had been married for fifteen years but was divorced way back in 1996. He had travelled extensively and moved around since finding himself single. He dated women but preferred to keep it simple and I could tell from the way he described his relationships that he found women easy to relate to. So was there anyone at all special? I asked, downing the dregs of my Guinness.

'Well, no, but I've had quite a few girlfriends and they're all still pretty cool with me,' he said. 'See for yourself.'

Majick took out his phone and began showing me pictures of a whole host of women. They were all shapes, sizes and colours but invariably very attractive. There was Mary from Ohio, Charlene from New York, Julia from Nebraska and Debbie from the Caribbean. On and on it went. Melba from Florida, Denise from Montana, Erica from Utah. The pictures were charming with cheery waves and smiles. There was not an ounce of the braggart in Majick's showing them to me. Instead, it felt as if they were a record of his life.

'If I had to say that there was one I really loved, it was this one,' he said. He sighed and showed me a picture of a young woman with bright eyes and a petite figure. 'It's all over now but I think I still love her.'

For a moment I felt sad. Majick had chosen the life of a rolling stone and being alone was one of the downsides. It went with the territory and the territory could sometimes be barren. Then, continuing to scroll through the pictures, he stopped.

'No, wait a minute,' he said. 'I almost forgot. I still really love this one. Yeah, I still love her too. It's her. Yep, s*he*'s the one.'

He carried on scrolling and I got up to get some more drinks before he had a chance to fall in love again.

By the time we got back to Lucky's the bar was filling up. Sarah had been right last night; there was excitement in the air. We had tables reserved at the front and I was pleased to see that Nacho was there. I was introduced to more of his friends but noticed that Rachel and Sarah were missing. Majick went to fetch some drinks and I had the fleeting thought that perhaps the police had found Sarah's boss buried under the patio.

Lucky's was cavernous but it was growing increasingly crowded as fans of the band arrived. There was a loud, good-natured atmosphere and a wide cross-section of types. As well as playing Dean's own songs, the bar expected Crash Meadows to keep the crowd happy with covers and that was fine with the boys; they were just as comfortable playing country as soul, rock or blues.

Drinks arrived in front of me with alarming frequency. Each time a new one appeared, I would look up and see a stranger over at the bar nodding and raising a glass in my direction. I had gained a certain notoriety as the Ten-dollar Guy and I would be lying if I said I wasn't enjoying it. In front of me now was a shot glass with a green substance in it which smelled vaguely of aniseed. I decided the least I could do to show my appreciation was to drink it. I raised the glass to the stranger and knocked it back.

Nacho gave me a dig in the ribs and told me the band were coming on. The lights went down and Crash Meadows took the stage, opening with 'Worlds Apart'. This begins with a deep and arresting riff by Medo and I began to understand what Majick had said about the way he played, as if always being comfortably within his limits. The fans loved it. Dean was moody and impressive, his voice deep and rich. If David Bowie likened Bob Dylan's voice to sand and glue, then Dean's was diamond dust and treacle. To his right, Daniel played bass, rhythmic and solid. At the back and in the dark was Hampton, head down and intense, avoiding panting looks from the women in the audience by hiding behind the brim of a very large cowboy hat. He was drumming at a thousand miles an hour but only occasionally did you see his face, when he came up for air.

They mixed their songs with numbers by Jimi Hendrix and Marvin Gaye, then kept the soulful mood alive with Dean's own 'Until Tomorrow'. When I first met the singer I told him

I thought his voice was made to perform Bruce Springsteen's 'Born to Run'. Halfway through the gig, and to my delight, the band played it and dedicated it to me. The crowd clapped and whistled and Nacho slapped me on the back while I blushed. On they went, playing songs by Smokey Robinson, Stevie Ray Vaughan and Otis Redding. They could change the mood whenever they wanted and take the audience with them, from their own material, to covers and back again. I was happily smashed and completely biased, but I decided this was a truly fantastic performance.

And then, as Spinal Tap might have said, they cranked it up to eleven. Dean began playing Pink Floyd's 'Comfortably Numb' and I gradually noticed all eyes turning towards Medo – the crowd had seen him do this before. The song is peppered with memorable but relatively short guitar solos; the Crash Meadows version involved Medo stringing one out for a full ten minutes. There were times when I tried to follow the fingers of his left hand moving across the neck of his guitar, forming chords from fret to fret, but I couldn't keep up. His note-perfect fingers moved faster than my eyes.

They closed the gig with that and brought down the house. It was one of the best live shows I had ever seen. When the applause died away I floated to the bar to buy drinks for the table and the boys. A girl I had been introduced to the night before waved at me from a perch near the front of the bar.

'Hi,' she shouted. 'Who you with?'

Oh, thank you, God, I thought. At last. I almost began hopping from foot to foot.

'Me?' I shouted back nonchalantly. 'I'm with the band.'

Well, what would you have done?

'Stay'

You said you were leaving
And I thought that I was dreaming
But you were nowhere, nowhere to be found
I beg you, don't go this way, please stay.
from 'Stay' by Crash Meadows

Dean offered me a bed for the night but I declined. We had been talking earlier in the day and I found out why so many of his most recent songs were moody and soulful. He had been through a messy divorce from his wife, Stephenie, and his were the lyrics of a man who knew he had lost something special. When I rolled into town, Dean and Stephenie were attempting a reconciliation. He was back in the family home, a one-storey, three-bedroomed house with a huge sweep of back garden where Neelah, his daughter, practised playing soccer. It was tastefully furnished and decorated and I guessed that although Dean was house-proud, the stamp on this home was probably Stephenie's. When I first met her I could see why Dean was fighting to rekindle the marriage. She was tall and slim with long, rich brown hair, blue eyes and tanned skin. She had brilliant white teeth and a straight, aquiline nose. She took one look at me, turned around and walked out.

That was earlier in the day when Dean had made a detour to pick up one of the guitars that hung like carob pods from stands and walls all over his home.

'Thanks for the offer, but I think the last thing your marriage needs right now is a drunken Englishman snoring on the sofa,' I said, my mind made up. Dean and I had become firm friends, grown intensely close in a ridiculously short period of time, and I wasn't about to blow his prospects.

The argument ended with us at Lucky's singing 'Happy Birthday' to Majick on the stroke of midnight. Medo played in the style of Brian May inducing vomit from the top of Buckingham Palace, then we all got out our presents. Dean and I gave him the rum we had bought earlier in the day, various women handed over little wrapped gifts and one or two whispered in his ear. He had been drinking and smoking weed and had a waspish glint in his eye. The bar was only half full now and I thought that was a shame, because the other half would surely have appreciated the gift that Crash Meadows had procured for Majick. It was a psychedelic, tie-dyed, full-body set of long johns which actually looked like a romper suit. Majick climbed into them like a giant baby on magic mushrooms and a small tear rolled down his cheek.

'Hell, guys,' he said, meekly. 'You shouldn't have. But thanks.'

The band might have been profligate with their gift, but they hadn't given Majick the night off, so once he had taken several slugs of rum and nipped to the car park for a few tokes, he threw up, fetched the van to the front of Lucky's and began loading equipment into the back of it. He was only able to get a parking space across the road and so the late-night traffic wending its way sedately past the Victorian façades of downtown Hot Springs was obliged to stop intermittently as an ageing hippie with long hair and psychedelic long johns staggered past with drums, amps, guitars and a variety of boxes.

The chaos of the night had meant that my goodbye to Dean had to be brief, and that was how I wanted it. I hadn't managed to get to the bottom of his sense of disappointment – or was it regret? – but I had grown to understand the man behind the songs and come to admire the person I found. We shook hands and embraced our farewell while Majick and the rest of the band wailed 'Cheerio' like Austin Powers.

When I told Nacho that I had turned down Dean's offer of a place to stay he nodded his approval.

'Man, you did the right thing,' he said. 'Dean's the kindest guy in town but –' he looked me up and down – 'I don't think Stephenie would have appreciated it.'

Instead, Nacho took me home with him, stopping at the motel to get my rucksack from the car. I would like to describe where Nacho's home was, but all I can say for sure is that it was on a piece of ground at the end of a journey that involved a car and some roads. There were two sofas in his living room and on the largest was an ill-looking man with the most horrendous cold. His name was Keith and he was Nacho's brother. The other occupants were a cat and a chihuahua whose names I instantly forgot.

I apologised to Keith for intruding on him and his malady at 3 in the morning.

'That's OK,' he said. 'Just better not shake my hand or you might get this cold. Can't seem to get rid of it.'

I nodded and shook his hand anyway.

Keith and Nacho were terrific company. It was hot and sticky and while Keith shivered Nacho took off his shirt to reveal a landscape of tattoos. He poured me a large vodka from a jeroboam-sized bottle and told me I could sleep on the two-seater. He took out a guitar and began to play; it seemed everyone could play around here. The brothers were clever and thoughtful and as I fell into a deep, fully clothed sleep on the sofa, with my boots hanging over one arm, a cat on my groin and a chihuahua nestling in my armpit, I was sure we would have had hours of great conversation if only I hadn't drunk that strange green shot about six hours ago.

When I woke up Nacho was asleep in his bedroom and I was relieved to hear that Keith was still alive, the phlegm in his nose and throat rattling elastically as he breathed in and out. I was seriously worried that I might have caught his cold and would have to bear it for the rest of my trip. I was supposed to have left at 9 a.m., intending to average sixty miles an hour in order to arrive in time for the delivery to Mr Ron Zoller's home by 4 p.m. I looked at my watch. It was 11.25. I spat out the cat and heard a yelp as I rose and sat on the dog. I had no idea where I was but I knew that some 400 miles away there was a ten-dollar bill that I was supposed to be following. I put my head in my hands and groaned.

My mobile was ringing somewhere at the bottom of my ruck-sack. Half asleep, I wondered whether a ten-dollar bill could make a call. 'Get off your fat ass!' it would have said. I answered it.

'Hey man! How's it going – where are you?' It was Dean.

'I don't know, but it's somewhere in Hot Springs.'

'What?'

'I'm at Nacho's.'

I heard him laughing down the line.

'That's great,' he said. 'Come over and watch the game with me and the boys. The Razorbacks are playing and we're having a barbecue at Medo's.'

'No, I have to go,' I said. I coughed and remembered I had smoked again last night. 'I should be on my way to St Louis and now I'm going to have to hire a helicopter to have any chance of getting there on time.'

'You got your car?'

Shit. No. I didn't even have my car. It was still at the All Seasons Motel. I was beginning to feel that I wasn't really keeping on top of things.

'OK,' said Dean. 'I'll pick you up in an hour.'

Surely I had blown it this time. The earliest I could possibly set off would be 1 p.m. That meant I could theoretically get to St Louis by eight. Then I would have to find Ron Zoller and, if he was out for the evening, begin following him and IA74407937A around the city – assuming he had not already spent it. I would have to find somewhere to stay and somewhere to leave the car, and I'd heard that some parts of St Louis were worse than Newcastle on a Friday night.

Dean came to pick me up and waved to Nacho and Keith as I said thank you and goodbye to them. It was 12.30 p.m.

'Good news,' he said. 'I've just spoken to Ron – the fantasy football guy – and the bill hasn't arrived. So you can come to the barbecue.'

I twisted and leaned with my back against the car door. He was being far too relaxed about this.

'*That's* what you call good news?' I asked. 'The fact that the ten-dollar bill hasn't arrived is *good news*? The fact that the ten dollars is *missing* is *good news*?'

'Yeah, well, it isn't missing. Remember the lady said it probably wouldn't get there before 4. It isn't there, so you're not late yet.'

I looked at Dean with something close to amazement. I was beginning to understand why I had wasted what probably amounted to months of my life waiting for the start of gigs that had never, ever begun on time. I was witnessing, first-hand, musician time-keeping. This, I thought, is how zoologists must feel in the presence of procreating pandas.

'OK,' I said, wondering if I could push it, 'at what point can we say with absolute certainty that I'm going to be late for the arrival of the ten-dollar bill?'

'That would be 4.01 p.m.'

'And where would I have to be at 4.01 p.m. to be deemed late?'

'At the barbecue with me and the band.'

Oh, fuck it. I offered to make the potato salad and we went to the K-Mart.

It had been some time since I had been in a supermarket and with the dead weight of a hangover on me I found it depressing. The strip lights hurt my eyes, the consumerism my sensibilities. Fat people walked like zombies from aisle to aisle in a silent procession born of habit rather than necessity. Crap junkies, food fixes. I felt sick. My head was swimming and my stomach was in knots worrying about the ten-dollar bill. *Worrying*. About a *piece of paper*. What was happening to me?

Within an hour I was back at Dean's; I didn't seem able to escape. He was standing on one side of the kitchen with tins of beans, ketchup, chillies, brown sugar and all manner of gloopy stuff to make his signature dish – barbecue beans – and I was on the other with potatoes, eggs, gherkins, dill and so on. He didn't have the appearance of a rock god and I didn't look like a respectable member of the Fourth Estate. I was beginning to look like a tramp.

We agreed we would never, ever tell anyone about this little domestic scene.

'You know, I really got into what you're trying to do,' he said to me, wiping his worktop and folding a flowered tea towel into a neat square.

'What do you mean?'

'Hell, just taking off like that. Just doing something wild and crazy. Just you, a backpack and a ten-dollar bill. It takes *cojones* to do something like that. Something you believe in – to follow your dream.'

I was beginning to see where this was going.

'It isn't exactly a dream,' I said.

(Did I tell you to peel the potatoes? You should always peel the potatoes for potato salad. The skin contains lots of vitamins but it gets stuck between your teeth.)

Dean put down his knife and looked at me. 'Well, why you doing it?'

He wasn't the first person to ask this question and I had never been able to come up with a satisfactory answer. Invariably I would say I was bored or curious. I often said, 'Because it's there!' trying hard to sound like Brian Blessed, which meant nothing but got people off my case. Sometimes I would say I was doing it for a bet, which was a lie. I told one man in a bar that I had to follow a ten-dollar bill around the United States of America for thirty days and thirty nights in order to inherit a billion dollars. He believed me.

I stopped chopping the potatoes.

'I think it might have something to do with my dad.'

'What?'

'My father . . .' I felt almost paralysed but couldn't stop talking. I had the strange sensation of feeling relieved and embarrassed at the same time. 'He died a couple of years ago and I took it badly. We were very close. I went off the rails a little. I couldn't do my job and quietly resigned from the newspaper I was working on before they could fire me. It took me more than a year to get over it and I woke up one day and felt better. I wanted to celebrate the fact and I think my dad would have approved.'

I wasn't entirely sure where this came from, but saying it felt cathartic.

'Shit. I'm sorry,' said Dean.

'No, it's fine.' I put a glob of mayonnaise on the potatoes and mixed in a couple of hard-boiled eggs and some lemon juice.

(When you add the chopped gherkins it lifts the whole thing. If you don't like dill, use tarragon.)

'It wasn't the fact that he died – I mean, I felt bereaved but that was normal. It was how. He was the toughest man I'd ever known but he died screaming in agony. Cancer. I had to wrestle him on to his bed ten minutes before he stopped breathing. He didn't want to die. He wanted to get up and he started pulling the tubes and wires out of his body. But we were afraid he would have fallen, so I stopped him. The last day of his life was the only day I was stronger than him. Wrestling him like that, forcing him down when he wanted to get up, played on a loop in my head. I didn't sleep for months. But I got over it. Life's good and if you can't just get up one morning and follow a ten-dollar bill, then what's the point? Can you pass the pepper?'

(Use freshly milled pepper but not too much. You can overdo it and get a bitter taste.)

Dean had become subdued. Through the open French windows I heard a crow and the rustle of dry grass. After a time he said, 'I should have gone to Nashville and I set off one day but then I turned back. If you want to make it in the music business, you have to go to Nashville. It isn't just country any more; it's rock, indy, R&B. It's where you get the exposure and where you learn from other musicians – where you cut your teeth and, if you're lucky, where you're discovered. But I didn't have the balls. I came back. I fell in love and started a family. I earn my living by playing most nights, which means most nights Stephenie is alone. It's always been like that and it's killing us. The band should have toured more, got outside Arkansas, but . . .'

This was the root of the unease I had sensed in Dean. He wanted to be successful but that meant being away from home and family. He was fighting on two fronts and something had to give. Right now, that was his music career. He would fight to keep his family together but he knew he couldn't have both. Whatever he chose to do, it was going to break his heart.

He poured the beans into a baking tray and put tin foil over it. The oven was at 160 °C. I gave him some advice that an old cowboy once gave me – to be careful about adding salt to beans while they're still cooking, because it makes them go hard and brittle.

Dean didn't say any more on the subject of the music business and I felt singularly unqualified to give him any advice about it.

'I think the trick is to decide what your ten-dollar bill means to you before you start following it,' was all I said.

Where's Alexander?

At around 5.15 p.m., just as I was wondering what my punishment would be for not travelling to St Louis (there would inevitably be some cosmic fallout), Ron Zoller called Dean.

Crash Meadows and I had been watching the game and enjoying the barbecue, and everyone had tucked into the food while the Arkansas Razorbacks overcame Texas A&M. Medo's barbecued chicken was the star of the show but the potato salad provided an excuse for the band to speculate on how the English – or, more precisely, Austin Powers – might pronounce the word 'potato'. Think tomato with a p at the front.

While Dean took the call, Daniel told me a story about Medo. Several years earlier, fed up with the music business, Medo had put down his guitar and moved to Memphis, vowing never to play the instrument again.

'We didn't see him for years and then one day I bumped into him in Memphis,' said Daniel. 'I begged him to play but he wouldn't. I stayed there and pleaded with him over and over again to pick up his guitar. I told him it would be a criminal waste of talent if he never played again. He was stubborn and said he'd never do it, never in a million years.

'Then one night a few of us took him out and got him totally drunk. We took him back to his apartment and put a guitar in his hands. He could barely stand up and there he was, looking at this thing as if he kinda remembered holding it but wasn't exactly sure what it was for. He was living in a square block with a courtyard outside and apartments on four sides. We arranged the speakers so they'd play out the windows and into the courtyard, then we switched on the amp, turned it to max and, for the first time in three years, Medo played.

'He played his first chords at 3 a.m. and didn't stop until 6. It was like he was born again. Hundreds of people must have heard him, but we never got a single complaint.'

Dean still had the phone to his ear and was listening to Ron Zoller. He was chewing his bottom lip and had a worried look on his face. I was feeling guilty because I hadn't followed the money. I had broken my own rules and felt fully deserving of any punishment that came my way, as it surely would. But I hadn't quite expected what happened next.

Dean put down the handset.

'The ten dollars,' he said. 'It didn't turn up.'

According to the UPS tracking website, IA74407937A was not delivered because its envelope had been incorrectly addressed. Dean double- and triple-checked with Ron Zoller and established that he had, indeed, addressed it properly. The problem for me was that it was a Saturday, UPS did not deliver on Sundays and Monday was Columbus Day, a public holiday. I had no idea whether its mercurial delivery operatives would be working on that day. All I got when I tried to call the UPS customer service department (whose very name is proof, if ever it was needed, that Americans really do have a highly developed sense of irony) was layer upon layer of cheery recorded messages designed to render callers insane and therefore ineligible to take out a lawsuit against the company.

What, I wondered, did this mean? Was the bill still in the capable hands of UPS? Or did UPS have a Wrongly Addressed Envelope Shredding Department which had obliterated it? Had the company just lost it? Or was it buried in mounds of undelivered mail at some far-off satellite sorting depot? Perhaps the sum of forty-two dollars and twenty-seven cents had not been enough to ensure the swift and safe delivery of something weighing slightly less than the air inside a gnat's anus. Perhaps I should have paid more.

I resolved that UPS stood for Useless Piece of Shit, but I also decided that the acronym applied more to me than to the mail delivery company.

Even Stephenie felt sorry for me. She and Dean invited me to stay with them and I accepted. The odd thing was that although it represented a disastrous turn of events, the failed delivery meant that I was still following the money. Sure, I wasn't moving, but neither, in the ethereal scheme of things, was the bill. It was in limbo – postal no-man's-land – and so long as I set off in the morning I could not possibly be late for its arrival. Either it would turn up on Monday and I would be there and ready to go, or it wouldn't and I would drive my car into the Mississippi.

I was already awake the next morning when Dean burst into the spare room. It was sunny again and I was watching shafts of light turn motes of dust into solid objects.

'Fantastic news, man!' he yelled.

I sat bolt upright. He looked ecstatic.

'What?'

'Stephenie and I are going to get married again!'

I blinked and for a scintilla of a fraction of a nanosecond I was disappointed that the great news had not involved the unexpected arrival of the ten-dollar bill.

Dean and Stephenie were going to remarry. That was, indeed, great news. I perked up, leapt out of bed and shook Dean's hand, shouting my congratulations to Stephenie as she emerged from their bedroom in a robe. We had a celebratory breakfast of eggs, bacon, potatoes and orange juice, during which the happy couple enlisted my help in trying to arrange for them to tie the knot in Paris. I said I would do whatever I could. The temperature rose swiftly and we moved to the veranda, where Stephenie fired off questions to me about the French capital. She was growing more and more excited by the prospect of her wedding. I was happy for them. I could think of nothing more wonderful than to see them in the shadow of the Eiffel Tower, repeating their vows in the presence of Neelah and the brother Dean had not seen since he was five. I thought we might even invite Ernie Schlatter along for the reception.

It was time to go and I began stuffing things into my rucksack, but Dean asked if I would play a little soccer with Neelah. After half an hour, when I began making moves to leave, Dean ushered me into his garage and demonstrated a bizarre and unexpected skill with an Etch A Sketch pad. He could draw anything on it; not just squiggles but real images. At the launch of one of his albums in 2008, Dean had dedicated all his first day's sales and an Etch A Sketch drawing of the *Mona Lisa* to a local children's charity. Someone bought it for 250 dollars. I stood up and said that this time I really did have to go, but he showed me some more of his guitars. Then he made me a sandwich. Then he asked me to hang around while he made me some fresh juice. Then he made me another sandwich.

After some minutes, I set a determined course for the front door. I had money to chase. It is difficult to describe how completely and irrationally sad this was. I jumped into my car mid-sentence and drove away on the cusp of crying. When I looked in my rear-view mirror, Neelah and Stephenie were still waving, but Dean had gone back inside the house.

I hadn't planned my route to St Louis. I had 400 miles to go, I had nowhere to stay once I got there and I knew very little about Ron Zoller.

I knew even less about the whereabouts of the ten-dollar bill.

Part II

Money (1)

According to the US Treasury Department's Bureau for Engraving and Printing, which produces America's paper money, more than 82 million ten-dollar bills were printed during my travels. On average, the BEP rolls out between 25 and 30 million bills of all denominations each day, with a face value in the region of 1 billion dollars. The cost of each bill comes in at just under ten cents, which is pretty good value considering the security features each contains. There is a variety of high-tech devices intended to make American money difficult to counterfeit, although that doesn't stop people trying. The Secret Service – which is responsible for tackling forgery as well as defacement of money – estimates that at any given moment 0.1 per cent of all the money circulating in the US is fake; that's about 780 million dollars. In the UK, the figure is proportionately higher at 0.3 per cent and 13.7 million pounds, and I assume this is because a busy counterfeiting operation can have a bigger impact on a smaller economy. Many years ago, before new security measures were implemented to stymie forgers, I spent a day with a Scotland Yard unit that was dedicated solely to dealing with dollar counterfeiting – a British police service department whose only job was to tackle crime related to the currency of another country. At the time, international police forces had a low opinion of dollar bills and the ease with which they could be copied, but that changed in 2003 with the introduction of bills with far more security features. These were first rolled out with the twenty and extended to the ten in 2006. They include colour-shifting ink, which can be viewed on the bottom right-hand side of the ten-dollar bill, where the number '10' changes colour from copper to green as the bill is tilted. There are also special watermarks, security threads woven into the fabric of the paper and micro-printed characters almost impossible for a forger to duplicate. The bills still do not feature the kind of holograms common in Europe and the jury is out on whether that is a shortcoming on the part of the BEP or a kind of sportsmanship which allows Europeans to feel smug about the flashier euro. British currency has holograms and you used to be able to get six dollars to the pound. Which would you prefer?

The BEP says that 95 per cent of all bills are printed to replace others that have worn out and been withdrawn from circulation for shredding. Bills of all denominations are composed of 75 per cent cotton and 25 per cent linen. The average life of a ten-dollar bill is eighteen months.

On the front of the ten is a portrait of Alexander Hamilton, the first US Secretary of the Treasury and one of the Founding Fathers. He is one of only two figures to grace currency who was not a president; the other is Benjamin Franklin on the hundred. Hamilton was born out of wedlock, the son of a plantation owner, on Nevis in the British West Indies in 1755. Despite his lowly birth, he went on to become a respected soldier and a brilliant lawyer, political philosopher and economist. He is often described by historians as the man who held most sway over George Washington and the formation of the US system of government.

Hamilton was an adulterer and some feel he wielded too much power (others say he abused it). As a non-president, his presence on the ten-dollar bill is not universally welcome, but at least he made it there ahead of Aaron Burr, a presidential candidate in the elections of 1800 who was beaten by Thomas Jefferson thanks to Hamilton's support for the latter. Burr became vice-president but never forgave Hamilton and in 1804 he challenged him to a duel. Mortally wounded, Hamilton died the next day aged just forty-nine.

I decided I liked Hamilton. He was an Anglophile and, to some extent, an underdog who probably experienced feelings of being an outsider. From time to time I found myself taking out a ten-dollar bill and talking to him.

Ron Zoller

(38° 38.381' N, 090° 02.093' W)

It was almost noon when I left Dean but I had already decided there was no need to rush. I still hadn't spoken to Ron Zoller and decided I wouldn't until around mail delivery time the next morning. In the meantime, I was feeling sorry for myself. I kept making friends and then having to leave them. I was homesick and lonely. I suddenly missed my partner, Suzanne, and I wondered why she ever put up with me.

'Darling.'

'Yes, darling.'

'I'm just popping out to America to follow a ten-dollar bill for a month. When I get back, I'll devote rather a lot of time to writing about it, probably at the expense of our time together and to the detriment of our relationship and bank balance, OK?'

'Righto, darling. Pick up some milk on your way back.'

I missed my bed. We have a big, soft bed with unfeasibly fluffy pillows that make you think you are in a pillow-lined womb furnished with central heating. We live in an old factory where someone – children, perhaps – used to make uniforms. You can still see impressions in the wooden floorboards where the machinery used to be. We don't have wallpaper because, apart from the exposed brickwork that forms the boundaries of our home, we don't have any walls. Only the bathroom. The rest of it, brightly lit by enormous windows that look over the City of London, is wide open and cavernous. And I missed it. I missed looking at the Gherkin through the west window and wondering why it wasn't called the Cigar. I missed my old oak desk and the layers of useless crap that I kept on it. I had cuttings on albinos and voodoo, shipwrecks and wild horses, baby kidnappers and mad inventors and I would write about them all one day. It was the football season and I was missing it. I missed Thai and Indian food and black pudding. I missed my friends, even the ones I couldn't stand. I missed selling articles to newspapers and then complaining about how little they paid for them, all shared with long-suffering drunks over pints of Courage Best. Or London Pride. Or Director's. God, how I missed pubs. How I missed the things I took for granted. Cooking. Taking a shower in the middle of the day. Cheese that did not have the consistency of plastic. Clean clothes. Earl Grey tea. Newspapers that had foreign news in them. Television news bulletins that had foreign news in them. Anchor men and women with double chins, thinning hair and bent noses. I think perhaps I missed them the most.

I had been on the road for less than two weeks. In the past I had been on assignment for months on end without thinking about home – it really was rather pathetic. I allowed myself to think I was feeling this way because my journey, and the friendships I was making, had become so intense. Saying goodbye had become regular and difficult and there might have been some truth in that.

I struck out east towards Benton and joined the I-30 on the south-eastern edges of Little Rock before taking the I-40 towards Memphis. When I left Dean's house, the mileage had stood at

1,267. The milometer was spinning fast and after a time the hills and woods around Hot Springs and Little Rock turned into flat prairie, the arrival of which heralded the departure of sunshine. Everything seemed suddenly grey and bleak. I wondered how much of this was down to my mood but later the day did grow prematurely dark. Perhaps I shouldn't have been surprised. After all, it was 10 October.

The journey took much longer than I had expected as I had underestimated the distance to St Louis; I later found it was nearer 460 miles. I was tired and bored. I stopped at truck stop after truck stop just for a change of scenery and to sit for a while with the truckers who did this for a living. There were showers in some and I wondered whether any had washing machines, but I didn't plan to linger that long. Other stops had small lounges where the truckers would sit and watch mindless TV or, more often, the endless streaming sport that bounced, jumped and sprinted its way out of the box. They were insular and when I first joined them I was tentative and smiled the way an outsider might at a clique, but they ignored me. They ignored each other. They were as lonely as I was.

About fifty miles short of Memphis I began to notice cotton crops. I must have seen cotton growing before but I could not remember when. I imagined legions of slaves picking it 200 years ago and more, and I shivered as smoke drifted in from stubble burning to the north. West of Memphis I took the I-55 north and at 5.45 p.m. I crossed the Missouri state line. The road ran almost parallel with the Mississippi, skirting Cape Girardeau and Kentucky to the east and then, as darkness fell, Illinois farther to the north.

At 6 I had more than 200 miles to go and by 9 I decided to stop for the night about forty miles short of St Louis. I figured it would be easier to find accommodation at a truck stop than to drive aimlessly into the city after dark. Up ahead was an intersection at hope-sapping Festus. I would sell my soul, I thought, for a bed one-half as comfortable as my own. I pulled off the interstate and into the floodlights of transport convenience at its junction with Highway 67. ARBY'S, DENNY'S, MCDONALD'S, TACO BELL. A mile or two away I found the Twin Cities Motel, with rooms decked out like log cabins. I registered and turned in for the night, reckoning as I slipped into unconsciousness that my bed at home was almost exactly twice as comfortable as this.

It was Columbus Day when I woke, the day people in America celebrate Christopher's arrival in 1492, though he actually landed on 12 October and when he jumped out of his boat he was not in as much hot water as I was. It was chilly but the chiselled weatherman on TV informed me that 84 degrees was predicted by lunchtime. I rang the local UPS office and listened to a message telling me to dial 1-800-DICK-UPS. I assumed Dick was in charge of lost mail, but I must have misdialled because I got a phone sex line. I tried again with the same result and the promise of some hot action. UPS, I thought, had plumbed new depths.

When I called the first number again I realised the message had advised me to dial 1-800-*PICK*-UPS. This sounded like a sex line too, but it actually got me through to a real human being who was working for the postal company rather than walking the streets. Although, of course, the two aren't mutually exclusive.

'It says here that a correct street number is required for delivery,' said the Real Human Being. 'UPS is attempting to obtain this information.'

'I can tell you exactly where to obtain that information,' I said.

'Thank you, sir. Where would that be?'

'On the envelope.'

'Well, sir, according to our records, an attempt was made to find the address but it didn't exist.'

'Well, the person who lives there has confirmed that the address on the envelope is correct.'

'There's no need to adopt that tone, sir.'

She was right. I was tired and scratchy and hadn't slept well under particularly abrasive bedlinen. I was adopting that tone rather too often, but I couldn't help it in the face of such corporate belligerence. I apologised and we agreed to speak in an hour. At that stage, she could not tell me where the ten-dollar bill was. I went for a coffee but didn't eat anything, even though I hadn't eaten since breakfast the day before. Then I drove into St Louis.

Somewhere on the outskirts of town I took a wrong turn and ended up in a loop on the I-270 before getting back on track with the I-64 heading east into central St Louis. Either side of the highway I could see that the city had green and leafy suburbs, but a high fence stretched the whole length of its approach and partially hid them from my view. In the distance I began to pick out tall buildings shrouded in haze, and then the St Louis Gateway Arch, at 630 feet America's tallest monument, a gargantuan stainless-steel structure built in the 1960s to reinforce the city's claim to be the gateway to the West. If you imagine the McDonald's 'Golden Arches', then take one away and colour the one remaining a matt grey or silver, that is what the St Louis Gateway Arch looks like. An enormous subliminal advertisement for a Big Mac.

I slowed down as Busch Stadium, home of the St Louis Cardinals baseball team, hove into view on my left, its name taken from the Anheuser-Busch corporation, brewer of Budweiser. The company – which makes almost half of all the beer drunk in

America – has its headquarters in the city and, inevitably, its presence touches on every aspect of local life. In a few short minutes, it was to touch on mine too. I pulled off the highway, lost myself in a series of random turns that brought me to some derelict industrial buildings next to the Mississippi and stopped. The river was wide, slow-moving and brown. I watched it for several minutes and felt the way you might if you were alone in a small boat on a vast ocean and a whale's eye suddenly rose out of the water to take a disinterested look at you.

I called UPS again.

This call was much friendlier than the first a) because the Real Human Being had been friendly all along and b) because I had stopped behaving like a pompous fool.

'Sir,' she said in honeyed tones filled with promise, 'we have located your item and it will be delivered by 10.30 this morning. The delivery man on Saturday was a temp and couldn't find the address. The regular guy has it now and he knows exactly where to go.'

I could have cried. I punched the air silently and thanked her for being so efficient and so kind.

I rang Ron Zoller at 9.20 a.m. to introduce myself and ask whether he was likely to be home until 10.30. If not, I would have another day kicking my heels while, unsigned for, the bill would be returned to the UPS depot and I would have nothing to do but dial 1-800-DICK-UPS all day. He answered, sounding very serious and more than a little puzzled. Dean *had* explained what was going on, hadn't he?

'Sure,' he said. He had a deep and authoritative voice and I felt a bit scared of him. 'It's just a little unusual is all. And I don't have to wait until 10.30. It just arrived. It's here.'

Just arrived? Arrived, just now? Just now – arrived?

'Yeah. It has some red markings in the corner. Did you do that? You know, some people say that it's illegal to mark money.'

I imagined for a moment that he had already called the Secret Service and there was a team of men in dark suits in his house, all wearing headphones and moving their hands in a circular motion to encourage him to keep me talking.

'We goddim! He's on the corner of Breadstick and Vine.'

And I would be arrested and thrown into prison with Mr Big and raped in the showers until I agreed to join the Bloods or the Crips. And I wondered whether any of Tookie Williams's gang would have read my interview with him and think I was a righteous dude and intervene on my behalf, commissioning a tattoo for my neck and taking me into his crew in return for unquestioned loyalty and a commitment to write all the prisoners' letters on B Wing.

I badly needed some sleep.

After a long silence, Ron said, 'You'll have to come to work with me. I'm leaving now. Meet me at Schmucks, it's at the mall, Clayton and Lindberg off Highway 40. I'm in a silver Pontiac.'

So I headed off to Schmucks, which I thought was appropriate, because I had felt like one for days now.

My first impressions of the city were very positive. It had lots of old red-brick colonial buildings and smart green municipal spaces, but I didn't have time to study them. I was in the wrong part of town and I needed to scramble in case Ron grew bored and drove off in his Pontiac.

It took me almost forty minutes to find him and when I did I was relieved. He was not scary at all. His deep voice had led me to expect a sharp ad exec or lawyer, someone ridiculously handsome and aloof, but he wasn't like that. He was in his thirties, about five foot nine, with short cropped hair and a goatee beard. He wore a grey T-shirt, white jeans and boots. He had a cheerful, welcoming face and when he held out his hand for me to shake, I saw in his eye a glint that made me think of Richard Dreyfus playing naughty or drunk or both. He reached into his wallet and brought out a ten-dollar bill.

'This what all the fuss is about?' he asked, holding it up.

I leaned forward and read the serial number: IA74407937A.

'Yes,' I said in a low voice. A strange calm descended on me. 'It is. I'm so very pleased to meet you.' And I shook his hand like a politician in a marginal.

I soon found out that Ron did not work at Schmucks, nor was there a place of that name. It was a Midwestern supermarket chain called Schnucks that I instantly decided was far superior to the food outlets I had encountered so far. It specialised in fresh and exotic foods which reflected regional tastes influenced to a large extent by the influx of European migrants – not least the French, who founded St Louis in 1764. It had a great deli counter, which is where Ron led me. He was picking up burgers for him and a workmate and he ordered one for me, too. With my sense of relief at finding the bill suddenly came hunger. Ron insisted on paying at the checkout and I thought it would be a shame if he and I and the ten-dollar bill parted company so quickly; he seemed like a nice guy. But he paid with a credit card, looked at his wristwatch and strode back to his car with me in hot pursuit. He was going to work, but didn't say where that was. Given that we were in St Louis and armed with some of the most attractive beefburgers in Christendom, I was hoping he would turn out to be the chief taster at the Budweiser brewery.

But his job was much more interesting than that.

During the journey to Ron's workplace I allowed myself to think of how close I had come to disaster. An inexperienced postal worker, an incorrect zip code and that would have been it. Nice try, no cigar. I had been lucky. I was so full of nervous energy that my hair touched the roof of the car as I followed. I would make sure I never lost track of the ten-dollar bill again. I would stick to Ron like a needy limpet.

We were still on the edge of town when the Pontiac suddenly turned right off the highway and down an unmarked track that wound past mature trees and a small creek. I was entertaining myself with the thought that perhaps my quarry was an inner-city lumberjack when we rounded a bend and something very strange happened. I found myself in the grounds of a stately home and I was in England and aged ten years old again. For a few moments, until I managed to gain some kind of fleeting orientation, I was on one of a dozen school trips that had taken me to Tatton Hall or Levens or any number of vainglorious piles from the eighteenth and nineteenth centuries. Central to this impression was a magnificent greystone house, the style of which was difficult to pinpoint but which brought to mind the words 'Gothic' and 'Germanic'. It was by no means a *Schloss*, but whoever built it had intended for it to endure. It was sixty or seventy yards long with grey gabled roofs. The tops of its doors and windows were arched, allowing for a misleading impression of great age, and there were black wooden shutters that dominated the windows and lent the whole building an air of regimentation and mild foreboding.

Ron led me through some outbuildings to the rear of the house and I stopped, my breath completely taken away. First, I realised that this must be regarded as the front of the house if its true grandeur were to be fully appreciated, because its doors opened on to flat lawns which reminded me of a miniature version of those outside Chatsworth House in Derbyshire. Second, as if Lancelot 'Capability' Brown himself had worked here, I saw that the gardens gave way to sweeping lawns descending like the nape of a horse's neck to a wide ornamental lake and a working fountain; its spray bent the late-morning light into brilliant splinters of primary colour. All of it – the craggy walls, the grey slate roofs, the pointing between the stone bricks, the tall and precarious chimney stacks, the wrought-iron balconies and wooden casement windows, no longer arched on this side, but with pediments – had been immaculately restored.

It was approaching noon and the sun was high now in a clear blue sky. Looking towards the lake, I saw maple and walnut trees, cedar, pine and oak. Leaves were turning but there was more than enough cover to blanket the sound of busy roads that could not possibly be far away. All I could hear was birdsong and I felt strangely flummoxed.

I turned to see Ron grinning, his face flushed.

'Incredible, huh?'

I nodded. 'I don't know where to start. What *is* this place? Who built it? Where exactly are we – is this still St Louis?'

'Hell, yeah. We're in Huntleigh. The house was built by Percy J. Orthwein, whose wife, Clara, was part of the Busch brewing family. It used to be owned by Marilyn Schnuck – it was her family's store that just made our burgers – and now Marc Bulger, the Baltimore Ravens quarterback, he lives here.'

It took me a while to take all of this in. The house had its roots in the success of Budweiser. It had been occupied by a member of the Schnuck family. And now a National Football League quarterback, the American football equivalent of Wayne Rooney or David Beckham, was the incumbent. I looked at Ron as if to say, *Pull the other one*, but he just smiled and beckoned me into one of the outbuildings. Surely he could not be serious?

Inside, shaded from the sun, was a big man with lumpen hands and smiling eyes. I wasn't surprised when Ron told me this man was from Irish stock, but when he said his name was Sean 'Paddy' McGinty – I mean, Paddy McGinty! – and the Irishman nodded in my direction, I decided they were clearly playing me for a fool. In any normal situation I would have smiled and walked out – I don't like being the butt of a joke – but I had to stick with the ten dollars. I had anticipated someone using it to lock me into a given – and possibly unpleasant – situation. Putting my balls in a vice, as Paul might have said. But winding me up about where I was and what was going on was leaving me feeling hopelessly out of sorts. Until now I had encountered nothing but kindness. Not for the first time, I felt like the most stupid guy in town.

'Oh, come on,' I said. 'Budweiser family? NFL quarterback? You're having me on.'

Ron held out one of the burgers he had bought and passed me a cold beer.

'Swear to God,' he said. 'Marc bought this place four years ago and Sean and I have been working on it ever since. Best job in the world. Marc is one of my footballing heroes and here we are, fixing up his home. Look around. Every day we get to come out here and enjoy this. It's a labour of love and, between you and me, I hope the job never ends. This is a beautiful house and Marc treats it with respect. Everything we do, we only use the finest materials and we work from the original plans. Sometimes I have to pinch myself when I wake up.'

I looked back at the house. It was locked today and a swimming pool where 'Capability' Brown might have sited a duck pond was covered in blue plastic.

I turned to face Ron and Sean and realised I was being paranoid and far too cynical. They were telling the truth. I have rarely seen two people looking so happy and so proud. Sean took a huge bite

on his burger and nodded his head in Ron's direction, as if to say,
He knows what he's talking about.

The Orthwein house had indeed been built by Percy J.
Orthwein between 1926 and 1929. When I returned to England
I found a posting about the sale of the house – before Marc Bulger
had bought it – on *St Louis Style*, a website run by local blogger
Ted Wight. 'It's an amazing house,' he told me over the phone.
'It used to be owned by Marilyn Schnuck and I think she liked
pink. I went there once for a baby shower and, well, there was
an awful lot of pink. The best part, though, was the basement.
It was all decked out like a kind of German *Bierkeller*, with a bar
and big barrels. I shouldn't have been surprised – it was built by
a brewing family after all – but, well, I was.'

Ted told me he thought there were French influences behind
the design but I think it was more likely that Percy would have
commissioned a building to please August A. Busch, son of
Adolphus Busch, who founded the beer empire. Adolphus left
Germany in 1857 and began brewing Budweiser in St Louis in
1876. Percy, president of an advertising company, had married
August's daughter, so building a house that reminded your beer-
making squazillionaire father-in-law of the motherland might
reasonably be seen as a shrewd move.

The architects of the house were Raymond E. Maritz and W.
Ridgely Young, but I discovered that the firm was no longer in
business so I could not mine its archives for more information.
Instead, Ted offered to call David Orthwein, Percy's grandson, to
see whether he would tell me a little more about the place. David
didn't want to be interviewed, but through Ted he told me that
the house was English-inspired and had been much loved by the
family. He recalled long summer days there as a boy and even fox
hunts attended by the upper echelons of St Louis society.

I asked Ted to tell David that it was being restored with genuine love and care by two men who took the utmost pride in their work. I was hoping that maybe David would see to it that Ron and Sean got a case of beer.

The Orthwein Kidnapping

The Orthwein house kept giving up secrets, the most dramatic, according to Ron, being the kidnapping of young Adolphus Busch Orthwein, Percy's thirteen-year-old son, on 31 December 1930. The boy was snatched from a chauffeur-driven car on the way to a New Year's fete. This was front-page news in almost every newspaper in the United States, many of them running this dispatch from the Associated Press dated 1 January 1931:

A widespread search was under way today for Adolphus Busch Orthwein, 13 year old grandson of August A. Busch, president of Anheuser-Busch Inc., and great grandson of the late Adolphus Busch, millionaire brewer, who was kidnapped last night by an armed negro. The boy, son of Mr and Mrs Percy J Orthwein, was kidnapped in exclusive Huntleigh Village about 7.30pm yesterday as the family chauffeur, Roy Yowell, was taking him to a New Year's Eve party at the home of August A. Busch at Grant's Farm. Huntleigh Village is in St Louis County.

'I left the house with Adolphus beside me in the car,' Yowell said. 'I drove down the private drive towards

Lindbergh Boulevard. A negro, standing at the left of the road, tried to wave me down but I didn't stop. He then climbed on a trunk on the back of the limousine and pointed a revolver at me. I could see through the rear window.

'As I halted the machine, he climbed down from the trunk, got on the running board and ordered me to give him what I had and give him the seat. I handed over [dollar amount illegible] and then he motioned me out of the way. Bub (the chauffeur's nickname for the boy) made no outcry. I said, 'Come along Bub' as I saw the negro was going to take the car, but he refused to let the boy get out of the car. He then jumped into the driver's seat, took the wheel and drove rapidly away.'

Witnesses later told police they saw the kidnapper bundle the boy into a smaller car a short distance away and, sure enough, the Orthwein limousine was found there.

The report continued, with some casual prejudice:

Friends of the family said they could offer no possible motive for the abduction other than ransom. They said the Orthweins had not employed any negroes for some time.

The Orthwein boy, an attractive youngster, is a skilled horseman for his age. He has won several prizes at shows. At his school he was 'an average boy in every respect', according to Principal Robert B. Thompson. His father is vice-president of an advertising agency, a member of the exclusive Racquet Club and a graduate of Yale. His mother was Clara Busch.

Mr and Mrs Orthwein were preparing to receive guests when they learned of the kidnapping. Mrs Orthwein became hysterical and today is under the care of a physician. August A. Busch, after a brief visit to the Orthwein home, went to police headquarters where he conferred with the Chief of Police and Chief of Detectives.

These were days when a ransom was often paid and successfully collected. One was offered by the Orthweins but the involvement of three remarkable men made its payment unnecessary.

The first was Pearl Abernathy, a real estate agent and a man of great moral fortitude in the face of what was about to become public disgrace for his family. He found out that his son, Charles, had kidnapped the boy and on 1 January he telephoned Percy Orthwein. In a later round-up of the case, *Time* magazine reported:

Next day Father Orthwein received a call from one Pearl Abernathy, negro realtor, who said: 'I know where your son is and I will trade your boy for mine.' Pearl was the father of the kidnapper, Charles Abernathy, 28, himself father of seven children.

Cried Mr Orthwein: 'For God's sake, is he alive?'

'I don't know,' said the negro, 'but if your boy is dead, I vow to kill mine in your presence.'

Mr Orthwein having agreed not to prosecute Charles Abernathy, both sons returned from a distant house. But local police, no party to the agreement, arrested Pearl Abernathy and sought Charles Abernathy, who fled.

Step forward Harry Thompson Brundidge, a reporter with the *St Louis Star*, the sort of hack you would be forgiven for believing existed only in gumshoe-style *film noir* – except that

Brundidge was the real deal, closing down organised crime operations, identifying murderers and nailing bent cops. Once, when pointing the finger at corrupt journalists in Chicago, Brundidge claimed to have travelled to Florida to ask Al Capone how many reporters he had on his payroll. Capone denied the interview ever took place but according to the reporter's account in the *St Louis Star* the meeting went like this:

> Brundidge: How many newspapermen have you had on your payroll?
>
> Capone (after a pause, a shrug): Plenty.
>
> Suddenly [Capone] leaned over, put his left arm around my shoulders and with typical Latin affection squeezed me and said: 'Listen Harry, I like your face. Let me give you a hot tip: lay off Chicago and the money hungry reporters. No one man will ever realise just how big it is, so lay off . . . They'll make a monkey out of you. No matter what dope you give that grand jury, the boys will prove you're a liar and a faker. You'll get a trimming!'

Many of his contemporaries believed Brundidge made up the interview, but he stood by it. What they could not take away from him was what he achieved in the Orthwein case. As the *Time* report says, Adolphus was returned unharmed to his family once Pearl Abernathy had an assurance (worthless, as it turned out) that his son would not be prosecuted. But that wasn't enough for Brundidge; he tracked down Charles Abernathy to Kansas City and ran a report with a front-page picture of the room where Adolphus had been held captive. Within two days he had extracted a full confession from Charles Abernathy and led police to him. The reporter got much deserved praise for his part in the case, but it took eight years for the role of a third, unsung, hero to emerge.

Ira L. Cooper had been one of the first two African-Americans to be recruited by the St Louis Police Department. That was back in 1907 and he had risen through the ranks to become the first black sergeant in the department in 1923, and then its first black lieutenant in 1930. When he died in February 1939, his fellow officers revealed for the first time that he had played a vital role in the recovery of the Orthwein boy. Cooper had been born in Mexico and on his death the *Mexico Weekly Ledger* ran a lengthy obituary which described numerous acts of bravery and undercover heroism:

Time and again Lieut. Cooper co-operated with local officers in solving local crimes. He seldom appeared in these cases, preferring to work behind the scenes. He was one of the twelve police officers in the world, one of only four in the United States and the only member of his race to have been given the 'Scotland Yard card'. This recognition was presented by the famous English police department only to crime investigators whose records were of such outstanding importance to merit such recognition.

One year he won the St Louis medal offered for the outstanding deed of bravery of the year. When Li Hung Chang, Chinese Ambassador to the United States, attended the St Louis World's Fair, some pickpocket stole his watch, a valued heirloom. Lieut. Cooper succeeded in securing the return of the highly prized watch. In appreciation of this success, regardless of a substantial reward, Lieut. Cooper has received each year a large carton of rare tea from the Ambassador.

Lieut. Cooper's life was more interesting than any piece of detective fiction you can buy. Not so many years ago, with a cringing criminal white man, sought by a mob, behind him, Lieut. Cooper alone held off a big crowd seeking to lynch the white criminal until police reserves came to his relief.

Most importantly for our interest in the Orthwein case, the obituary reveals, almost in passing:

His ability to lend a sympathetic ear to gossipy confidences of his own race and his quiet, unassuming manner enabled Cooper to pick up information on important cases, which subsequently earned him the reputation as one of the leading detectives on the force. In such a manner, he learned that Pearl Abernathy, negro real estate dealer, was the father of Charles Abernathy, who kidnapped Adolphus Busch Orthwein . . .

Because county authorities were in charge of the investigation, Cooper's role in the case was never made public, but officers last night recalled it was Cooper who went to the elder Abernathy and persuaded him to telephone the Orthweins and promise to return the Orthwein boy. Later, Charles Abernathy was captured in Kansas City and was convicted.

I found it sad that Ira L. Cooper had not received the credit he deserved in the Orthwein kidnapping case, but also uplifting that his skills and talents had been appreciated by the St Louis force such a long time ago. There was certainly routine and institutional prejudice at the time he was appointed – black officers in St

Louis, for example, were not allowed to wear uniforms until 1921 – but ultimately Cooper flourished in a meritocracy. It might seem impressive that the first black police officer in the UK was PC John Kent, who walked a beat in Carlisle as long ago as 1837, but that appears to have been a fluke. The next black officer to be appointed in Britain was Norwell Roberts, by the Metropolitan Police, 130 years later. It was not until the appointment of Mike Fuller to the Kent Constabulary in 2003 that Britain had its first black police chief.

I decided it was time I left Ron and Sean to their work. Ron would have no opportunity to spend the money until later that night when, he said, he would be taking me out for dinner, so I jumped in my car, took another breathless look at the Orthwein house and headed for downtown St Louis.

Not for the first time or the last, I had to decide whether to book a room. If I did and the ten dollars were passed to somebody leaving town, then it was a waste of money and – if I left my gear in the room – an added complication. I was too tired to make a decision so I drove down to the Mississippi and parked at Laclede's Landing, a cobblestoned riverfront district named after Pierre Laclede Liguest, who founded a trading post on the river in 1764 and named it St Louis after King Louis IX of France. Here warehousing that once stored tobacco, furs, food and alcohol now housed restaurants, bars, theatres, hotels and shops. I looked at smiling groups of people enjoying lunch and was mildly pleased to see the value they still put on tobacco, furs, food and alcohol.

St Louis' early history as a frontier town attracting the brave, the smart and the foolish fascinated me. The ebb and flow of its fortunes as the region passed from French to Spanish to American control threw up heroes and villains in equal measure. This was the America of steamboats, trappers and traders rather than wagons, farmers and cowboys. As every American schoolchild will tell you, it was from here that America's greatest adventuring heroes – Meriweather Lewis and William Clark – set off to explore the West in May 1804. Lewis and Clark were tasked by President Thomas Jefferson to travel to the Pacific Ocean, map their journey, find out what and who inhabited the lands between, collect plant specimens and, if they could, find a navigable waterway across the continent, the Northwest Passage that had eluded our friends Marquette and Joliet on their Mississippi journey. Travelling with a team of around thirty trained men, they followed the route of the Missouri River, traversed the Rocky Mountains and made it to the Pacific and back again in just over two years. Theirs was a remarkable achievement; they prepared the way for expansion to the West and established peaceful relations with more than two dozen indigenous tribes, without whose help the expedition would probably have failed. They did not, however, find the Northwest Passage, which wasn't discovered until the early part of the twentieth century way up in the Arctic and was navigable only with the help of an ice breaker.

I returned to my car and as I drove around the city I became more interested in the fortunes of St Louis in its recent past. From its founding until 1830 the city's population grew slowly to around 5,000 people. Over the next century, however, its significance as a port and growing industrial centre attracted waves of immigrants – largely from Germany and Ireland – and the population exploded to 575,000 by 1900, reaching its peak of 856,000 by 1950. And since then it has been in decline. At the last census, in 2010, the population was put at 319,000 or 8.3 per cent lower than the previous count ten years earlier. I was reminded of Lebanon and its shrinking fortunes, but that was different. That was a farming community; this had been a bustling city.

I drove up and down Market Street, Pine and Chestnut, and along 4th Street, Tucker and Boulevard. Then I parked and walked and walked. I liked the feel of St Louis – it had age and presence – but it also felt moribund and lacking in confidence. As the day wore on, I went to the foot of the Gateway Arch and craned my neck to take in its scale, feeling its smoothness and solidity. It really was quite remarkable. I walked back down Walnut Street past the court buildings and City Hall and by the time I reached my car it felt as if the city was emptying. Night flight. I decided to check into a hotel.

Ron lived in Caseyville, which was over the Mississippi to the east and so I headed across the Poplar Street Bridge and drove until I found a Motel 6 at a characterless intersection in Collinsville, next to Caseyville. The room I was given was clean but bland. I looked around my bed at walls decorated so as not to interest or offend guests; the pictures were probably bought by the case. Outside, the day had turned grey and I could have been anywhere. I sat on the bed and looked at my watch.

Ron would not be finishing work for a while and we had made no plans to meet. If he found the need to spend the ten dollars on his way home he had promised he would call me and now that I knew my way around, I could be there in minutes. In the meantime, I noticed the room had a microwave oven. I washed a pair of socks and underpants, wrung them out as much as I could and put them in the microwave. I knew this was a stupid thing to do but I was bored. The oven filled with steam and I lost my nerve. When I pulled out the socks they had shrunk. I had forgotten they were for hiking and contained man-made fibres.

I had melted the plastic in them. I sighed, threw them in the bin and went outside for a smoke. It was safe to say that I had started smoking again. I watched the traffic pass by and made small talk with the girl on reception. She told me her boyfriend was English and had grown up in a place called St Helens on Merseyside, where I had lived as a child. I smiled and said, 'Wow. Small world.' I didn't have the heart to tell her what a disappointing little town St Helens was.

That night Ron and his wife, Sandy, took me to a bar and we had a pleasant dinner. They were excellent company and I was intensely grateful that they had decided to include me in their plans. The way I was feeling, a night alone at the Motel 6 would have seemed like rock bottom. Ron was an American football nut – hence the fantasy football league – but he was keen to learn about English football too, which is unusual for an American sports fan. Those who did not follow soccer usually disliked it intensely. He had grown up in Salem, the state capital of Oregon, but had moved around more than most, finding jobs in southern Oregon, New York, Biloxi, Mississippi, Westminster, California, Cape Girardeau and Missouri, before settling in St Louis. At first, I had imagined Ron to be a tad formal, but he wasn't. He had a terrific sense of humour and constantly seemed on the lookout for harmless mischief. Add to that a passion for talking about sport and politics and I felt that I had found something of a soulmate. We shared an interest in beer and while Sandy probably grew increasingly bored – though wonderfully stoic – Ron and I grew increasingly loud.

Ron's team was the Oakland Raiders, but his boss – Marc Bulger – had played for the St Louis Rams between 2000 and 2009 and was regarded as one of the team's all-time great quarterbacks (he was certainly one of its best paid, at more than 10 million dollars a year). Ron had watched him from the stands and then met him face to face at the Orthwein house.

'Meeting your heroes is a dangerous thing to do,' he said. 'They have a habit of disappointing you, but Marc was the opposite of that. He amazes us almost every time we meet him. If we're at the house demolishing a wall, he'll pick up the biggest hammer and join us in our work. At first, we thought he was just trying to humour us, but when it became normal we realised he wasn't. And he never talks down to us.

'There was one night when he was holding a birthday celebration in town and all the city's bigshots were there. But I was late and he noticed Sandy was on her own and feeling embarrassed by it all. He excused himself from his guests and went over and talked to her, making her feel comfortable until I arrived. That was typical of the man.

'It reached a point where Sean and I would sometimes rib him about joining in our work and one day we were installing some plumbing in a bathroom and he was messing it up. We were joking with him and suddenly he said, "OK, I'm not very good at your job, now let's see if you can do mine." He began drawing football plays on the wall and we just froze. In American football, each player has to know exactly which moves to make and where to be for each play called out by the quarterback, but the quarterback has to know all the moves for every single player on the team. The plays were so complex that we just shut up, amazed. It was a fantastic insight into the mind of a quarterback and I suppose we felt privileged to see it.'

I tried to imagine Premiership footballers behaving like this, being so kind, so intelligent and considerate, but decided I would need an imagination much more powerful than the one I possessed.

Ron asked for the check and insisted on paying. He did it

with plastic and the ten stayed in his wallet. I left a cash tip and we made our way to the door. Outside, rain was coming down in torrents.

A smiling Sandy drove us home as Ron and I argued about the evils of money in sport. They dropped me off at the Motel 6 and Ron said he would call when he planned to spend the money. I stood in the rain for a while, my mouth open, swallowing deeply and hoping that I might freshen up, but all I managed to do was resurrect the smell of damp dog and with it memories of Ray and Clarence, Nacho, Majick and Dean.

Chum and Cake
(38° 35.460' N, 090° 20.452' W)

M arc Bulger did not want to talk to me. Ron telephoned
to say this the next morning. I looked at my watch. I had
slept for eight hours.

Pulling myself upright in bed, I remembered that I had
asked Ron to request an interview, not to talk about football but
about the Orthwein house and architecture in general. Typically,
quarterbacks are intelligent people and so I thought this might
appeal to Bulger – an interview with a journalist that was not
about football – but I suspect he thought I was slightly unhinged.
I would probably wait until he showed me some original cornicing
in a vestibule and pull a knife on him. Another kidnapping at the
Orthwein house.

I reached for my microwaved underpants and felt a twinge of
satisfaction. They were clean and dry. What a terrific start to the
day.

'Thanks for trying,' I said. 'You spending the money today?'

'That's for me to know . . .' He began laughing like a maniac
and put down the phone.

I wasn't sure whether I should have been alarmed by this.
After some initial reticence, Ron had become a great supporter

of my quest to follow the money and he wanted me to succeed, but he had asked me the night before what I would like him to do with it. In accordance with the rules, I told him that it was up to him and when he began discussing options I put my fingers in my ears and shouted, 'Lalalalalalalalalalala . . .' This was possibly the intellectual low point of the evening. My real concern was that Ron was cooking up something special and I didn't want him to do that. If normally he would have spent the ten dollars on a haircut, then that is what I would have preferred. But what could I do?

I showered and luxuriated in the feel of fresh underwear next to my skin. My jeans were leaning upright against a wall and I cracked my way into them and pulled a bedraggled T-shirt from my rucksack. I shook clouds of dust from my jumper and pulled it over my head before reaching for my socks. I was sure they would have held water if I had put them to the test.

It was cloudy with a wind chill outside but I had only ten yards to walk to a Denny's. I was famished and ordered fried eggs, hash browns, bacon, mushrooms, toast, apple juice and endless cups of coffee.

My spirits had risen, but within a couple of hours they began to fall again. I drove into St Louis but couldn't relax. I might receive a call at any moment to say Ron was spending the money. The sun peeked from behind grey clouds and the temperature rose rapidly. I went back to the motel and washed some more clothes with the intention of drying them in the car *à la* Hot Springs, but this time I would leave a window open. I packed again and realised how much I had come to loathe this process and the act of checking and double-checking that I had not lost my journals, my computer, my camera, their chargers, their cables and memory sticks. And each time I filled my rucksack it felt heavier.

I checked out, telling the girl at reception that she really should visit St Helens, and sat in the car feeling out of control. All along I had thought the existential nature of my journey was its most appealing feature. I was living from moment to moment, milking it, and my choices were taken from me. I went where the bill went. Now I was beginning to see that the burden of making choices had been removed but not the consequences of the choices made for me by the ten-dollar bill itself. Or, more accurately, by its carriers. (Was I endowing it with life? Monetary anthropomorphism?) I felt powerless to make decisions. Not where I went, when I could lie down, take a bath, or even go for a walk. I needed to be ready to move at all times. Today, made nervous by Ron's phone call, all I could do was sit and wait in my car. I put on a Crash Meadows CD and closed my eyes. The hum of traffic at the Collinsville interchange was like a lullaby and I fell asleep.

The phone rang. It was Ron and he was cackling.

'Hey, man, you're going to have some fun!'

Oh, God. I was afraid of this. Fun.

'What do you mean?'

'OK, well, there's this radio show hosted by a guy called Dave Glover on 971talk.com radio and he's really funny and, well, I'm going to buy one of his compilation CDs with the ten dollars and I've spoken to one of his producers and told them about you. If it works out, then I'm going to suggest that Dave asks all his listeners what he should spend the money on – and then you can follow it!'

I sat in silence. This was in danger of becoming a circus. I liked Ron enormously but this was not what I'd had in mind when I set out to follow the money. This would clearly not be a journey that the bill would have made had I not been following it. I wanted to implore him not to do this, but that would be a breach of my own rules. I found myself asking again, What could I do? How could I change my fate? What, I wondered, would Sartre have done? It didn't take long to decide. He'd have had a drink.

I went to a bar that had Wi-Fi and looked up the show on the Internet. It was consistently at the top of the St Louis radio ratings and seemed to be a mix of comedy, serious discussion, celebrity interviews and japes. Listeners were divided over whether much of this was juvenile or brilliantly hilarious, but at least it wasn't the Mancow. The show began at 4 p.m. and I listened online with the dread expectation that at any moment Dave would tell his audience about a ten-dollar bill he had acquired and the strange man who was following it.

'Hey, we got Bubba on Line One. Hello, Bubba, and what do you want to talk about today?'

'Hi, Dave, first-time caller. Love the show.'

'Thanks, Bubba – we know there are other radio stations out there.'

'Well, Dave, it's about that ten-dollar-bill competition you got going there. I reckon you should spend the money at a brothel and then the Limey could spend some time hangin' with the crack hoes.'

'That's an imaginative idea, Bubba – are you suggesting I frequent houses of ill-repute?'

(Studio laughter.)

'On Line . . . hey, we got a joker here, folks. George Washington on Two. George Washington? That the best you can do, George?'

(Studio laugher.)

'Well, Dave, if you were married to my wife, you'd use a false name too.'

'We don't do wife jokes here, George. Line Three – Barbie. Well, hello, Barbie – you blonde and beautiful?'

'That's what they say, Dave.'

'Well, what can we do for you today, beautiful?'

'It's about the ten-dollar guy. I have a friend who makes shark chum. Why don't you buy some shark chum, Dave? Then the ten-dollar-bill guy could help my friend grind up the chum for a while – they use rotten herring and mackerel and blood from my daddy's slaughterhouse. My daddy slaughters pigs, Dave.'

(Sound of a hooter and fire tender bells.)

'That's a doozy, Barbie! OK, gang, put that one on the YES pile. Have a great day, Barbie. Who's on Line Seven?'

'Hey, Dave, it's di Angelo.'

'Hey, di Angelo, what's up?'

'The ten dollars, Dave. Can't you donate it to a leper colony?'

(Hooters, alarm bells . . .)

But none of this happened.

I rang Ron.

'The producer didn't even call me back,' he said, crestfallen. 'Wanna go for a beer tonight?'

I checked back into the Motel 6, made up some stories about St Helens to entertain the receptionist, and went out with Ron to a sports bar at Fairview Heights. The highlight of the evening was the appearance of a man in a kilt. I asked whether he was wearing it in the traditional fashion and he knew exactly what I meant. He hoisted it up and showed the bar his penis.

Ron still had not spent the ten dollars.

All I could think of when I woke on 13 October was the film *Groundhog Day*. I felt as if I were caught in a loop and couldn't get out of it. I had breakfast at Denny's again, packed again, checked out again, described the aesthetic and architectural beauty of St Helens at reception again, and sat in my car. Again. It had been cold last night and I woke with a stiff neck and a headache. I had bags under my eyes and reddened beer cheeks. No sane person would let me follow them in this state.

The phone rang. It was Ron.

'Hey, man, you ready to roll?'

I croaked yes. Ron told me to meet him at a particular café in Webster Groves, ten miles south-west of the city, and I headed off. We sat outside at first but it was too cold and so headed back into the warmth of the café. After a short interval a tall, slim man with spiky hair and spectacles walked in and surveyed the room as if looking for someone.

Ron shouted, 'Syd?', and the two shook hands.

Syd Rodway was the musician husband of Erin Bode, a local singer who was making waves in the Midwest and whose voice had captured Ron's heart. Ron had emailed Erin's band through their website to ask how he could get hold of an early copy of their latest CD, *Photograph*, which was to be released the following month. Syd had replied this morning, saying Ron could buy one personally if he would come to this café at this time. I found it reassuring that even as online digital music sales were booming, musicians were still prepared to sell CDs out of the boot of a car. I bought Syd a coffee while Ron rummaged in his wallet, pulling out a ten and a five. The ten was IA74407937A. I handed Syd his coffee and shifted in my seat as Ron explained to him that I came with the money. It was 11.15 and there was a churning sensation in my stomach, like orange juice on milk. Ron would soon be gone and uncertainty would return.

He got up and shook my hand.

'Gotta go to work,' he said.

I grinned and we hugged. He had been such good company. I hadn't laughed so much in years.

'Would you have spent the money like this if I hadn't been here?' I asked.

'Yes, swear to God. You'll believe me when you hear her voice.' He paused before turning and said, 'You keep in touch.'

Syd watched this love-in with something approaching bemusement. He was forty and, in common with Erin and other members of her band, had been classically trained at Webster University's Community School of Music nearby. They performed a mix of jazz and folk – Syd said Joni Mitchell meets Paul Simon – but it was Erin's voice that people were talking about.

'It's calm and clear,' said Syd. He was serious and intense and I felt obliged to maintain eye contact the whole time he spoke. 'People say it's angelic. Our relationship aside, she really moves me when she sings.'

Unexpectedly, Syd asked me whether I knew Danny Baker, the BBC broadcaster. I said I knew of him but we had never met. Syd explained that someone had played their music for Baker, who immediately fell in love with it and featured it every day for a week on his BBC London show before interviewing Erin by phone.

'I think he might be our biggest fan,' Syd said, and smiled.

But the band had not made a breakthrough in either Britain or the wider US, something which, once I'd had a chance to listen to the music, I found difficult to understand. Erin did indeed have the voice of an angel and her band members were highly accomplished musicians. Unfortunately for me, Erin was out of town and the band had no gigs planned. Only days earlier they had performed for 4,000 people at an open-air festival not far from where we were drinking our coffee.

Syd and I chatted and after a while we moved to Cyrano's Cafe, where the band sometimes played and which he told me was renowned for its desserts. The café was situated opposite the Webster Groves Opera Theatre and itself had the feel of an art space, with wide windows, mosaics on the walls, concrete floors and wooden tables. Syd knew the proprietor, Charlie Downs, and told him about my mission. Charlie was tanned and always seemed to be laughing. He struck me as something of a free spirit and he immediately chuckled at the idea of randomly following money around the country. Within seconds he began hovering around our table and calling for the most exotic and dangerous-looking desserts I had ever seen, all made by Charlie's wife, Carolyn.

'Try this,' he kept saying, 'and this . . .'

We had caramel brioche bread pudding with cherry bourbon sauce, key lime pie, peach melba, carrot cake and a chocolate gateau topped with more whipped cream than I had ever seen in one room.

When we were finished and I asked for the check Charlie wouldn't take any money. It was his way of supporting me. I looked over at Syd and he shrugged his shoulders as if to say, 'Good people'. I offered my thanks, even if I had made myself feel a little sick.

Syd had a rehearsal and I was wondering how far away it would be when he thanked Charlie and said, 'If you won't take our money, the least I can do is leave a good tip,' and he gave the ten-dollar bill to our waitress. He said goodbye, wished me luck and headed off into the sunshine, leaving me to say hello to Deneva Elvins, who was twenty-five and had been working at Cyrano's for two and a half years. She was wearing a black T-shirt and skirt and had dark hair tied back to emphasise high cheekbones and kind eyes. She seemed too intelligent to be a professional waitress but she was clearly happy; and, anyway, who was I to judge? I didn't have a job of any kind.

I had asked Syd and Charlie about St Louis, the sense of abandonment I had felt there and about its plummeting population. They told me about the desire of people to move out to the suburbs after the war, to own their own home and escape from what was then a heavily industrialised and polluted city, and how the population of the County of St Louis grew as that of the city fell in a process called suburbanisation. The city had been no stranger to race problems and while the wealthier whites moved out to upmarket places like Webster Groves, Kirkwood, Brentwood, Shrewsbury and Clayton, many poor blacks were left to occupy increasingly neglected areas of the city. At the same time, restrictive covenants prevented black people from buying homes in white areas and reinforced policies of segregation until as recently as 1949, when they were outlawed following a US Supreme Court ruling. After that, white flight took hold and between 1950 and 1970 60 per cent had left St Louis.

Deneva, who lived in the city, was more positive about it. An outflow of young people twenty or thirty years ago was now being reversed, she said. Old warehouses were being reclaimed by young urbanites. There was a great ethnic arts and music scene and an unshakeable sense of pride in the architecture of St Louis, its free museums and its many beautiful parks, churches and restaurants. As a city dweller, I found myself rooting for St Louis.

Deneva was working the late shift and was heading home after that, so we agreed to meet when she came back into work the next day. If the need to spend the bill arose in the meantime, she would let me know and I would be there in a flash.

I drove around aimlessly for a while, found a grim motel in Kirkwood and had an early night.

Paul Huning
(38° 35.023' N, 090° 20.059' W)

There was some truth in what I had told Dean, but I had not really set off to follow money as some kind of weird tribute to my dead father. The certainty that he would have vicariously enjoyed the exercise shored up my resolve to do it, yes. But was I following the money just for him? No, of course not. Time and again I returned to the theme of boredom. Was I bored at home? Yes. Not with my relationship or my life in general, but with work. I felt I had squeezed the life out of it. Only the year before I had set off up the Amazon with an Italian photographer friend of mine, Domenico Pugliese, to write about the Cinta Larga tribe, who were fighting against miners illegally extracting hundreds of millions of dollars' worth of diamonds from their land. There were horrible massacres, gems as big as your eye and fearsome warriors in bloodied battledress. But after three weeks of negotiating, the Cinta Larga refused to let us on to their reservation. Domenico, a passionate and fearless photojournalist, was furious. I was bored. So we headed off, uninvited, to see the Santo Daime, a Shangri La-type religious community way upriver from Acre. They had told us not to go but we went anyway; their followers had spread to

Europe and their sacrament, ayahuasca, was a hallucinogenic tea that was regarded as a Class A drug in almost all European countries. On the way we saw rare pink dolphins and were caught in ferocious thunderstorms. We became stuck in tiny tributaries blocked by trees that had been felled by lightning. Each time our progress was halted by one of these, we climbed out of our canoe, stood on the fallen trunk and hauled the boat over it, being careful not to topple into the piranha-infested waters below. I remember feeling mildly amused by this, and then bored by our lack of progress.

When we reached the community, its members actually welcomed us and allowed us to partake of the ayahuasca, which was brewed from the root of one plant and the leaf of another. While Domenico, a man pure of spirit and clear conscience, had a wonderful time soaring towards his soul, I had visions of women with beards and wrestled to close bulging red doors behind which I had locked away a cocktail of guilt, regret and unresolved grief. When it was all over, I felt slightly less bored than when we had arrived.

'You know, man, you should take uppa the parachute ting,' said Domenico.

We were waiting at a hospital on the edge of civilisation after he had developed an enormously swollen neck and looked like a rugby player with mumps. The doctors had been convinced that he had contracted malaria but, mercifully, it turned out only to be a particularly vicious infection.

'I don't get that,' I replied. 'Why jump out of a perfectly good aeroplane?'

'Mountain climbing?'

'I don't want to climb anything higher than a bar stool . . .'

He had another plan. He knew a government unit that used

to fly into the rainforest to arrest – or, more often than not, shoot – illegal loggers who were using the indigenous population as slaves. We could fly in with them and free some slaves. Maybe take some pictures of loggers having their heads blown off. It sounded promising. He called his contact and came back shaking his head. 'No raids a-plan,' he said. 'But he say wait and maybe something come up.'

We waited. I got bored and went home. Domenico went back upriver and took pictures of the religious followers brewing ayahuasca. They let him shoot on one condition; that he drank ayahuasca the whole time. He spent seven days hallucinating and took the most wonderful photographs. They were brilliantly sharp even though he could barely focus. I admired him for that. I still do. I would have been bored after a couple of hours.

I was lying in my motel room smoking in the dark. I had not been bored so far, but I was getting there. It was 5 a.m. Having an early night had been a mistake. I hauled myself out of bed, showered, dressed and drove to midtown St Louis, where I cruised the streets like a burglar. I was struck by how beautiful so many parts of the city were. I pulled up on Grand Boulevard near the Fox Theater and went into the City Diner for breakfast at 7. Breakfast seemed to be the only meal I was eating, so I made the most of it.

During the morning I visited the Cathedral Basilica of St Louis and found myself bedazzled by the mosaics adorning its walls and vaulted ceilings, glowing gold in shafts of sunlight. Behind the cathedral were imposing grey mansion blocks and beautiful red-brick houses on tree-lined, broad streets. I wanted to see more of the city but I couldn't relax. I rang Deneva mid-morning but there was no reply, so I decided to head back to

Webster Groves and park outside Cyrano's. I put on an Erin Bode CD I had bought from Syd and wondered how deluded or in love a person would have to be to become a stalker. It was such a crushingly dull pastime.

Just before lunch, Deneva arrived for her shift.

'Hey,' she said. 'I'm glad you're here. It's my husband's birthday and I want to buy something for dinner tonight.'

She led me over two streets to Old Orchard Avenue and a growing sense of busyness and noise. The air temperature had fallen but the sky was blue and a white sun shone on golden leaves that were at last beginning to drop on to the street. Along the length of the avenue were stalls selling everything from empanadas and soap to organic vegetables and cakes. Down one side were pork roasts and burger stalls, vendors of cookies, olives, bread, dried pasta, nuts and fruit. There were flowers and pumpkins, kettle corn and honeycombs. Children's hats and decorated mirrors rubbed up against wind chimes and paella. The smells of Mexican food and American barbecue melded into one delicious autumnal whack on the head. At the end of the street was a bar called the Roadhouse and outside two musicians were playing blues. All in all it brought me out of my fug as surely as a snap of smelling salts.

Deneva browsed for a while until she came upon Paul Huning, a fifty-four-year-old apple grower from Union, Missouri, who was selling apples and everything to do with them. He had apple juice, apple butter, apple cake, apple sauce, dried apples and apple pie. Deneva bought a pie to take home for dinner and she paid with IA74407937A. Paul raised an eyebrow when I explained that I would have to follow him back to his orchard, but he didn't seem too fazed by the prospect. Union was about thirty-five miles away. This was not as far as I would have liked – I felt trapped by the gravity of the city – but it was a start. Perhaps now the bill would begin to move again.

I gave Paul my number in case he had to pay out IA74407937A in change, then I had a stroll around the market and down back towards Cyrano's, where there was a village bandstand and growing numbers of people enjoying picnics from the food and drink they had bought. I walked on up Big Bend Boulevard towards the university, where signs advertised the merits of not one, but two theatrical productions. Not bad, I thought, for a relatively small campus. Over the road was a dance studio where young girls in tutus were practising ballet steps. As darkness began to fall, I doubled back up Old Orchard Avenue to see if Paul still had the money. When he said he did I went to the end of the street and watched people drinking coffee under fairy lights at the Big Sky Café. From the other end of the road I heard a brass band strike up and inside my head I recalled the voices of English friends who had insisted the American Midwest was a cultural wasteland. It wasn't even a weekend; this was an average Thursday night.

Paul did not give out the money in change, so when he packed up for the night I followed south-west along the I-44. He went home to his wife and children and I checked out where he lived to see whether there was anything that might tempt him into a late-night spending spree. There wasn't. We had agreed to meet the next day, but he asked me not to turn up until noon, as he would be looking after his four-year-old son until then and didn't want to be disturbed. I found a motel in an isolated spot off the I-44 near St Clair. There were no temptations for me either, so I drove to a gas station and bought a bottle of wine and a turkey sandwich.

I noticed that the mileage on the clock stood at 1,978.5.

Paul was an outdoorsman. He had joined the National Forest Service, a part of the Department of Agriculture, responsible for more than 190 million acres of woodland, in 1978 after gaining a degree in forest management from the University of Missouri in Columbia. Three years later, he went on to join the National Park Service, which manages America's fifty-eight national parks, and moved to Alaska where his love of the wild flourished with the seasons and the landscape.

'I loved the cold winters and the cool summers,' he said. 'I loved the skiing and walking the trails, the fishing and white-water canoeing.'

We were sitting under an awning at the back of a 2,600-square-foot wooden frame house that Paul had designed to be energy-efficient. There was plenty of sunshine here even in the winter, and he had fixed it so that south-facing windows somewhere in the house drew in the sun's warmth from dawn till dusk all year round. The house was built on concrete with insulation between gypsum walls and a PVC shell. There was no need for central heating, with wood-burning stoves providing hot water and any extra warmth that the sun could not.

He had met his wife, Sara-Beth, in Anchorage. She had been training as a medical technologist – a biomedic working in analytical and research laboratories – and he was happy to move with her as her career progressed. They left Anchorage and set up home in Seattle, Washington State, then Coeur d'Elene in northern Idaho, before moving back to St Louis County in 1999. Sara-Beth then landed a job at St John's Mercy Hospital in Washington, about twelve miles away, and they bought five acres of land, later extended to ten, on which to build this house. They moved in in 2002 and Paul had been planting apple trees ever since.

His orchard took up just one and a half of his ten acres.

He took me through a gate in an eight-foot fence designed to keep out deer and we walked along his rows of apple trees. The varieties he had originally planted sounded familiar: Braeburn, Granny Smith and Enterprise. Only a fourth, Arkansas Black, was new to me. Later, he planted Galarina, Liberty, Pristine and a second variety of Enterprise. For a time he had Golden Delicious, but they didn't take. In all, he had some ninety trees, with each producing an average of 500 apples a year.

For the family, Paul had a garden growing cucumbers, peppers, okra, green beans, corn, sweet potatoes, beetroot, strawberries, kiwi fruit and blackberries. There was a paddock in which two horses grazed, and around the edges of the orchard he showed me trees growing plums and three types of hickory nut – pecan, shaggy black and bitter.

It all seemed perfect, yet I couldn't shake off the feeling that something was wrong.

Paul was tall and slim with a brown, taut face and piercing eyes that appeared unworn in the way that mine were. He wore a pale blue polo shirt, black jeans and a black baseball cap and was very precise when he spoke. He was interested in the European view of America and it was clear there were elements of it with which he disagreed. He did, however, admire Europe's attention to detail when it came to social rights, welfare and engagement. People in love with nature often bear a strange malevolence to their own species. Not Paul. He was concerned for the welfare of his fellow man and we chatted for some time about the demise of the unions and the exploitation of workers that this had caused. He also told me that he had been a great admirer of the Anheuser-Busch corporation and the way it looked after its employees with decent salaries and benefits. Since a 52 billion dollar hostile takeover by the giant Belgian brewer InBev in 2008, the new company's cost-cutting policies had resulted in 2,000 job losses, cutbacks in pension contributions and the abolition of life insurance for retired employees. Calling to mind the Ronald Reagan era in much the same way as British liberals invoke Margaret Thatcher's, Paul talked about a diminution of rights and salaries running in tandem with the crushing of the unions. Automotive workers at Ford and GM had suffered, he said, and people like his father, who used to work at the Boeing headquarters in St Louis. 'They were the last good union-protected jobs,' he said.

The war in Iraq was bullshit, and so was Afghanistan – an excuse to enrich the military industrial complex, he said.

Paul was smart and entertaining but he seemed angry. Not angry crazy, but angry concerned, and I found that interesting. His arguments were cogent and well put, endowed with more weight by dint of the fact that he had no self-interest; he was an apple grower who lived almost untouched by the consequences of the matters he was discussing. But I still wasn't sure why he was quite so wound up.

Paul had been looking after his son, Benjamin, who was asleep when I arrived. Later in the afternoon, Sara-Beth came home with the couple's seven-year-old daughter, Julia, a lovely ball of energy who fizzed with curiosity and excitement. I was introduced to Sara-Beth and felt a little awkward. She looked tired and I began to think about leaving; I didn't want to intrude and could keep tabs on the bill from a distance, but then Benjamin saw me and began hauling over his toys one by one, explaining how each worked and what, in the mind of a child, it could do. He was a force of nature with a head of thick brown hair and a cherubic face. He had on a blue T-shirt and blue and white board shorts. Not to be outdone, Julia pulled out her dolls and all their outfits for me to admire.

Paul stopped talking and sat quietly while the children steam-rollered me. Sara-Beth went inside and I could hear the sound of groceries being unpacked and put away. We talked about the horses and Julia told me their names and how she cared for them. Benjamin jumped on my knees to demonstrate the advantages of one toy over another. After a time, Paul asked me inside to look at his photographs. Over the years, he had developed a passion for nature photography and he had become highly accomplished. His pictures of rivers, mountains and forests had been framed and hung on the walls. They were displayed off the main living area, which also incorporated an open kitchen. This was ample and made larger by a pitched roof that stretched, uninterrupted, to the full height of the house.

A little while later, Julia appeared with a framed photograph measuring about eight inches by ten and she put it on my lap. Paul saw it and fell quiet. It was a picture of a younger Julia with a girl who looked two or three years older than she did. About her age now.

'What a lovely picture,' I said. 'You look very pretty in that. And who's this? She looks very nice.'

'This is my big sister,' said Julia. 'She died.'

She said the word 'died' with a sad and falling inflection that left me almost paralysed. I glanced up for a cue from Paul or Sara-Beth, for a sign or a look that might say, 'It's time you left.' But there was none.

'Her sister drowned three years ago,' said Paul, looking into his lap.

I gleaned from him that it was freak accident in the garden involving a paddling pool, but I didn't pry further. Her name was Laura.

Julia wanted to talk about it and it seemed that her parents felt this was a healthy thing for her to do – cathartic perhaps – so off she went to various rooms, returning each time with more and more photographs of her big sister.

'She's beautiful,' I said. 'I think it's wonderful that you keep so many pictures of her.'

Julia smiled and her face took on a look that was at once sad and stoic.

'Do you remember her well?' I asked.

'Yes, she was my best friend. I miss her.'

After some time, Julia put down all the photographs and stopped talking about Laura. She went over to her mother and they hugged, then the little girl ran out to play with Benjamin. I felt that Paul and Sara-Beth didn't want to discuss Laura's death and I was embarrassed that it had been brought up in front of me. This was a loving family building a special life, but I couldn't begin to imagine their heartache. I offered my condolences and left. Paul asked me to call him in the morning.

Outside, the sun was falling fast. Its dying rays painted the wings of horseflies, making the air seem flecked with silver and gold. I drove aimlessly for perhaps an hour, feeling numbed by the events of the afternoon and humbled by the enormity of the disaster that had befallen the Huning family. I had burdened them with my lame and frivolous enterprise.

The countryside was beautiful. There were stout brick farm-houses set back from the road, most with paddocks and horses, some with cattle grazing on knee-high pastures. Suddenly, the landscape began to look very English, reminding me of the Cotswolds, and I felt wretched and alone.

Shaw Nature Reserve

(38° 28.927' N, 090° 49.454' W)

Ihave an unfortunate talent for finding a good bar, but invite me to book you a decent room for the night and I rarely fail to disappoint. I sat on the bed in my latest, surrounded by empty beer bottles, and tried hard to remember when I had last stayed in such a miserable billet outside a Third World country or a war zone. I couldn't. This had walls made of breeze blocks with one coat of unevenly applied paint, a dirty and sticky floor encrusted with dead flies, a cracked sink, a shower with no pressure and a selection of furniture that had been made from bricks, lengths of wood and cannibalised cupboards and cabinets. My bedside table should have been a linen basket, my desk a vanity table. And so on.

I had fallen asleep on top of the bed. Would that make me less likely to have been bitten by bedbugs? It was a consolation that I decided to embrace, as the discovery that you could dry underwear in a microwave oven had been welcomed as a good start to the day. I would be positive. Day 16 would be a better day than day 15. I cleared up the beer bottles, placing some of them into a plastic bin in the room and others in the boot of my car to be disposed of later. In the unlikely event that someone should clean my room, I didn't want them to see how much I had been drinking.

I left the motel as early as I could and drove up and down a section of road that used to form Route 66 (the route having been diverted along a newer stretch of highway). I found myself whistling the tune and felt, selfishly, mildly better about my situation than I had last night. It was a bright morning again but now each day was dawning colder. The air temperature was low but forecast to rise to 68 degrees later, which I reasoned would be classed as a heat wave back home.

My phone rang. It was Paul calling to say he was taking the children to a nature reserve and asking whether I wanted to tag along. Of course I did.

We met on the forecourt of a bank and Julia, Benjamin and I waved urgently at one another through our car windows while Paul stepped out to take some cash from an ATM. He came back and leaned in through the driver's side of my car.

'You ready to go?' he asked.

'Yes,' I said. 'Paul, about yesterday . . .'

'Heck, it's OK . The kids like you and, well . . .'

There wasn't really much either of us could say. Paul jumped into his Blue Honda and sped off with me in pursuit towards the Shaw Nature Reserve in Gray Summit, about ten miles to the north-east on the I-44. The reserve is an extension of the Missouri Botanical Garden, which is located in St Louis. In the 1920s, botanists were so worried about levels of coal smoke in the city that they feared the pollution would kill their living collection of plants, particularly orchids, at the botanical gardens. Plans were made to move them to a new reserve and so the Shaw was created.

Today, it includes 2,500 acres of Ozark border landscape,

thirteen miles of hiking trails, a fifty-five-acre 'pinetum', which includes conifers and meadow plants from around the world, and the five-acre Whitmire Wildlife Garden, which features grasses, trees, shrubs and wild flowers native to Missouri and the eastern US. Inside the reserve are natural and cultivated examples of savannah grasslands, marsh wetlands, tall grass prairie and flood plain forest. In other words, everything that Paul loved could be found in one place, under one sky.

We parked our cars and went into the Visitor Center. Paul wanted to take Julia and Benjamin for a walk but first they had to pay the attendant, Judith Hunt, for day tickets. I was like a watch spring that had been wound too tight, but Paul didn't use the ten. Instead I waited impatiently while the children played and their father perused the shelves of the centre's bookshop. I sat on a chair in the corner of the room and fidgeted. And then I saw him heading back towards Judith Hunt.

'Could I get this please?'

I jumped up and looked over his shoulder. He was buying a second-hand book called *A Field Guide to the Grasses, Sedges and Rushes of the United States* by Edward Knobel and he was paying five dollars with IA74407937A. It was 1.12 p.m.

'I guess you'll stay here now,' said Paul. He wore a steely grin and I squeezed his hand in a way that I hoped conveyed my gratitude and my apologies for crashing into his life. The children spun from behind me and Paul told them to say goodbye.

Judith Hunt had a puzzled look on her face.

'You're *what*?'

'I'm following that ten-dollar bill.'

'But why, honey?'

'It's a long story. Will you help?'

'Well, sure I will, but I hope you got lots o' patience. You could be here for quite some time.'

Judith described herself as the Visitor Center dogsbody, but her correct title was Visitor Center Attendant. She had worked as a volunteer for nine years, taking money and giving advice, and she was very proud of the reserve and the happiness it brought to visitors. Today, she was in the company of Bob Bryan, a maintenance worker.

Bob nodded at me. 'You one o' them eccentric Englishmen?'

'Yes,' I said, smiling. 'I suppose I am.'

Judith told me that most of the people who came walking at the Shaw were members who needed only to show her their card. I quickly saw what she meant. Walkers popped in, made small talk, flashed their membership and then were gone. No money changed hands. I sat down and had a chat with Judith.

'We get a lot of very nice people here,' she said. 'They come down from the city and sometimes you can see that they have come to walk away some troubles. But usually when folks leave they are in a good mood. It's nice to be a part of that.'

I stood up and put my hands behind my back to avoid looking at my watch. Perhaps Judith might let me read one of the books here. *The Mighty Mississippi*, *Voyages of Discovery*, *Songbird Journeys*, *The Last Great Adventure of Sir Peter Blake* . . .

I was beginning to think that the last sounded promising when there was a commotion and Judith called out, 'The Wilderness Wagon is about to set off. Why don't you jump on? I'll call you if I'm going to give out this bill. To be honest with you, I think you're stuck here till Monday.' Today was Saturday.

The Wilderness Wagon was a flat-bed trailer with plastic seats and a green tarpaulin roof and it was pulled by a people carrier. I couldn't figure out why they didn't just put the people into the people carrier, but I had to admit that the wagon was a splendid way to see the edges of the reserve. Our guide was Jim Jackson, a mine of information dressed in a brown checked shirt, blue jeans and a baseball cap. As we passed varieties of trees and wild flowers, Jim would point them out and name them. He told us about the history of the reserve and explained that it comprised five run-down farms that had been neglected and were growing wild. He pointed out purple thistle, bush honeysuckle and pawpaw trees, sugar maple, ponderosa and Scotch pine. He told us that on one weekend a year there was a deer hunt to control the population but that this year numbers hadn't warranted one. And he drew gasps when he told us that the reserve was home to black rat snakes that could climb trees. Jim was a volunteer; he did this for the love of it.

Halfway round the Wilderness Wagon's circular route was an opportunity to climb down and walk the couple of miles back to the Visitor Center. I looked at my phone and it had a full signal so I felt confident enough to chance it. There were quite a few hefty people on board the wagon and I waited to see if any would wobble off, but none did.

I don't usually walk more than a mile without some Kendal Mint Cake and a set of crampons, but it was such a lovely day that I reckoned I would be fine so long as I didn't come face to face with a black rat snake. The sun had climbed high in the sky, but it was not too hot. Underfoot, the crunch of leaves was evidence that autumn had finally arrived.

I realised that I had spent so much of my trip surrounded by spectacular countryside but because of the nature of my journey I had not been able to enjoy it, to get into it. Now, with grass under my feet and nothing but the sound of birds to break the silence, I began to think how sad that was. As I walked under hackberry and hickory trees, I noticed I was being followed by a robin. We both stood still for a while, but I was the first to move. I looked at my watch and headed back to the centre.

Judith told me nobody had needed change while I was gone, so I sat down. Then I went for a stroll round the car park. Then I came back inside again and had a walk around the building.

Near the lavatory was a sign on which was a quote from Søren Kierkegaard, the father of existentialism. Taken from a letter to his daughter, it read:

> Above all, do not lose your desire to walk. Every day I walk myself into a state of well-being and walk away from every illness. I have walked myself into my best thoughts and I know of no thought so burdensome that one cannot walk away from it. But by sitting still, and the more one sits still, the closer one comes to feeling ill. If one just keeps on walking, everything will be all right.

When I returned to Judith, she was looking very pleased with herself. In front of her were a bright-eyed man and a woman holding a camera, and they both turned to face me.

'Here you are,' said Judith. 'Here's the feller you need to see.'

The man to whom Judith was talking was called Nathan Walker. He was paying for entry to the reserve for himself and his wife, Jennifer, who was outside in the car with their six-year-old son, Lucas, and four-year-old daughter, Allison. He was also paying admittance for the woman with the camera, Sarah Lough. She was a photographer and she had been commissioned to take some pictures of the family.

Nathan was given IA74407937A as part of his change. He

smiled, held out his hand to me and said, 'Why don't you tag along?' So I did.

We went outside and I was introduced to Jennifer and the children, who showed absolutely no interest in me, which came as a welcome relief. I remained convinced that I was not particularly good with children or animals. Jennifer was cheerful and friendly and all three adults seemed immediately intrigued by my journey, asking lots of questions that I found difficult to answer. Sarah said she didn't mind me taking photographs of her taking photographs of the Walkers, but once her work began I kept out of her way.

It was almost 4.10, which I thought was a little late to be taking portrait photographs in a forest, but once Sarah had lined up the family as a group, then mum and dad, then the children holding hands and grimacing, then individually, all bathed in golden evening light, it was clear that she knew exactly what she was doing. She photographed them walking between young trees, knowing they would be silhouetted by the sunset, and led them to the porch of the Bascom House, a restored two-storey farmhouse built in 1879 by Thomas William Bouldin Crews, a former Confederate colonel whose family had farmed the land. This farm was one of the five Jim had told us about on the Wilderness Wagon and the house was now a museum.

The Walkers were clearly a tightly knit family. Allison was a photographer's dream and reminded me of the little girls on the labels of Pears soap my mother would buy when I was a child. She would occasionally appear bored but had the knack of springing into life at the appearance of a camera. Lucas was spirited and wilful and did not enjoy having his picture taken. Nathan seemed calm and solid, and while Judith had told me that many people came here in search of peace, I somehow felt that Nathan enjoyed peace wherever he went. Jennifer had a round face with translucent skin and smiling eyes. Her shoulder-length black hair fell on to a flowered blouse while she fussed over the children, negotiating tired tantrums out of Allison and overcoming Lucas's lack of interest in the project (he was creditably devoid of vanity) with gentle comfort and persuasion.

When it was all over we walked back to Sarah's four-wheel drive and Nathan told me that he and Jennifer were missionaries. I had never encountered a missionary before and had always imagined them lashed together in pairs, standing naked in cooking pots. Whenever I met particularly religious people I always felt vaguely grubby and was convinced that they could sense my unease and see me draped in sin like some kind of glowing ectoplasm. I felt this way now but smiled casually and tried to give the impression that some of my best friends might be missionaries.

Jennifer whispered something to Nathan about church, but they evidently thought better of inviting me along and instead asked me to meet them at their home in the morning.

'What about the money?' I asked. 'Will you be spending it tonight?'

'No, we're having a quiet family dinner tonight,' said Nathan.

By that, I took him to mean a church family meal. I was quite disappointed that they had not tried to convert me but reasoned that it was a Saturday and even God had taken a day off.

I felt lucky to have met Nathan and Jennifer. They arrived at 4 p.m., just as the Visitor Center was about to close. Judith's earlier prediction that I could be there until Monday was based on the expectation that the ten would most likely be used to pay for food deliveries at the beginning of a new week. It would have been a long wait. Instead, I had enjoyed a pleasant couple of hours walking, visiting the Bascom house and anticipating a carefree evening.

The only downside – and I couldn't quite believe this – was that the Walker family lived in Washington, Missouri, just to the north of Union. I had travelled there last night for a change of scenery and that was where I had found my dreadful motel. It seemed the gravity of St Louis County still had me in its grip.

I drove east towards the city and found a section of Route 66 that looped off the I-44. Route 66 seemed fragmented and complicated. It was dusk now but the glow of the sun below the horizon turned the sky the colour of a blood orange. I drove towards the Six Flags amusement fair and past RV parks and run-down shacks at the side of the road. From time to time exotic motorcycles whizzed by, their drivers looking as puzzled as I was about Route 66 – though most of the time I couldn't see past their beards and sunglasses. I turned round and headed back towards Union, Washington and St Clair and found a Budget Lodging off the I-44 that was set back from the road and quiet.

The room was modern and clean and it had a heater, which was a blessing since the night-time temperature was falling fast. After I had checked in, I drove into St Clair and bought myself some ribs and tubs of potato salad and coleslaw. I found some Camembert and bread in a supermarket and added a bottle of Australian wine. I would have a feast in my luxurious room. The Walkers seemed thoughtful and reliable and not the sort to engage in frivolous or unexpected spending. In short, I could relax.

I began running a bath and put on the television to watch a movie. How normal! I had half of the wine in the bath with the ribs, coleslaw and potato salad while reading P. G. Wodehouse. After I finished off the rest of the wine with the bread and cheese I decided to turn in and reached for the bedside lamp. It was then that I noticed a book on the bedside table. It was the Bible and it had been left open at Psalms 8: 'I will both lay me down in peace and sleep: for thou, Lord, only makest me dwell in safety.'

I closed it, switched off the lamp and fell into a deep and contented sleep.

God (1)

The blue-shuttered Walker household in Whispering Oaks Drive was only a five-minute hop from where my nightmare motel had been and as the couple answered the door I was wondering whether I would remain in orbit around St Louis forever. They looked a little troubled and I assumed that was my fault, my dark thoughts on my lined face. Jennifer offered me a cup of coffee and we went out to the back porch and sat in the sunshine. The couple appeared worried, as if they were about to tell me I had been made redundant or, at the very least, had some flesh-eating disorder. They glanced at one another and then back at me. They didn't seem very comfortable.

'It's about the ten-dollar bill. Did we tell you that we bred goats? Last night, one chewed its way through the screen door and, well, it just about ate Jennifer's purse. Your ten dollars was inside. We've been up all night waiting for the goat to poop but so far nothing has come out. I'm sorry.'

I have no idea why I was thinking this and I suspect I might have smiled a little at the thought of the kindly Walkers waiting for the goat to make a *cash deposit*, before Nathan actually spoke, rousing me from a thousand-yard daydream. I was doing this a lot.

'I'm sorry, Nathan, what did you say?'

'I said we love your project but we realised last night that we know so little about you. Where are you from, what's your background –' he leaned forward – 'your faith . . . your church?'

I had been worried that this might happen and had resolved in advance to tell the truth as far as I could. I did not want to lie about being amoral and godless, but neither did I want these very nice people to be frightened off by me, as I might lose sight of the ten dollars that way. I needed *co-operation*. In my own defence, I felt that there was some kind of symbiosis going on: I was clearly a person in need of saving and, while they had the ten dollars, Nathan and Jennifer would be in a position to give it their best shot. On the other hand, I wanted to stay as close to the money as possible, so I didn't want to give the impression that I was beyond redemption.

Nathan and Jennifer were thirty-two and had attended the same school. She was now a full-time mom, though she had studied the leisure industry at college and had worked in it for a time. He was an electronics technician and a co-founder of a local Internet service provider, but he was giving it all up to become a full-time missionary with FamilyLife, a Christian organisation dedicated to preserving and promoting marriage. It had a network of thousands of couples around the US who held conferences, workshops and talks aimed at helping people stay together and pray together. And Nathan and Jennifer were working hard to become another of these full-time couples.

'Shame I didn't know you guys before I got divorced!' I blurted.

They didn't find this very funny. I coughed and decided not to crack any more jokes. We moved to the living room because it was so hot outside and I asked them about their faith. There was no mileage in discussing mine. What had so interested them in saving other people's marriages?

'I think I got into it when I began working part-time as a youth director at our church, St Paul's,' said Jennifer. 'The kids there are seventh- to twelfth-graders – thirteen to eighteen years old. Over the past five years, we've been seeing more and more kids coming through with some very tough issues, acting out in inappropriate ways, struggling with promiscuity, drugs, alcohol, self-mutilation . . .

'When we dug into their personal situations, there were invariably problems at home. The divorce rate now is around 50 per cent. Commitment is fragile and the children suffer when their parents split – you see some terrible custody battles. There was one seventeen-year-old girl who was kicked out by her father but her mother had no home. The girl was trying to get through her final exams to improve her future prospects and she ended up living with a stepsister. She was striving to make her life better, but there wasn't a parent in sight. The family had completely broken down. Stories like this broke our hearts, but to do anything about them would have involved going to families and we didn't know how to do that. Then we heard about FamilyLife and went on their Weekend to Remember. It's a three-day getaway – no kids – where you find out how to strengthen your marriage. We had been married seven years at the time and we had two small children and thought we were OK, but we hadn't realised how far we had grown apart. It really worked for us and we wondered how much heartache we might prevent if we could persuade other couples, couples with real problems, to try it, to work on their marriages through Bible study and encouragement.'

Jennifer had me until she suggested you could save your marriage by reading the Bible. If you were forced at gunpoint to spend so much time reading the Bible that you didn't have time to cheat on your wife, then maybe. Otherwise, I wasn't convinced. But I was captivated by her honesty and conviction. What struck me was a sincere desire to use religion as a practical tool to help others rather than just bask in the glow of one's own beatification.

'My parents were happily married and they fostered three kids,' she continued. 'One was called Lenny and he was eight years old. One year, his mom said she was going to work really hard to bring him home for Christmas and he was so excited about that. Then, the week before Christmas, his mom rang him up and she said, "Lenny, I have some good news and some bad news. The good news is that Mommy has gotten married again and she is really happy. The bad news is that Mommy's new husband doesn't want a family . . ."'

'Another of the foster kids was called Debbie. She was eleven or twelve and her mom struggled with drugs and alcohol. She would have weekend binges and lock her kids in the closet or in the bathroom for two or three days. My mom told me that when Debbie came to live with her, she would find food stashed away in the closets and hidden behind the toilet. The girl had been planning ahead and couldn't imagine a world where she wouldn't be locked up like that.'

I was still trying to imagine the damage done to Lenny and Debbie when Jennifer said, 'God has put a fire in my heart to try to help kids like this.'

In Europe, God is dying. This is a difficult concept to broach with Americans as, particularly in the Midwest, it is hard to find one who might not find it offensive. A 2009 Gallup poll established that 45 per cent of Americans attended church at least once a week. A UK poll for the relief and development charity

Tearfund in 2007 found that only 15 per cent of Britons admitted attending, not once a week, but once a month. The figure is even lower in Hungary, France and Denmark. An earlier Gallup poll conducted across Europe found that 55 per cent of Swedes, 52 per cent of Norwegians and 49 per cent of Danes regarded God as 'an irrelevance' in their lives. However, far from being godless societies in the traditional sense of moral breakdown and amoral chaos, these are countries with low crime rates and social welfare policies that might have come straight from Matthew, Chapter Five, the Sermon on the Mount. Go, one might say, figure.

In the US, concluding a presidential speech with the words 'God Bless America' is considered de rigueur. European politicians who invoke God in any way are considered barmy. This is arguably the subject politicians on both sides of the Atlantic skirt around most when they meet; the gulf in attitudes is so wide that it is not even worth talking about. Several years ago, in an ICM poll for the BBC, 71 per cent of Americans agreed with the statement, 'I would die for my God or beliefs.' In the UK, only 19 per cent of people agreed with it. God, they reasoned, could fight his own battles.

One question demonstrated that a large minority of Britons were not simply uninterested – or even disinterested – in the concept of a God; they actually felt that worshipping one was bad. Asked to consider the statement 'The world would be more peaceful if people didn't believe in God', 91 per cent of Americans disagreed while only 63 per cent of Britons did.

I was moved by Jennifer's motives and her desire to improve the lives of other people. Apart from Relate (which used to be called the Marriage Guidance Council), few people in the UK cared about marriage as an institution. The Church, of course, but then only dwindling numbers of people gave a damn what the Church thought anyway. After speaking to Jennifer it seemed obvious that if your focus was on helping children, you should first help their parents. The only thing that was moot was the methodology.

'I had a difficult childhood,' said Nathan. We had been sitting in silence, digesting what Jennifer had said about Lenny and Debbie. 'My dad was the primary provider and that was his focus. Monday to Friday he worked away. When I saw him he was very busy and didn't make much time to connect with us. One day when I was eight I had basketball practice and my mom couldn't make it that day. I was excited because I thought my dad would be there instead. I kept looking around but I didn't see him. At the end, everyone ran over to a loved one, but there was nobody there for me. I thought he must be in the parking lot, but he wasn't. I felt abandoned and sat on a kerb and just cried. Cars stopped to offer me a ride but I said no, I was waiting for my dad. Eventually, he came and I wiped my eyes, but it was obvious he didn't understand why I was so upset. He found it difficult to express love.

'When he was four, his mom died and his dad didn't do such a great job of raising him. Before he was sixteen my dad had moved out to be on his own, wandering from YMCA to YMCA. Later, when we were born, I know that he loved us but he had no blueprint for how to be a father; how to show it. He knew no other way. Since Jennifer and I have been married, a lot has changed in him. He sees how I treat our children and he spoils them. He's much more emotional, and I think he looks back to how my childhood was and he thinks about that. Maybe he wonders what he would have done differently if he had his time again. I love my family and they love me, but I now see the things that I missed out on and I want it to be different for my children. I want all fathers to show love to their children and their spouse. There is more to being a father than providing a roof.'

He said that when they were in their teens, he and his brother attended a youth group where the leaders became, for Nathan at least, role models.

'Later, when it came to making serious decisions, I remembered admiring the way they behaved and thinking, "This is what I want my family to be like. I want my family to be a role model – not just getting 'em there, buying 'em things and sending 'em out into the world." There is so much more to life than material possessions.'

The Walkers wanted to change society one couple at a time and to do that they were becoming missionaries for Campus Crusade for Christ, of which FamilyLife is a part, based out of Little Rock, Arkansas. But before they could, they had to find sponsors, something they described as 'developing a partner team', who would make donations to Campus Crusade, until a certain target had been reached. Then, and only then, Jennifer and Nathan would be allowed to report for work. Their partners would continue making donations to Campus Crusade, which, in turn, would set up an account to cover the Walkers' wages, accommodation, food, furniture, cars and so on. Any surplus would sit in the account and be used if donations slumped. I asked how much their target was and Nathan said it amounted to 'a God-sized task'.

'But God already knows who our partners are going to be: He waters, provides the seed and the sunshine and He will bring them to us,' he said. 'During this process of developing partners we get so much closer to God.'

This period of raising money seemed to me to be stressful and cruel. If an organisation wants to employ people in a full-time role, then it should pay them. Nathan was taking a course with the Institute of Bible Studies as part of his application, but wasn't spending all his time counselling couples. Instead he was mostly providing IT and Internet support. I felt that this amounted to a job and he should have been remunerated for doing it. In my experience, evangelism and money was a mix that often turned sour.

In this case, I was wrong. FamilyLife is a respected not-for-profit organisation with not a whiff of scandal about it. I simply didn't like seeing the pressure the Walkers were under. I didn't agree with their goal, I didn't share their faith, but I knew decent people when I saw them and they reminded me of fish out of water, gasping. They could see that I had problems with the fiscal side of the operation, because I kept asking questions about it. But they answered as best they could, realising that they were losing me bit by bit.

'Hey!' Nathan said suddenly, raising the mood. 'Do you like apples? We're taking the kids to an orchard. Hey, kids!'

There was an instant explosion of activity, a gathering up of coats and boots, bags and toys, and laughter returned to the Walker household. I was beginning to think I could darken a room merely by calling a phone in it from a thousand miles away.

But at least I had started praying.

'Dear God,' I said. 'Please don't let the ten dollars go back to Paul Huning. He's a lovely man, Lord, but I want to go to Disneyland. Or Vegas. God, could the ten dollars please go to Vegas?'

A Surfeit of Apples

So that is how I came to visit two orchards in three days. The second was called the Thierbach Orchard, was run by Susie and Otto Thierbach, and was situated four miles north of Marthasville on Highway 47, about fifty miles west of St Louis. It was a much bigger affair than Paul Huning's and at weekends the Thierbachs put up an inflatable castle for kids, carved out mazes in fields of honeysuckle vine, rape and corn, and provided slides, goats to pet and ponies to ride. Depending on the time of year, you could pick your own apples or peaches, pumpkins, cherries, strawberries or blueberries. And admission was just three dollars. Nathan paid with IA74407937A and I experienced a familiar sensation of falling. It was 4.35 p.m.

Susie's mother, Laverda, took the money inside the orchard's store while I explained to her father, Bob Puyear, just what was going on. He appeared to be late middle-aged and wore jeans and a denim shirt. I suspect he was older than he looked, but right now he was frowning, and that aged him.

'That bill – that bill there?'

'Yes, sir.'

'Laverda – young man wants you to take good care of that ten dollars.'

Laverda was slight and she had an appealing bird-like face and greying wavy hair cut around her ears. She stood behind a red wooden counter and smiled as if she were impressed and uninterested at the same time.

The note was in her custody for just three minutes before Paula Morriss from Washington, Missouri, received it in change from the purchase of four bottles of water. Paula was fifty-four and enjoying a day out with her fourteen-year-old daughter, Alleasha, her sister and a friend. Paula was a big lady who had my number straight away. She put on an English accent that was so good I thought she was a native. We went outside and sat on a bench and she gave me a drink while we chatted about her; in particular, her voice. She said she sometimes sang at Stovall's Grove in Wildwood, Missouri, a venue made famous by the Missouri Valley Boys, who had been playing there in a rolling line-up for more than sixty years. Honky-tonk and country had been pounding from the roof of Stovall's Grove since 1930. Today, it is a registered historic building in Wildwood, but it has existed longer than the neighbourhood itself.

'I sometimes sing there on Saturday nights,' Paula said in between sips of cold water. 'It's a fantastic venue with a wonderful history. Makes me shiver just to think about it.'

But isn't country music dying out?

'Hell, no. We get more and more young people every year. Country's enjoying a real resurgence in popularity.'

'Go on,' I said. 'Give us a song.'

And she did. Paula stood up and sang 'You Ain't Woman Enough (to Take My Man)' by Loretta Lynn.

I was pondering this choice of song when Alleasha came over and stood in front of me.

'Who the hell are you?' she asked forcefully. And, leaning into my face, she said, 'Ah like pie.'

'You do?' I mumbled. 'That's terrific. What's not to like about pie?'

Alleasha did not look fourteen. Alleasha looked about twenty-one. She put her thumbs in the pockets of her jeans and began dancing a jig. 'Ah like pie! Ah like pie!' Then, in my face again: 'Ah'm a redneck and proud of it. What you think about that?'

I turned and looked at Paula, hoping she would rescue me.

'Oh, don't you mind her,' she said after a while. 'She's just at that age.'

I would never fathom children. The Terrible Twos. The Pie-Eating Fourteens.

Paula told me that she had a twenty-nine-year-old son who was a professional cage-fighter and I realised that the back of my throat was dry. Was it the afternoon heat? Or was it the prospect of spending a night eating pies and wrestling a man who could probably kill me with his thumbs?

At exactly 5.09 Paula decided she was thirsty again and went back into the shop to buy drinks for everyone. Kindly, she bought me a root beer and paid with the ten-dollar bill. She was a terrific sport but I would be lying if I said I wasn't relieved. I would not have to eat pie or set foot in a cage; I would live to follow money another day.

The bill went back into the hands of Laverda and was tucked away in the cash register. The family would be locking up soon and I realised I might have to come back and pick up the journey tomorrow morning, assuming they wouldn't let me sleep in the store. I took a stroll around it and marvelled at the variety of apples. There were Blushing Gold and Jonathan, Wiresnap, Gold Rush and Mutsu. On the shelves were jars of salsa made from pineapple, red raspberry, mango and corn.

I nodded to Laverda that I was going outside to join Susie Thierbach for a while. She and Otto were the orchard's owners. Susie was attractive and patient in a sleeveless blouse and I could read in her eyes that she knew my questions were superficial. When it came to apples, I had learned everything I ever would from Paul Huning.

At 5.49 I was called back into the store to find a dark-haired man in a pink shirt looking from Laverda to Bob to Susie to a ten-dollar bill and back again. He had bought a can of soda.

'I have to *what*?' he asked. 'But I'm flying to Chicago.'

Chicago. I looked up and whispered, 'Thank you, God.'

His name was Darrell Mikulencak, he was a thirty-nine-year-old financial adviser and he was less than enthusiastic about taking me along with him.

'I really don't think I'm the man for this,' he said after we had shaken hands. 'I live in Chicago. I'm flying back there first thing tomorrow morning. I mean, that's not what you want, is it?'

'It isn't up to me,' I said. 'It's up to Alexander Hamilton.'

'What?'

I pointed to the portrait on the bill.

'Oh, yeah, sure. But, I really don't think . . .'

'Look, I promise I'll be no trouble,' I said. 'Are you likely to spend the money tonight?'

He said he wasn't. He was staying with his girlfriend in St Louis this evening and would catch his flight in the morning before heading straight into work. Might he spend it at the airport? Or at work on a cup of coffee? A newspaper? But he said he wouldn't. 'I'll be working through the day and won't have anything to spend it on until I finish,' he assured me.

This meant two things. One: Darrell didn't want me to follow him back to his girlfriend's house or to his office – that was why he put me at arm's length until after work the following night. Might he have spent the ten dollars sooner if he had not had to make this trade-off? We will never know, but it wasn't my problem.

Two: if I didn't have to catch up with the ten-dollar bill until the following evening, I wouldn't have to fly. I could drive the car. I swapped contact details with Darrell, who seemed uneasy. I think he suspected a scam.

'See you in Chicago!' I shouted.

I thanked Susie Thierbach, her parents and the Walkers and ran to my car before Darrell could change his mind. I had about 380 miles to drive on top of the 2,135.9 already on the clock.

I climbed behind the wheel as the sun was setting. I would return to north St Louis and head north-east on the I-55 all the way to Chicago. I was on the road again and felt free and elated. I turned the key in the ignition and listened for the sound of the engine. There was no time to waste. It was too dark for sunglasses but I slipped mine on anyway and put my foot hard to the floor for a celebratory wheel spin. I was in my own road movie. I cranked up 'LA Woman' as loud as the system would go and then I stalled the car.

I headed due north on Highway 47 before turning east on the I-70 and the I-270 to its junction with the I-55. This took me just north of Ron's home and back into Illinois. By 9 p.m. I had done 120 miles. I was feeling tired and decided to pull over on the edge of Litchfield. I checked into America's Best Value Inn and seriously doubted that it was, but my room was clean so I felt disinclined to argue. Somewhere nearby, a railway track crossed a road and through the night I would hear endlessly long freight trains clickety-clack over sets of points. Each time this happened, the driver would sound the train's air horn. I had once thought that this was a criminally inconsiderate thing to do after dark until an old railway man I met in a bar in San Francisco told me that the driver had no choice in the matter; that he was required by law to sound his horn a quarter of a mile away from any road crossing. During a long and sleepless Californian night I came to the conclusion that a horn from an unseen locomotive was the loneliest sound in the world.

I woke refreshed and relieved that Darrell would be on his flight. That meant I would literally be following the money again. I was aware that for some twelve hours I had been ahead of the bill, but I hadn't fretted too much over that. As yet, nobody had established the International Money Chasers' Federation with its rules and exceptions. All I had at this point was a minimal set of basics and I was trying to adhere to them.

I packed, checked out and drove to Jubelt's Bakery Restaurant nearby. It was filled with the heavy smells of freshly baked bread, pastries and bagels. I ordered hot black coffee and an American breakfast and watched the world go by with a rising sense of contentment. It seemed I had stumbled once again on to old Route 66. The Route, which John Steinbeck referred to as the Mother Road in *The Grapes of Wrath*, was no longer officially designated as part of the US Highway System – it had been overtaken by newer, wider interstate highways – but the obsession with tracking its meandering course was still as powerful as ever. In Missouri, very close to Paul Huning's orchard, I had tried following its path for a while, but it stopped dead at a small basin overgrown with tall grasses. Embedded in the dried mud were dozens of tyre tracks where disappointed and confused drivers had made U-turns. I picked up Route 66 again briefly after meeting the Walkers at the Shaw Nature Reserve, and here it was once more, following or spinning off sections of the I-55 like a dotted line that had been cut by a child. When it was established in 1926, Route 66 ran north-east to south-west from Chicago, through Missouri, Kansas, Oklahoma, Texas, New Mexico, Arizona and California. Since its removal from the official highway network in 1985, its survival had been assured by individual states which signposted sections variously as Historic, Old or State Route 66, and by its designation as a National Scenic Byway. Though I doubted the bikers at Jubelt's would be singing 'Get Your Kicks on National Scenic Byway 66 . . .' over beers that night.

I finished my breakfast and headed back to the I-55. The sky was grey and there was a sub-zero wind. The hot sunshine of Arkansas seemed a lifetime away and I felt excited and sad at the same time. The crops were gone this far north and the fields on both sides of the road were flat and dormant. I sped past Springfield before the road turned north-east again towards Lincoln and Bloomington. After Springfield the landscape bore depressing signs of industry. I passed an old chimney stack spewing out smoke or steam just as the clouds burst overhead and it began to rain. Beyond Lincoln the ground was dark brown to the horizon and lightning tines danced and crackled soundlessly on the soil. Five hoardings flashed by on my right, claiming in sections that Chicago was number one in America for gun crime. I had never been to Chicago and found myself a little unnerved by the thought that someone should advertise a city in this way. Just after a signpost for Peoria – which I had previously thought was a disease that could send you mad – I saw another set of hoardings which read 'When danger calls, sonny, that rabbit's foot won't save no bunny'. I assumed the Chicago tourism office was not responsible for these signs, but I thought it should consider having a word with the folk who were. Perhaps at gunpoint.

Much later, after Pontiac and Dwight but just before the bridge over Des Plaines River near Channahon, there was more heavy industry and an Exxon oil refinery. I had felt like a pinball being bounced in and around St Louis, but already I was beginning to miss the beauty of Missouri, Arkansas and Kansas. I would be entering a great city soon and must leave behind thoughts of plains and wild prairies. It was a welcome change of scenery but I was a little melancholy nevertheless. Chicago would surely have a greater gravitational pull than St Louis – would it ever loosen its grip on the ten-dollar bill? Would I finish my journey there? Or would some coin toss or fickle fancy take IA74407937A out into the wilderness again? I would have to wait and see.

My Kind of Town

At 4.23 p.m. exactly I hit a traffic jam, my first since leaving London. It lasted a full minute and had me groping around the car for a paper bag into which I could hyperventilate. I had turned into a country boy. The sun had come out and it burned away clouds that might otherwise have obscured my first sighting of the Chicago skyline, which seemed strangely forbidding. I was convinced that the twin communication masts on top of the Sears Tower, which sparkled black in the afternoon glare, gave the building a demonic look. It was like a confident bully surrounded by shorter acolytes. *Come and have a go*, it seemed to be saying . . . *if you think you're hard enough.*

Two hours before I had called Darrell on the number he had given me but was put straight through to voicemail. He did not call me back. I gave it an hour and rang again, leaving a cheery message to the effect that I couldn't remember whether I had left my number last time, so here it is now! But that was a device designed to make it sound as if I was not actually *hassling* my quarry. Me? Hassle? I do not *hassle*; I leave messages with information you can use. Such as my phone number. So, hey, why not dial it?

This was so transparent it was embarrassing. Now, half an hour after the second call, I was nearing Darrell's home at about the time a financial adviser ought to be leaving for the day, and he still hadn't called. Should I ring again? I felt like a thirteen-year-old deciding whether to chase a girl. If you had called and she hadn't called back, then that was it. You should move on. But the inner workings of a thirteen-year-old fizzing and popping with hormones were nothing compared with my head.

Darrell would have gone into work and told his colleagues about the guy he met who was following him and this – this! (flourishes IA74407937A) – ten-dollar bill. All his workmates would have laughed and told him he was a putz. It had to be a scam, or I was a serial killer. He would have turned white, realising that he had given me his address the night before, and now he was avoiding me. He would never go home again. One of his banker friends would be lighting a cigar with the bill and having the temerity to call me a stalker at this very second, just as I was driving slowly past Darrell's apartment.

This was in a large and imposing house directly across the street from Wrigley Field, hallowed home of the Chicago Cubs baseball team, one of the most venerable (though unsuccessful) in North America. I sat for a while a short distance from Darrell's front door, like a cop on a stake-out. Except I wasn't eating doughnuts and chocolate. I was smoking again. Nerves.

Restrictions around the baseball ground meant that I could not park for long, so I fired up the engine and drove round the block. The streets behind Darrell's were intimate and tree-lined, filled with a variety of sturdy and expensive-looking houses, some made from wood, others brick or brownstone. As an area dominated by sport, it reminded me of the streets behind Arsenal's old stadium at Highbury in north London and I felt briefly at home. I hadn't expected anywhere in Chicago to be this pretty. Later I was to find that I was hopelessly ill-informed as usual, but I went easy on myself and blamed those roadside hoardings. NUMBER . . . ONE . . . FOR . . . GUN . . . CRIME.

It was 6.50 and there were 2,520.7 miles on the clock. I called Darrell again but there was no reply. He had cold, cold feet for sure.

To kill some time I telephoned Paul Coleman, Dean and Ron one after the other. I told them about my situation and they each offered to help in their own way. Dean wanted to ring Darrell and, assuming the call would go to voicemail, leave a reassuring message saying what a nice chap I was. He might even sing it. Paul offered to leave a more forceful message intended to encourage Darrell to pick up the goddamn phone. And Ron offered to jump in his car with a baseball bat to sort out the problem once and for all. By that, I assumed he meant he would put in some batting practice at Wrigley Field after having a quiet word with Darrell. I thanked them for raising my spirits but declined all offers of help. It was 7.30 and I drove around again. Periodically, I would pull over and have a smoke before moving on when people began looking at me through their blinds. It was now very dark.

I had a contingency plan for the loss of the bill which I would be reluctant to put into operation but which just might work. Wherever I happened to be when I lost sight of the ten, I would contact the local newspaper, radio and TV stations and ask for help. It would be an irresistible news item: *Have You Seen This Bill? English Reporter in Lost Cash Drama*. I had pictures of the bill, its markings and serial number. If it had not left the immediate area, then there was a good chance that someone would find it in their pocket. I could offer a reward of ten dollars . . .

This might work even in a cold-feet scenario. The bearer of

the bill would spend the money eventually – probably sooner rather than later as they would want to be rid of the damned thing – and it would be back in circulation. I would then follow the person whose attention had been drawn to the ten dollars by the news coverage I had generated. If this worked there was every likelihood that I would be insufferably smug and best avoided.

But it wouldn't work if one of Darrell's banker friends really had used it to light a fat cigar.

Dean had suggested that if that happened, I should simply give another ten-dollar bill away at exactly the spot where mine was last seen and begin following it. But that didn't seem right. If I couldn't follow IA74407937A then I would go home. It was as simple as that.

I was annoyed at myself for lighting another cigarette when my phone rang. It was 7.51. I heard Darrell's voice. If I hadn't been sitting down, I would have hopped from foot to foot.

'Hey, man,' he said, sounding relaxed and in good spirits. 'Sorry I didn't get back today – I've been so busy and then I came to the gym and switched off the phone. I forgot about you!'

Mentally, I was going Mwah! Mwah! Mwah! into the mouthpiece, but I tried to stay calm. I was still in business, still on the move, still following the money. Having confirmed that he had IA74407937A in his possession, Darrell said he was going straight home after the gym and planned to turn in early as he had been up at dawn to catch his flight. But I didn't mind a bit. This was what he would be doing anyway, even if I weren't parked fifty feet from his house like an itinerant psycho.

'Shall I see you in the morning? Or at lunchtime?' I asked.

'I'll call when I'm going to spend the money,' he said. 'Get some rest. You've had a helluva journey.'

I'd had a helluva ride.

I had nowhere to stay and began cruising for motels near Darrell's home, but those I saw looked run-down and uninviting. I was desperately tired but had no desire to lay down my head in another fleapit. I followed signs for downtown and as I drew closer my weariness fell away. Chicago was the antithesis of St Louis: it had problems of its own but was not burdened with the sad phenomenon of urban flight. The city rose ahead of me, glowing in the dark. I drove aimlessly, feeling at home with the buzz of it. Somehow I found myself near the Opera House and was glad again to be in a metropolis. There were young urbanites spilling out of cool bars and fusion restaurants, limousines pulling up outside hotels that reeked of solidity and money, audiences decanting noisily from shining theatres and, in the darker places, the homeless, drawn to the big city and crushed by the unbearable weight of it.

I pulled over at several hotels and quickly left them. Their rates were two, three and four times my budget. I drove north and stumbled upon the Inn on Lincoln Park, which was situated between the park of the same name and the neighbourhood of Lakeview. It was the most expensive place I had stayed on the journey so far, but it was also the most comforting. Before I checked in I noticed that it was located close to a host of bars and restaurants, but I resisted the temptation to go out. It was only 10 p.m. but I was hungry and tired, so dialling a local food delivery was clearly the best option. I ordered lasagne from a nearby restaurant, had a glass of wine, set my alarm for 6 a.m. and went to sleep. I had heard that these money men had a habit of rising early.

It was still dark when I woke but the sun soon rose sharp and bright in a pale blue cloudless sky. I showered, dressed and packed my bags reluctantly. I liked it here but had to be ready to scramble at a moment's notice. I explained my situation to the hotel receptionist and asked whether it would be better to leave my car here or try to find parking in the financial district where Darrell worked. He told me to leave the car. I could be back here in a taxi in ten minutes, whereas I might need to take out a mortgage for a downtown parking space.

I had coffee and a doughnut for breakfast and walked down Diversey Parkway to North Sheridan Road and Lincoln Park, where I caught a bus, ostensibly to the Art Institute of Chicago, which I intended to visit. But I simply couldn't stay on board after seeing Lake Michigan for the first time. I climbed down from the bus and made my way to Oak Street Beach, which had been raked and cleaned. The air was crisp and autumnal. This is something that Chicagoans must take for granted, but to find oneself in brilliant sunshine on a beach in October, with crystal blue water to the left and an iconic skyline towering to the right, was simply breathtaking. The beach was deserted save for the occasional jogger and lovers walking hand in hand near the waterline. A bag lady was searching trash cans unaware that gulls were wheeling above her, hoping she might unearth some scraps. Lake Michigan was still and flat to its eastern horizon and an unlikely sense of peace descended on me. I was next to the water but felt I could reach out and touch the city. It was quiet, with only a soft hum of traffic and the random echo of car horns bouncing and fading through the canyons of skyscrapers.

I called Darrell and went straight to voicemail. All I could say was hello in plaintive tones that might remind him that I existed. He had work to do and I felt guilty impinging on that, but I couldn't bear the thought of him forgetting that he was carrying something precious to me; something he might pull out of his wallet and spend at any moment.

Farther along the beach a group of students had rigged up a low tightrope between two poles and were practising balancing and somersaults. I sat for a while watching them until they asked me to try for myself. Their names were Ben, Mary, Joseph, Sam and Alissa and they ranged in age from nineteen to twenty-one. They were so open and generous that I felt unable to say no, even though I fully expected to take a tumble. Ben explained that what I was about to try was actually called slacklining, as it used a kind of flat nylon webbing rather than rope. I stepped up but could do nothing to prevent the webbing from oscillating wildly from side to side and I fell off. Ben took my hand and I managed a few steps before bouncing a little and jumping down. When most teenagers would have mocked the pathetic old bloke who was toppling from their high-tech tightrope with rather too much gusto, these didn't. It was a generous attitude I was to encounter again and again. I had begun to fall in love with Chicago.

Alexander Hamilton's Day Off

There was nothing I could do except take a look around, so I did. I walked north to south along Michigan Avenue, the Magnificent Mile with its swanky shops, wide sidewalks and flower beds, over the Chicago River, through Millennium Park and on to the Art Institute of Chicago, where I had intended my bus journey to end. There was a confidence about the city that I had rarely encountered outside New York, Paris and London (whose qualities were diverse anyway). The Chicago I had seen in films appeared somewhat dour, but this gleamed with a swagger and elegance that I had not expected. I knew it would be impressive, but not quite so impressive as this. It was grand in scale while feeling people-friendly. At Millennium Park I stood in silent admiration of the pavilion designed by Frank Gehry, with its curves and swirls reminiscent of his Guggenheim Museum in Bilbao. I was struck by the thought that on Gehry's first day at school, his mother must have forgotten to pack a ruler, and he decided never to take one. A stone's throw away was Anish Kapoor's *Cloud Gate*, a seamless and shining stainless-steel sculpture that had come to be called 'The Bean' because of its shape. Its reflective distortion of the city seemed apposite, reminding me of all the misplaced assumptions with which I had begun each leg of my travels, not least this one. Fleetingly, I thought I might be in danger of learning something.

As usual, I did not know how long the luxury of being a tourist might last, and no visit to Chicago would be complete without a ride to the top of the Sears Tower, once the tallest building in the world. I looked around and could see its upper floors, so I struck out in its direction. I reckoned it was five or six blocks west along Monroe and then two or three south. I admit I wasn't concentrating, excited by everything I saw and trying – pointlessly – to compare Chicago with New York, but I realised after half an hour that I was no nearer to the tower than when I started. I knew it was more than a hundred storeys high and, as a trained observer, I expected to be able to locate it; it wasn't exactly small. But the closer I felt I came to it, the more geometry and scale conspired to hide it from me. I walked around and around, fully aware that all I had to do was stop and ask somebody, but I felt foolish. ''Scuse me, I'm looking for one of the largest man-made structures in the world. It's about spitting distance from here. Could you tell me where it is please?' So on I walked, like a mapless male motorist who refuses to ask for directions.

After a while, I stopped for a drink and a hot dog, inexplicably the first of my trip, and wondered what American tourists must think when they asked for one in the UK. There was no comparison. I felt revived and set off again to find the tower, this time resolving to swallow my pride and ask for help. After a few yards I saw a man in a smart commissionaire's uniform and approached him rather meekly.

'I'm very sorry,' I said, 'but this is going to be the dumbest question you'll hear all day. I know it's here somewhere, but . . . ahem . . . I can't find the Sears Tower. Could you point it out?'

He smiled.

'That is not a dumb question, sir, because it would not be possible for so many people to be that dumb.' I had no idea what he was talking about, but then he explained. 'I get it all day, every day. Your problem is that it isn't called the Sears Tower any more. It was renamed the Willis Tower in 2009.'

I suddenly felt that the name Willis was terribly familiar. In fact I was sure I had already walked past a building called the Willis Tower. I looked over my shoulder just as the commissionaire pointed to a door three yards behind me. 'I think you'll find that's what you're looking for,' he said. I wondered whether he had been put there simply to redirect people like me. As I stepped through the door I realised he had managed to steer me there without making me feel completely stupid, which was an achievement in itself.

I hadn't been this excited since my visit to the Gangster Museum of America back in Hot Springs. The tower's elevators whizzed up at something like 400 miles an hour to an observation deck on the 103rd floor of the building, but first there was a brief film about its construction and the history of modern Chicago.

The shape of the city centre was largely determined by a great fire on 8 October 1871 which consumed four square miles and killed somewhere in the region of 300 people. It had also left 100,000 homeless. The conflagration was a tragedy that might have brought a lesser city to its knees, but Chicagoans rose to the challenge with the kind of spirit that saw Londoners through the Blitz. They rolled up their sleeves and got on with rebuilding. As soon as the ground had cooled enough to begin clearing up, foundations were being laid for the future Chicago. Developers and industrialists borrowed huge sums of money and some of America's most talented architects relocated here as the city grew stronger, from the ashes. Before the fire, good rail transportation and the Illinois and Michigan Canal, which provided a link from the Great Lakes to the Illinois River when it was opened in 1848, had made Chicago the country's most important market for food and construction commodities. The canal allowed onward travel to the Mississippi and the Gulf of Mexico, taking ships across the portage identified by our friends Marquette and Joliet way back in 1673. Lumber, grain, meat, iron and steel were all channelled through a state-of-the-art Lake Michigan harbour for onward shipment or manufacture. It all meant that the city was too important to be allowed to fail. As building progressed, Chicago continued to boom, and during the next two decades the cost of city centre land increased tenfold to almost a million dollars an acre. That meant the only way to make real estate financially viable was to build higher and higher. And this led to the birth of the skyscraper. Architects and engineers designed buildings that would no longer be supported by ever thicker foundations and brick walls, but by an internal steel skeleton that was much lighter. The Home Insurance Building, designed by William Le Baron Jenney and finished in 1885, was regarded as the world's first skyscraper because of its use of a steel frame, which made it one-third the weight of similar structures built from masonry alone. Weight – within reason – would no longer be the nemesis of height.

Fast-forward almost a century and it would have seemed odd, at the opening of the Sears Tower in 1973, if anyone had mentioned the fact that that first skyscraper was a paltry ten storeys high. The tower commissioned by Sears, Roebuck & Co., then America's biggest retailers, boasted 110 storeys and was, at 1,451 feet, or 442m, the tallest building in the world, surpassing the 1,368-foot-high World Trade Center's North Tower. It remained so for an impressive twenty-five years, until it was overtaken by the twin Petronas Towers in Kuala Lumpur. (At the time of writing, the title is held by the Burj Khalifa in Dubai which is almost twice the height of the Sears/Willis building, standing at 2,717 feet, or 828m.)

The elevator took one minute to reach the tower's Skydeck on the 103rd floor. I worked out that if the building had been laid down horizontally – which would have done nothing to alleviate Chicago's shortage of commercial office space at the time – it would have taken Sir Roger Bannister about the same time to cover the distance.

I had a particular reason for coming here. I knew I was unlikely to see Darrell or the bill for some time; it seemed he was a workaholic and although I was prepared to follow him at lunchtime, I was secretly betting he didn't do lunch. If I was right, then that meant I would have a free day, just like one of my heroes. *Ferris Bueller's Day Off,* a movie about a student, wise beyond his years, who skips school in order to squeeze every ounce of joy from a single day, was one of my favourite films. Ferris had come here to the Skydeck, put his forehead to the glass and watched the people of Chicago, like ants scuttling about their business, 1,353 feet below. But he was not the only person to do this and over the years the glass around the Skydeck had been almost permanently dotted with hand and forehead prints. When the Willis people took over, they decided to make it easier for people to look down. Looking out was easy, and on a clear day you could see for fifty miles, east over the lake to Michigan, to Wisconsin in the north-west, Indiana to the south-east and south-west over the plains of Illinois.

But looking down was harder, as Ferris had discovered for himself.

Willis solved the problem by commissioning the building of four glass boxes that protruded four feet from the western façade of the tower. Collectively, they called this the Ledge, and I wanted to stand on it.

The observation level is a wonder in its own right, particularly if – as I was – you are fortunate enough to visit on a fine and clear day. I put a quarter into a telescope on the north side to get a better view of Wrigley Field and Lincoln Park Zoo. To the south I squinted at Soldier Field, home of the Chicago Bears football team, and Chinatown. Down close to the west was Greektown and off to the east, over Monroe Harbor, was the calm blue of Lake Michigan.

I queued politely for a turn in one of the glass boxes, but as I drew nearer I realised I was in no rush to get to the front. When you reach the fine line where the solid opaque floor ends and you step over on to the glass outside the building, with an unobscured view to the ground far, far below, there is a moment when nothing at all matters except blind faith in mathematics and engineering. Around me echoed the screams of girls and women whose friends and partners were pulling and shoving them on to the glass against their will. As aversion therapy for vertigo, it left something to be desired.

I loved it. I looked down between my dusty feet and found the sense of walking on air, high above the city, exhilarating. I wondered whether birds felt this superior when they saw us rooted to the ground, lumbering against gravity, anchored and graceless like lummoxes.

Back down on the street I called Darrell and went to voicemail again. I said I was downtown.

For the rest of the day I tried to behave like a tourist but found my velocity stunted by weariness and anticipation. I walked and walked around the Loop of the central business district, visited expensive shopping malls, sloped under the elevated railway, mooched up the Navy Pier, which was essentially a theme park for children, bounced in and out of a couple of bars, made my way back to the lake and sat next to Ohio Street Beach watching joggers who had just finished work. They looked terribly disapproving when I lit a cigarette.

Would Darrell ever call? I took a ten-dollar bill out of my pocket and looked at Alexander Hamilton. What would you do? I wondered.

It was growing dark and I felt increasingly guilty being surrounded by joggers, cyclists and people on skateboards. When I saw a man swimming in the icy lake, I turned tail and dipped back into the city along East Chicago Avenue and past the headquarters of the American Dental Association. The building was cracked and discoloured, which came as a terrible disappointment.

I had settled down to a beer in a bar called Pippin's Tavern when Darrell finally called. He suggested we meet later at his home. I arrived at eight and he took me to a bar in Wrigleyville, a few hundred yards from the baseball stadium. I could tell he wanted to be friendly, but there was also a residual mistrust that I would have to work through, and if I had been in his shoes I would have felt exactly the same. I might not even have turned up. He worked for J.P. Morgan, the investment bank, advising clients on everything from pensions to share portfolios. He had a thousand clients with an average of a quarter of a million dollars to invest and he had been successfully advising them and earning their trust for fifteen years. He took pride in his job and seemed to care about the welfare of the people he advised. It struck me that I had no right to find this surprising. A journalist judging a banker.

And then the financial collapse of 2008 hit him like a twentieth-floor suicide.

'God,' he said. 'It was awful. I had experienced bad times – I'd been through 2000 and 2001, when the dotcom bubble burst – but this was far worse than that. I had my worst year ever and so did my clients. A lot of them were seniors with what you call "401K" pensions. They're company retirement plans that workers can draw down on from the age of fifty-nine and manage themselves. When times were good, they would take my advice and then come on down to my office and have a coffee and take credit for how well their money was doing. I was happy to let them. But when everything turned sour, they didn't want the blame. They put that on me. Some of them actually blamed me for the collapse of the world economy and they were very, very angry. There were times when I was afraid to walk to my car. Some would come and visit me and at times it was like being a therapist; they were ruined and needed someone to talk to. I really felt for them but there was only so much I could do.

'I advised them to hold their nerve – the market would recover over time. But they felt burned and a lot of them got out at the bottom. They would no longer listen to me or to anyone else. Everyone suddenly became risk-averse. I left my own investments, but I have time. My younger clients have time to recover too, but the older ones don't. They could be dead before the market gets back to where it was before the crash.'

The cynic in me had wondered whether bankers like Darrell secretly despised their clients for their ignorance, but he didn't. He seemed deeply concerned. He reckoned that between September 2007 and February 2009, the average investment portfolio lost 60 per cent of its value, recoverable if you happened to be fifty-nine, but financially catastrophic if you were sixty-five.

When it was time to leave, Darrell insisted on paying for our drinks and pulled out a credit card. I left a tip in cash. I could see the ten-dollar bill in his wallet, but it stayed there.

'You use plastic a lot?' I asked.

'All the time.'

We strolled down to a bar called Trace, where I felt obliged to buy the drinks after Darrell's generosity. I began talking to a slightly bohemian couple and Darrell told them about my mission.

'Get outta here!' the woman said.

'No, I'm not kidding,' said Darrell, and he produced the ten-dollar bill. 'You can be part of it. Hey –' and he pointed to a small Thermos flask she was clutching in her hand '– I'll buy your flask for ten dollars.'

I felt like someone in a slave auction and half expected the woman to start squeezing my arms and probing my gums.

'Sure!' she said. 'And I get the ten-dollar bill – *that* ten-dollar bill?'

'Yeah, but you gotta take him with you. He comes with the deal. You have to let him follow you round until you spend it.'

The couple giggled and whispered, but their laughter subsided as quickly as their enthusiasm. It was as if they had been drunk and suddenly became sober. They looked me up and down.

'Naaahh – but, hey. Good luck!'

Darrell could be my financial adviser any time he wanted. He could read people.

'You knew they wouldn't take it, didn't you?' I asked.

'Yep,' he said.

We said goodnight and I headed on back to the Inn on Lincoln Park to check in all over again.

Money (2)

It took two more days for Darrell to spend the money while I went slowly insane. Each morning I checked out of the hotel and explored, venturing further into Chicago's satellite villages and suburbs in the growing belief that my services as a money chaser would not be required. Darrell was not doing this on purpose; he just didn't use cash.

Although I wanted the money to move faster, I had no reason to complain. The American website wheresgeorge.com, which went live in December 1998, invites visitors to register serial numbers of bills of all denominations so the bills' progress can be followed. So far, more than 190 million have been recorded on the site, a number so vast that statisticians have found it useful as a tool for modelling how people move. If a dollar travels from A to B, it is usually because it is in someone's pocket. In 2009, statistics from wheresgeorge.com were even used to predict the movement of swine flu. Researchers who took part in that project found that the upper end of an average nine-month journey was 500 miles. I had done more than four times that in three weeks. We imagine that money flies and wheels insanely around us, but the fact is it doesn't. How many times have you left a ten-pound note or a twenty-dollar bill in your wallet for days on end? When you do spend money, how often do you take it to your local greengrocer or newsagent a couple of hundred yards away? And if it isn't on a main road, what is the likelihood of the note going any further than the wallet of the next person who receives it in change? Someone who might be your neighbour?

And consider the effect of plastic on the journey of paper money. During my ten-pound note escapade, I was frustratingly becalmed twice. The first time was perhaps understandable: we were at a private members' golf club where everyone had an account. It was obvious from the start that we might have problems, as everything was simply signed for. But the second time had me utterly confused. We were stranded at a petrol station where the ten-pound note got stuck in the till for around twelve hours. How could that be? Well, if someone filled up with fuel, they usually paid with plastic. If they paid with cash, then most likely they were buying a small amount of petrol – say, ten or twenty pounds' worth – and they had the correct money. If they came in for a pint of milk or a newspaper, they used coins or a five or a ten. You rarely buy a pint of milk with a twenty-pound note.

In the UK, the use of plastic overtook cash at the end of 2004. In the US, this happened in 2006.

Chicago's little districts, self-contained and with some beautiful architecture, reminded me of London's. Clapham, Islington, Dulwich and Hampstead might be swapped for Wicker Park, Lakeview, Lincoln Park or Wrigleyville. I drove and strolled, impressed with the restaurants, shops and bars, all welcoming and interesting in their own way. Chicago was as infuriatingly attractive as those rarest of people, the ones who were cool without trying.

I had to explain to the staff at my hotel why I kept checking in and out, and they joined in the spirit of the thing. In the end, my stay there extended beyond Darrell, and the uncertainty of where I would sleep was removed by the kindness of the receptionists, who kept a room open for me each day, even if the rest of the hotel was fully booked. I thanked them, but they couldn't possibly understand how much stress this relieved me of. I had my phone, my car and my bags packed at all times, but it meant that Chicago became for me a place of rest after weeks of chaos.

I ate food from around the world, exciting and reviving my taste buds. I bounced around the city, sampled its bars and galleries, listened to jazz and comedy, feasted in Chinatown and Greektown and realised that although I wanted to be on the road again, I also didn't want to leave. I loved New York but I found Chicago and Chicagoans more welcoming than New Yorkers. I told them this but I think they already knew it. It was something in which they took pride.

I seized the opportunity to have my clothes laundered properly and was in such a good mood that I didn't make a fuss when my jeans came back with a raggedy tear in the backside. I put them on, looked in the mirror and laughed. If I had been twenty years younger, they might have seemed trendy. As it was, I looked like a middle-age man with his arse hanging out of his trousers. I could have bought another pair but, strangely, I felt this would have been cheating. I didn't know why, but it felt like stoicism and that had been lacking in me.

On the third night that Darrell had the bill, he stayed in. On the fourth, we went back to Trace and he gave the money as a tip to the barman, Adam Antonucci, in the early hours of day 22. We said our goodbyes and by the time he left I felt Darrell had finally come to believe that he was not at the blunt end of a scam. If I'd had ten dollars to invest, I would have given it to him.

I ordered another drink and tried to get to know Adam, but it wasn't easy. Trace grew busier as the night wore on and he was on a 4 a.m. shift. The money was in his pocket but there was still time for him to use it, to repay a debt to a customer or a member of staff; to pop out and buy cigarettes or spend it on a cab or to lose it.

After a while he came to my end of the bar holding the note above his head. Oh, God, I thought, he had changed his mind.

'Here, you take it,' he said. 'I can't bear the responsibility.'

'You want to quit? You want to back out?'

I was quivering on my bar stool. What did all this mean for continuity? For the purity of my journey? He was slim and handsome, with cool long hair and a sculpted goatee and sideburns. If anyone was going to ruin this trip I wanted them to be a pathetic loser. If someone this cool abandoned it, then that would make *me* the loser . . .

'No,' he said. 'I want you to take it into protective custody. I don't trust myself. I'll lose it or spend it and I'll forget to tell you when I do. I finish at 4 and I'm taking my bike home. I'll sleep till 2 or 3 tomorrow afternoon. Call me then and we can talk.'

Protective custody. I liked that. I liked it even better that I had found someone who trusted himself less than I did.

I would have just one more drink.

As the volume in the bar increased, I fingered the ten dollars in my pocket and wondered who *I* could turn to for protective custody.

I met Adam early the following evening at the Firkin and Pheasant pub on Diversey Parkway, not far from my hotel. The pub had four types of English bitter, so I told him that his choice of venue was inspired.

'So,' he said, 'what do you want to do?'

'That's up to you.'

'What do you mean?'

'Well, wherever you go, I go. That's what we'll do.'

'No, no, no,' he said, wagging his finger. 'I have a date.'

'Great. I'll come too. Is she a looker?'

'No way, man. You are not coming on a date with me.'

'Don't you think she'll understand?'

'That's not the point.'

'I think it is. What kind of a person wouldn't understand if you brought along a ten-dollar bill and the man pursuing it across the United States of America? Are you sure she's the right person for you?'

'You are *not* coming on a date with me.'

'Where are we taking her?'

'We're going for dinner at . . . nah, nah! No way!'

'I could sit at the next table. She need never know I'm there. If you spend the money, I'd be gone before she even noticed.'

'Absolutely not. I am *not* going to let you blow this for me.'

'What if I just sit in my car and stare at you through the window?'

'No!'

I handed over the bill.

'Hereby released from protective custody. What do you want to do now?'

'Let's have a drink,' he said, and I had an awful feeling he was going to stand her up.

Adam told me an amazing story.

He was thirty-five and even though he was originally from

Chicago he had been something of a drifter. He was a qualified youth worker, specialising in wilderness adventures for problem kids – fishing, camping, outdoorsmanship – but he had always worked bars in between his more serious jobs. He had lived in West Virginia, Washington State, Arizona, New Hampshire, Hawaii and Illinois.

'Thing is,' he said, 'as a barman, you have a shelf life. There comes a time when bar owners don't really want you around. You aren't good for the image of the bar. They want someone *younger.*'

'You're kidding me . . .' He was so handsome. I couldn't believe that anyone would disqualify him in this way.

'No, really. It's even worse for women; they hit their shelf life earlier. It really isn't fair. You want a bartender's job after that, then you have to actually *know* someone at the bar. I came back a couple of months ago because my sister had gotten ill, and I'd been away for a while – my contacts weren't so good any more and I was struggling to find a job. One night I was just sitting at the bar in Trace, wondering what I should do next, when I realised I was kicking something under my stool. It was a woman's bag; her purse. I picked it up and shouted to the guy behind the bar, telling him what I'd found. Next thing this woman runs up and gives me a big thank-you kiss. It was her purse and the guy was her husband, the owner of the bar. They were called Jason and Jenny.

'So I get talking to Jason and explain that I'm looking for a bartending job, but I can see that he doesn't need anyone. We talk about my past and I tell him I went to Prescott College in Arizona and studied outdoor leadership. Then I tell him about the time me and some of the other students were taken out into the wild for an emergency medical trial as part of our course – you know, it's a pretend scenario where someone's been injured and you have to fix them up. We hiked up into the mountains to search for this person who'd been "injured" and we stumbled upon this guy who told us he had fallen down a cliff the day before. He had some nasty injuries – broken bones – and he was badly dehydrated. At first, we thought this was a really convincing exam with some pretty good special effects. Then we realised this guy was for real and so were his injuries. We saved his life. Pure chance. That was ten years ago.

'Well, Jason stood up behind the bar and looked me straight in the eye. "I know that story," he said. "That was my best friend, Eric." And he gave me a job on the spot.'

I mean, what are the odds?

I had promised Adam the night before that allowing me to follow the money wouldn't cost him a penny, so when the bill came for pints and pints of beer followed by shots, I dutifully picked up a sixty-dollar tab. I knew what was coming next; he would leave the ten dollars as a tip at the bar. That was two bartender tips in as many nights, but mine was not to reason why.

I paid the bar manager, Megan Schneider, and Adam handed over the ten-dollar bill, explaining that I came with it. Megan was young and had a broad, friendly smile. She looked too young to be in charge of such a big venue and I was sure she would certainly not have time for me. I shook her hand and said goodbye to Adam. It was just after ten o'clock on Friday night.

'Sorry, but I'm going to be boring,' she said, biting her lip. 'I go home tonight and then I'll stay there all day tomorrow packing for a big trip. I won't be buying anything. I'm going to Michigan on Sunday to hunt deer with my dad . . . We have a cabin there . . . It's in the woods . . . We hunt with bows and arrows . . . Near an Amish community . . . Hey – you could come!'

Could it *be* more boring?

God (2)

You should never encourage an Amish man to get into a pissing contest.

I was mentally filing this in the folder marked: 'You Offended Him But I Think You Got Away With It' as John Brenneman stared me out, refusing to answer the question I had just put to him.

We were standing in one of his barns, him wearing dungarees, white shirt, boots and straw hat, me with my waterproof coat, torn jeans and underpants with the footballs on, and I had just been admiring two Amish buggies. They were black with oilcloth sides to make them waterproof and their weight was supported by generous springs to give a comfortable ride on unmade roads. Only a couple of hours earlier I had followed something similar in my car and chuckled when I clocked it doing thirteen miles an hour, faster than the average speed of traffic in London. John had told me that one of these buggies had been made by his younger brother, William, and the other by a man called Levi Yoder. The two men made all the buggies for the community of 120 families.

'Who makes the best ones?' I asked, grinning. 'Is it William? I bet it is. Go on, you can tell me!'

But John just stared at me. Showing a preference for one person's work over another's would have been rude and inconsiderate. Encouraging one man to boast that his work was better than another's would have been worse. It would have fostered vanity and that was something with which John had no truck.

The smile on my face seeped away like mercury through a grater.

It was day 25, a Monday, and I was in Morley, Mecosta County, in rural Michigan. I had not seen Megan since the night of day 22 and I was in big trouble. I had taken Saturday off and called her in the afternoon to make arrangements for travelling to her father's cabin. The call went to voicemail so I left a message and she didn't call back.

On Sunday morning, the day she was to travel, I tried again and again but there was no reply. I was afraid we were getting into creepy territory and felt very uncomfortable.

What had happened? It was obvious. She had called her father and told him that a guy in her pub was following a ten-dollar bill that she had been given as a tip and so she had invited him up here, the middle of nowhere, to stay with them in their isolated shack. Megan was aged twenty-four. Her father would have fallen silent for several minutes when she told him this.

'Let me get this right,' he would have said, eventually. 'We are going to our cabin in the woods, far from any other habitation, with no electricity, running water and, perhaps more importantly, NO TELEPHONE LINE OR CELLPHONE SIGNAL, and you have invited a complete stranger, someone who is certifiable – he is following a goddamn ten-dollar bill for Chrissakes! – to stay with us in our cabin bristling with hunting weapons? Have I just about got that covered?'

'Uh huh.'

Megan had told me the general area where their cabin was located – near the townships of Morley and Stanwood – and that the nearest town was Big Rapids, but finding the actual cabin would be impossible even if I had wanted to try, which I didn't. There's creepy and there's psychotic and I didn't want to be either. It was only a ten-dollar bill.

I was sick of the inside of my hotel room and surveyed my packed rucksack and the plastic bag I used to carry my boots. What should I do? Stay in Chicago and wait for a call that might never come? Or get on the road again, head for Big Rapids some 200 miles away and see what happened next? If Megan and her father decided they didn't want a stranger in their midst, then I would see a gloriously beautiful part of America and call it a day.

It was time to check out anyway and if I was going to make this journey it would be better to make it in daylight when I could see my surroundings. My mind was made up.

I headed south out of Chicago, skirted east along the bottom of Lake Michigan and swept into Indiana – my fifth state after Kansas, Missouri, Arkansas and Illinois. Ugly and industrial Gary crept up on me, the landscape around it stained with chemical plants and trailer homes. A dead skunk lay at the side of the road and the funk around its body seeped into my car, heavy and cloying like burnt rubber. The weather was perfect for driving, dry and sunny with a cloudless sky. It was cold outside, but inside I was warm and my spirits were high. The route turned north, first on the I-94 and then on the I-196, and followed the contours of Lake Michigan at a frustrating distance, so that glimpses of its placid blue waters were welcome but rare. Past Portage the trees grew thicker and there were high forests of red and brown, russet and gold. At exactly 2.03 p.m. I crossed into Michigan, my sixth state, and was struck by the number of deer carcasses lying at the side of the road. They had bounded fatally into headlights from woods of ash and maple, poplar and birch.

The road ran east of Benton Harbor and the countryside opened up to reveal farmland and a hardy vineyard. There were more pine forests now, growing darker green as grey clouds began to roll across them, low and chill. The route turned inland, heading east towards Grand Rapids, and suddenly there were signs for Holland and Zeeland. At the side of the road were substantial wooden houses painted olive, beige and pale yellow. And, slowly, one after another, red Dutch barns came into view. I skirted Grand Rapids as the sky turned grey and continued north on Highway 131 towards its smaller sister, Big Rapids. The clouds burst and through driving rain I could see that the countryside grew lovelier and more unspoilt with each mile travelled. The road rolled and pitched gently through forests turned rust and orange. And as dusk fell the light from them rendered my progress surreal, as if I were moving through a glowing tapestry woven from threads of brass or bronze. Dusk failed as I crossed into Mecosta County and found the centre of Big Rapids, uninspiring in the dark with only the lights of its retail parks to guide me – WalMart, K-Mart, Meijer. I bought some cheese and a salad, battled through fierce rain to a cheap motel and turned in for the night.

I hoped that Megan had missed the worst of the weather.

And so I found myself with John Brenneman. I had heard nothing from Megan that morning and came to the conclusion that my journey was over. It was a shame, but I had had a good run and, frankly, I couldn't blame her father for not wanting their peace shattered by an outsider. I would stay another night and do some exploring. I was excited by the proximity of an Amish community and wondered whether they might tell me about their way of life. My hotel receptionist said that the Amish were often to be seen in town in their horse-drawn buggies, the men dressed like John, the women in dark blue woollen dresses, pale blue aprons and white bonnets. Their handiwork was admired and valued. Their best craftsmen made furniture, jewellery and rugs and their carpenters were sought after by locals who wanted a new porch or a roof fixing that would last. Out in the countryside, stalls in front of their wooden clapboard homes sold honey and vegetables, pumpkins and fruit. One man was renowned for his butchery skills, another for the quality of his leather halters and saddles. I headed south to take a look for myself.

I had driven through this landscape in darkness the night before. In daylight, it proved to be wide open, fertile and lush with corn swaying in the breeze. It was a fresh, bright day with blue skies and thin cloud travelling fast in lofty streams. Long, straight roads cut through the landscape and every mile or two was a farmhouse backing on to well-tended pasture or fields of grain or pumpkin. The Amish houses were easy to identify: either on the porch or on the lawn were long washing lines of clothes drying in the wind. They had large families and there would be row upon row of white shirts, dungarees, blue dresses and aprons. At the side of the road were yellow diamond-shaped warning signs imprinted with the silhouette of an Amish horse and buggy. I had seen such signs many times before, but usually they bore the image of a deer. I stumbled upon a school and slowed a little. It was playtime and the girls were on one side of a field outside their classroom, holding on to their bonnets in the wind, and the boys were on another, clutching their straw hats. Several stopped what they were doing as I passed and waved at me. I waved back and sped up.

I found myself awkward in a different way from how I had felt with the Walkers. They were taking their beliefs out into the world and although I found the subject matter uncomfortable, Nathan and Jennifer were only too pleased to discuss it. The Amish did not evangelise; they just wanted to be left alone to live their lives. I would approach carefully and if my presence was not wanted I would turn round and go back. But how to make the first move?

I stopped at a large white house by the side of the road that had a stall laid out with peppers and spinach, a variety of squashes, apples and gourds. Alongside the gourds was a sign that explained how to dry them out and turn them into bird boxes. It was all for sale underneath a white awning. A smiling Amish woman came out of the house followed by a straggle of young children. They were shy and curious and hung on to their mother's skirts. I bought some apples and two bracelets made from string and beads, but I had no idea what to say next. It seemed ridiculous to explain that I was an interested foreigner and would love nothing more than to sit down and have a conversation. Instead, I explained that I wanted to buy a rug. Buying rugs took time and everywhere I had ever haggled for one – in the Middle East, the Far East, South-East Asia and North Africa – the encounter had been accompanied by tea or coffee and friendly discussion.

The woman directed me to a farm about a mile away where, she said, someone might be able to help me. I drove up slowly. The farmhouse was painted white and near to it was a cavernous red Dutch barn. The doors were open and I could see two men inside in the Amish dress. One was on a mini Caterpillar bulldozer, which puzzled me; I understood they shunned modern technology. I got out of my car and approached the older of the two. He smiled and waved and walked towards me to save my having to negotiate a sea of mud. I shook his hand and explained that I had heard someone here made rugs.

'Ah, yes,' he said, with something approaching an Eastern European accent. 'That would be Gideon. Gideon makes good rugs.'

He called over the younger man and we also shook hands. Gideon had a broken-toothed grin that blazed out from a bushy beard and no moustache, which gave him the air of a New England whaler. He had lived a different life from mine, with different stresses and strains, but I guessed he was about twenty-five. He jumped into his buggy and I followed for some two miles until we arrived at a small, run-down farmhouse with grey, peeling paint. Gideon showed me to an outbuilding where he kept a small hand-made loom surrounded by mountains of brightly coloured wool.

'I only have three finished rugs at the moment,' he said, and laid them out before me.

They were rich and heavy, and of a better quality than I had expected. While I decided which to buy, Gideon told me that there were about a hundred families in the Amish community but they generally kept themselves to themselves. He didn't mind talking about their way of life, but there was someone better at it than him. A man called John Brenneman, who lived on 5-Mile Road and made furniture.

I chose a cheerful rug which I resolved to put under my writing desk at home. It cost twenty-five dollars. Then I asked whether I could take a picture of Gideon holding it near his loom.

'No, I'm sorry,' he said. 'You can take as many photographs as you want of our homes, my buggy, our fields – anything. But we don't like being in the pictures.'

There was a horse in a small paddock outside. Gideon saw me looking at it.

'That's Betty,' he said. 'Why don't you take a picture of her?'

So, with Gideon's permission, I draped the rug over Betty and took a photograph. Then I thanked him and made to leave.

'Where are you from?' he asked.

'London. England.'

'What's it like to live there?'

I looked over Gideon's shoulder and saw stalks of corn shimmy in the wind, changing colour as the breeze danced over them. There was no sound except the soft rustle from the fields, like ears of barley poured from a sack or rice on taffeta.

'It can get busy,' I said. 'I don't think you'd like it.'

He seemed pleased by this and gave me his goofy smile, waving as I turned and walked to my car.

John Brenneman was sixty-two but he looked much younger and fitter. He had a big white beard and a weathered face that exuded health and vitality. He was broad-shouldered and his arms were strong. He worked a 120-acre farm for corn, oats and hay, and he had a herd of cows whose milk was sent off every day and made into cheese. If this weren't enough, John was one of the community's ministers and he made much of its furniture. I thought briefly of the hours I wasted each and every day.

We were standing at the back of his house underneath rows and rows of billowing dungarees, pinafores and dresses, socks, shirts and underwear. He introduced me to his wife, Sarah, who was holding a young child. She looked tired but also happy. They had had twelve children.

'We originally came over from the Alsace-Lorraine area in the 1600s and 1700s,' said John. 'Many of the original settlers had been working the land of other people and they wanted farms of their own. They were Christian people of very strong faith and there were constant problems when they were ordered to join armies and fight in the wars of the region. We believe in non-resistance as Jesus taught us.'

I thought back to my classroom history lessons and was familiar with the tensions of the region on the border between Germany and France, tensions which erupted into the Franco-Prussian war of 1870, long after John's ancestors had left. I had visited the region as a young reporter and was taken by the population's laissez-faire attitude to their nationality, sometimes German, sometimes French. Even today, they have a confused – or relaxed – attitude to identity, something perhaps best reflected in their wines: French in the pursuit of perfection, Germanic in taste.

'They first settled in the east, in Pennsylvania, and then spread out to other regions as their need for land grew. This particular community settled in 1982 after spreading out from Ohio, Delaware, New York State and Wisconsin. There were good prices for the land at the time, but now they are very high and it's hard for the young ones to make a living. There are about 120 families, eight schools and five churches, though we don't have churches as you might think of them; they are people's homes.

'We try to have a simple life and we survive on the foods we grow and the animals we raise. We have our own meat, crops and vegetables. We are self-sufficient. I think people once thought we were a little strange, but now they are coming round to our attitudes to food. Some of the talk of GM crops and seeds scares me. Everything we eat is natural. We work hard and we look after our neighbours.'

I asked him about the traditions of barn-raising, where the whole community would turn out to build a house or a barn for a newly married couple, to give them a head start, and John said that this was still a custom.

'These are wonderful days,' he said. There was a wind which nipped at my ears. As John spoke, I pulled up my collar. 'The foundations are laid first and everything for the barn is made in advance and then assembled on the farm in one day. Everybody helps. We make a celebration of it: the women make food while the men build and the children play. It is all about being a good neighbour.'

I asked John to describe a typical day. For him, it began at 4.30 a.m.

'I milk the cows and do other chores like feeding the livestock, then we will have breakfast. In the summer I go to the fields and work the crops, in winter I am up cutting wood and repairing the buildings. We have three good meals a day, the last being at around 9 p.m., then it is time to retire. I am very happy with my life, but it is becoming a struggle. The prices for milk are low, the price for feed is high. My biggest fear is for our children's future.'

Sarah had been away doing her chores but now she joined us. I could hear the sound of a generator and asked John why the Amish would not drive cars but would use motors and the small bulldozer I had seen. I knew they didn't use electricity. He smiled.

'We are basically living the same way as our ancestors did 200 years ago. We don't use cars; we have our horses and buggies. But we do use trains and buses for transportation. We don't use tractors but something like the small machine you saw is allowed.'

John led me to the generator that I had heard. It was hooked up to a washing machine with a small gas pump. I looked across to Sarah and she nodded at the machine and flashed me a look of mock-relief.

Her days began at 5 a.m. with heaps and heaps of clothes washing. I could not imagine how she could have managed without this simple piece of technology. She would start the day by loading the machine before preparing breakfast for her family. Caring for John and the youngest of the children was a full-time job in itself.

John said a local council of ministers conferred on what was and was not acceptable in terms of labour-saving devices and would then ask the Amish church council to decide, but very few things were ever deemed acceptable. Not that they asked for guidance on a regular basis; he said he couldn't remember the last time something new was admitted. They stayed away from junk food and television, read the Bible and tried to adhere to its teachings as much as they could in the modern world. Being neighbourly saw them through most of their difficulties, he said.

The community's ministers and preachers were chosen by lot. John said this was in accordance with the Book of the Acts of the Apostles, in which Jesus chose the men who would spread His word. Every two weeks the homes of the preachers were used for prayer meetings.

'It's much simpler than having a church,' said John.

People outside the community later told me that this avoided property taxes, because homes were also deemed places of worship. It might have been a cynical observation, but it was the only one I encountered. Contrary to Hollywood depictions of the Amish being ostracised or victimised by local bullies, Gideon and John told me that they were treated kindly and with respect by the ordinary folk of Morley, Stanwood and Big Rapids. Certainly when I spoke to them, the locals seemed to enjoy having gentle God-fearing people living on their doorstep.

John took me into his workshop and I was sent reeling by the smell of wood and oil. Tools hung from the ceiling and walls like the inside of an obsessive magpie's nest. He made rocking chairs and wardrobes, tables and cupboards, each from oak, pine or cedar and hand-carved with a workmanship I had not seen since I was a boy. I sat on a rocking chair fashioned from curly maple. The detail was astonishing. He made them in batches of four over a two-week period. I bought a box from him made from oak and pine to put on top of my writing desk; it would hold my pens and notebooks and the other flotsam that seemed to gather all by itself from one day to the next.

I had been asking all the questions, but then John asked me what I was doing, and no matter how hard I tried to explain, he simply could not understand. I showed him a copy of the original article I had written about a ten-pound note.

'What's a ten-pound note?' he asked. But he couldn't get a grasp on it. 'Is it like a ten-dollar bill?'

I said it was exactly like a ten-dollar bill.

There was a sudden commotion and John ran off down the pasture. A gate had swung open and his cows were pouring out, thinking milking time had come early, and we chased and rounded them up in the mud.

He was busy. It was time to leave.

I thanked John and Sarah and he meandered away without ceremony, off to do some more chores, not waving. I felt richer for the experience but wondered how much I had disrupted his day. He didn't seem to mind. There was a cart full of bright orange pumpkins at his gate, a yellow field beyond and buzzards catching eddies in a clear blue sky. Half a mile down the road I stopped at a lane that skewed off at ninety degrees. It was perfectly straight and stretched, seemingly without end, as far as I could see. At the junction was a sign that read 'Dead End', and I wondered how it must feel to raise children where even endings fell short of defining your horizons.

Fear and Loathing in Big Rapids

When Hunter S. Thompson went on his big road trip in *Fear and Loathing in Las Vegas*, he found himself wired, wasted and paranoid at a hotel hosting a conference of district attorneys. His brain had been mashed, pulled, stretched and pummelled by LSD, cocaine, ether, tequila, rum, amyl nitrate, marijuana, mescaline and a variety of 'uppers, downers, screamers and laughers'. He was travelling with his psychopathic Hispanic lawyer in a high-end rental car he called the Great Red Shark and the sun was shining. He had a lot of material. When I went on mine, Big Rapids was hosting a state-wide conference on *weatherisation* – double glazing and home insulation. I was standing in the car park of my motel smoking with Big Steve, Little Steve, George, Eric and Kimble, drinking their home-made blackberry wine. They were weatherisation guys and they told epic stories about draughty doors and windows, leaky roofs and inappropriate heating systems. The merits of PVC against hard wood were sliced, diced and served up on the salty debating table of energy efficiency. I took a drag on my cigarette to take away the taste of blackberry and looked across to my car. It was a Toyota Corolla. Slyly, I positioned myself behind Big Steve and used him as a break against driving rain and sixty-mile-an-hour winds. According to the news, 26,000 people in Michigan were without electricity.

When I could take the glamour no more, I went to bed.

It is very difficult to describe the look on a hotel receptionist's face when, as you are checking out and paying your bill, you ask whether they have a room for the night. I did this nearly every day. Usually they would just cock their head to one side and give me a straight answer with a puzzled look on their face. It was nearly always yes; nowhere in Christendom is October a particularly busy month. Very rarely did they enquire as to what I was up to, and I supposed that was why they were hotel receptionists and not particle physicists smashing atoms to pieces at the Large Hadron Collider in Switzerland.

But today was different.

'There is one room tonight, but then you'll have to leave. We're fully booked for the rest of the weatherisation conference. Every hotel and motel in Big Rapids is full. You didn't know about the conference? Everyone knows about the conference.'

I looked at the receptionist with faux bashfulness and drew imaginary circles on the reception desk with a forefinger.

'Oh, heck, I realise I should have known about the conference but – can you believe this? – I forgot. I've been out of town on a big academic project.' I looked over my shoulder and leaned forward, whispering. 'It's about the movement of cash around the country. I can't say too much about it, but how it moves through Big Rapids could prove crucial. Come on, you must have one room, just a little one?'

But after tonight, he didn't. By tomorrow, he reckoned, the nearest motel with a vacancy could be forty miles away. I decided to take this one tonight, checked back in and dumped my gear. It dawned on me that nobody had ever offered *me* a job at the Large Hadron Collider.

The location of my future accommodation was important because I was off to meet Megan, her father, Jim, and the ten-dollar bill. Megan had called the night before and apologised for disappearing from my radar but there had been something of a disaster. When she and her father arrived on Sunday, they found their cabin had been ransacked by thieves. All their hunting gear was stolen, amounting to more than 20,000 dollars' worth of equipment. Food had been taken, a clock and even the contents of a jar of sweets. Jim and Megan had spent the following forty-eight hours reporting the matter to the police and their insurance company and restocking the cabin, their weapons, food and ammunition.

We met at a restaurant in the centre of Big Rapids, a pretty old town with one main street and broad satellite roads and avenues lined with colonial-style houses and ancient trees. On the edge of town was a large university campus and the usual selection of retail lots. I was nervous when I walked in. I was about to meet a hunter whose twenty-four-year-old daughter I had followed for more than 200 miles after meeting her for five minutes in a bar. If I had been him, I would have given me a good kicking.

When I had first met Megan, she wore big lacquered hair and lots of corporate meet-and-greet make-up. Now she was dressed down with her father. They both wore jeans, fleeces and boots; he had a baseball cap, her hair was tied back with an Alice band. She was much prettier without the corporate look. She gave me a warm welcome and I stepped forward and held out my hand for Jim to shake. I felt like a spotty youth on a first date. Jim was slightly severe in appearance and did not smile. Given what he had just been through, I was astonished he was here at all, and I said so.

I thought it wise to pull out my credentials, the original ten-pound-note magazine article and my press pass. If I was going to butcher Jim in the middle of the night, the least I could do was give him a name to scream as the lights went out.

'It's a terrible thing,' he said. 'Years of collecting equipment gone, just like that. This is a nice town, but like everywhere else, there's bad people who do things like this. The cops think they've got them but I don't know whether we'll get anything back. Punks.'

Jim was sixty-five and a retired steel worker from Taylor, Michigan, twenty miles south-west of Detroit. He was slim and about five foot ten with a well-proportioned face and taut, weathered skin. I would have put him at about fifty-five. He had piercing blue eyes that fixed you when he spoke and I thought he looked a little sad, but not from losing his possessions. He didn't smile much and I wondered whether he would rather I wasn't there. But he wasn't judging me and I liked that. I felt he was the sort of man who never lied and never let you down.

It was immediately clear that Megan and Jim were close. She was showing him off and I thought that any man whose daughter was that proud of him could die happy. Megan had an older brother who was not interested in hunting and two older sisters who were staunchly feminine and preferred not to get their shoes dirty. She was the antithesis of that. From an early age she had loved the countryside and hunting with her father in the cold, rain and mud, sitting in mildewed forests while the wet dusk surrounded them in uncompromising silence. Because that was how you hunted with bows and arrows. Silently. Jim and Megan dispelled my assumption that you crashed through the undergrowth like Robin Hood in Sherwood Forest, nailing Bambi with every arrow you pulled from your quiver. No. You sat and waited. If you coughed, the deer were gone. If you moved, they saw you. If you breathed heavily, they smelled you and melted away. If your equipment creaked or groaned, if your boots squeaked, if you sneezed or scratched an itch, they vanished into the gloom. It was a battle of wits and I guessed that was the challenge.

'My dad bought forty acres here when he retired,' said Megan. 'It has a little cabin on it. There's no running water or electricity, no plumbing and no telephone. You can only hunt for an hour and a half, maybe two, when the deer come out to eat at dusk and before darkness falls and you can't see them any more. We sit up in trees and wait for a clear shot, but it's very rare that you get one.'

They respected the countryside and the animals. They never shot does because does produced the fawns, and they never shot bucks unless there was a clear shot behind the foreleg and through the heart and lungs (isn't this what Rick told me way back in Lebanon?) . When they did that, death came instantly – even with a bow and arrow – and their discipline was such that they never broke their own rules. It meant they were lucky to achieve one or two kills in a whole season and when they did they used all the animal for meat. I had no problem with hunting where it was not gratuitously painful or profligate. After all, I ate meat and believed complaining about the death of animals while chewing on a burger seemed the height of hypocrisy.

We ate chilli and swigged Coca-Cola while Megan talked excitedly of last season and her moderate but skilled success with the bow.

'Anyway,' she said, glancing at Jim, 'we've got a lot of fixing up to do tonight, but we'd like you to come over tomorrow and hunt with us. You could stay in the cabin. If not having water or electricity and using a hole in the ground as a toilet doesn't bother you, then you'd be welcome.'

I was beside myself, and not just because it would get me away from the weatherisation conference and potential homelessness. I'm sure some chilli ran down my chin as I said yes please.

So, at dusk the following day I am sitting on a wooden platform in a maple tree with Megan. It is windy and the platform is swaying somewhere between gentle and violent. She is armed with a 300-dollar carbon-compound bow and a quiver of arrows at sixty dollars a dozen that look as if they could penetrate a tank; the bow's forty-five-pound tension fires its missiles at 280 feet per second. We are wearing padded camouflaged coveralls and I have a woollen full-face balaclava that has shed some fibres into my throat. As these tickle, tears are rolling down my cheeks and my nose is running. I need to cough, sneeze or choke but the imperative of silence has been drilled into me and I don't want my first hunting session to result in a spoiling for Megan. It is growing darker and my eyes are playing tricks on me. Did something just move in the undergrowth? Is that an *elf*? The smell of decaying leaves is sweet and pungent; the sense of oneness with nature strangely complete. I cannot remember feeling so alive, every sense slapped out of indolence and turned to max. I move my head from side to side, watching, one degree at a time, feeling a part of something, not just observing. I am amazed by Megan's poise and control, scanning, scanning. We sit for an hour, maybe more, swaying, choking. Below is a trail well trod by the deer, but the fading light seems a dimension short – logic tells me the forest floor is twenty feet away but it could be fifty. There is a faint chorus and I hear a crow, a grouse, a blue jay. I am gagging now but you will have to shoot me before I will surrender to it.

Gently, Megan nudges me in the ribs and begins to stand and pull back her bow, kissing its taut nylon string. In the process, she nods and I follow the line of her gaze. I can see nothing. The stillness is massive, the silence brittle. With a controlled grace, she lowers herself back into a seated position and leans across to me, whispering, 'There. A doe and a fawn. No shot.'

And as if a veil has been pulled from my tired urban eyes, I see them, not as complete deer shapes, but as contours and lines that read snout, foreleg, eyes. The fawn has its face in the ground, the doe is still, watching, suspicious, alert to the power of ten. A rush of excitement wells up in me, not as a freshness of experience but as understanding. *I get it.* And then, with the bob of a tail, they slide into the undergrowth and are gone.

I had arrived earlier in the day with low expectations. Jim had drawn me a map and I found the cabin with ease, tracing south along lonely roads and pulling off on to a track that led to the Schneiders' home from home. The cabin resembled something between a chalet and a shack. It was in three sections: a basic living area with a table, an oil-burning stove and a portable two-ring gas burner for cooking. Hung on the walls were five or six deer skulls with small antlers, the result of previous seasons' hunting successes. There really weren't many, which emphasised the kind of sport in which the Schneiders were engaged: a blood sport with not very much blood. The outer walls were constructed from PVC panels and the roof at the centre slid lower to the left and right to form two more rooms in which were basic cots for sleeping. The bedroom to the left was already built when Jim bought the place and the one to the right had been added by him. The bedrooms were chilly and a little damp, though the centre section was as warm as a deer's muzzle from the heat given off by the stove. Outside was a large picnic table and a trestle loaded with bottles of water and beer. There was a low chiller cabinet kept cold from a generator that was fired up at night, and which provided power to a small television set in the right-hand bedroom. Nothing would stop Jim from watching football and baseball in the evenings. In the camp was a gorgeously silver streamlined trailer next to a flagpole with a hoisted Stars and Stripes, several outbuildings for storage and, some fifty yards from the cabin, a small wooden privy that resembled a phone box. This had a ledge with a toilet seat above a hole in the ground. Each time you went, you were required to dump a trowel full of lime into the darkness below. On the rear wall was a sign that read 'Fasten seat belts'.

I wasn't allowed to hunt; I didn't have a licence and in all likelihood I would have shot myself in the foot, which would have made hopping from one to the other a painful experience. But Jim and Megan had bought a new toy, a Ten Point 1,000-dollar crossbow, and they set up a target and let me shoot at it. I hit the ring outside the bullseye with my first shot and tried not to hoot when their beagle Charlie joined me to pull out the arrow.

Over piping-hot coffee inside the cabin, Jim and Megan were telling me about hunting deer – about how their sense of smell was their most powerful defence; about how they could scent meat-eaters up-wind and about their innate skill as a quarry – when Jim's oldest friend and hunting companion arrived. His name was Glenn Waddell, a retired Ford car worker from Detroit. He was a big man in every sense and the cabin seemed smaller from the moment he walked in, round-bellied and moustachioed. He flashed a huge smile at Megan and gave Jim the smallest of nods, but he ignored me completely. It was clear he was no pushover – I would have to earn his respect. I liked him immediately and in my mind I was already calling him Big Dog. He was hard as compound fibre but I suspected he had a soft centre.

I had taken along beer and wine and asked if I could cook the evening meal to show gratitude for the Schneiders' hospitality. I enjoy cooking and, like a fey city boy at an Islington dinner party, I prepared chicken in a tarragon sauce with vegetables and sweet potato mash on the two-ring stove before we went hunting. When I served it up, Megan gushed compliments but the two old hunters grimaced and chewed, flashing disapproving looks at one another. I really could be very stupid in the most simple of situations. *Poulet avec sauce estragon à la Michigan hunting shack.* I still shudder, but it didn't spoil the evening. We drank the beer and wine and the three told hunting stories and swapped tips on new equipment while the stove pumped out its heat. Later on Megan lit a bonfire and we sat outside under a clear and complicated sky, the stars as bright as any I had seen from Missouri or Arkansas or Kansas. By the time we slipped into our sleeping bags for the night, Glenn had begun to grunt at me and acknowledge my existence. As the lights went out in the room we were sharing, I could have sworn I saw him smile.

The Deer Hunters
(N 43° 29.741' N, 085° 24.182' W)

The next few days assumed a pace of their own. We would rise early, put on layers of clothing on top of the ones in which we had slept, shiver, stretch and splash a little water on our faces in the cold outside. There was nowhere to spend money and I began to forget about the ten-dollar bill.

Megan had a degree in advertising from Michigan State University but more importantly she had a thirst for knowledge. We discussed books and travel. She had been to Europe and wanted to see more of the world, fearlessly, voraciously. The pub-restaurant that she managed was a large and busy concern, seemingly much too onerous for a twenty-four-year-old to handle, yet she was the boss and on the rare occasions when she found a signal on her cellphone, I would hear her discussing problems with her staff. It seemed that Megan had a good rapport with them and they called her Marge in Charge. She was slim with brown hair, clear skin and deep brown eyes. She had a waspish sense of humour and seemed reassuringly indomitable.

Jim was a Vietnam veteran and I guessed it was his experience there that made him appear sad. Megan told me he didn't talk about the war but something awful had happened to him, something worse even than being shot through the stomach, which he had been (cruelly, I had badgered him to show me his wound – the bullet had entered his stomach and exited his back). I found myself drawn more and more to Jim. There were men in Vietnam towards whom others would gravitate. They were skilled or lucky talismans and, for the superstitious, being in their proximity meant you wouldn't be cut down by a sniper or a bomb. I suspected Jim was such a man.

On day 28, we were in his wood and he was showing me the signs of deer courtship: a broken twig at antler height which had been chewed by a male to leave his scent and, directly below, some marks scratched in the ground on which a doe had urinated. He had come to his own conclusion that the annual rut lasted just seven days, always from 3–10 November. It was a time when, like clockwork, bucks became careless in their pursuit of does. There were three tree platforms, or blinds, in Jim's wood, and we walked past the one in which Megan and I had sat the night before, being careful to avoid the paths used by the deer.

'If they get your scent on that, you can forget about seeing any deer for some time,' said Jim.

The wood comprised mainly oak, white pine, which was Jim's favourite, and Australian pine, which he described as being no good for anything; it was too spindly and its wood made poor furniture. It was good cover for the deer, though not as good as the young beech trees. I wanted to spend as much time with Jim as I could.

The next morning, Jim, Megan and I went for breakfast at the American Legion club in Morley. It was a cold, grey day and the legion was warm and empty. It resembled any one of dozens of British Legion clubs I had visited. I ordered corned beef hash with two eggs, coffee and toast while the waitress made small talk and hovered around our table. I don't know whether it was the surroundings or my gentle persistence, but after a while Jim told us what had happened in Vietnam.

'I'd always been a hunter and I guess that was useful when we had to go out on patrol,' he said. 'I was used to tracking animals and knew what to look for on the ground, to see signs of danger where the VC had been and how to find them if we were on ambush. That kind of led to me going on point and then I ended up with my own platoon. I took great care of my men and I did my best to keep them safe, using everything I had learned in the woods.

'But one day we got a new commanding officer and he was kind of aggressive. He ordered us to patrol an area that I knew was just too dangerous, and I told him so. He wouldn't listen, so that night we went out on patrol and we were ambushed. I got shot and some of the other men were wounded. I was medevaced out and that was the end of the war for me.'

Megan was looking across the table at her father, her hand over her mouth. She knew something like this had happened and she had even discussed some aspects of the episode with me, but she had never heard her father talk about it. Jim had begun to well up but he took a deep breath and carried on.

'A while later he made them do it again,' he said. 'It was *still* too dangerous. Most of them were killed. They were my friends and I wasn't there to take care of them.'

He stood up and walked across the club, wiping his eyes, his shoulders heavy with a burden that wasn't his to carry but which he had heaved and shunted around for most of his life.

I expected to return to Chicago with Megan and the money

when she had to leave for work on 29 October. Either that or I thought she might use the bill to pay for her train ticket from Grand Rapids and I would pick up the rest of my journey from there. But the night before, she fell into an argument with Glenn over the outcome of a World Series baseball game between the Texas Rangers and the San Francisco Giants which resulted in a ten-dollar bet which Glenn won. Megan settled it with IA74407937A and suddenly I was on the trail of Big Dog. I had been looking forward to a bath and some Chinese food back in Chicago or Grand Rapids, but now I would be staying in the woods as long as Glenn was. I said an emotional goodbye to Megan and resolved to stick to the Dog like glue. I could see immediately that he didn't like the responsibility.

'It's a goddamn crazy idea if you ask me,' he said. 'I might just go and spend it somewhere without telling you.'

On my third night in the woods, a nephew of Jim's came to hunt so I was told to sit with Glenn in the second blind. He wasn't too happy about having a rookie around.

'You ain't gonna take your cigarettes, are you?'

I told him I wasn't that stupid and had learned a huge amount from Megan and Jim.

'You know you gotta sit still? You don't move, you don't breathe, you don't make any sound at all. You got that?'

I nodded and climbed into my camouflage. Glenn frowned.

Once up on the blind, the platform creaked and groaned under our combined weight and I wondered how much it would hurt to plunge twenty feet into moss and lichen.

'Sssshhhhh!' said Glenn, as if my thoughts had penetrated the silence. And the waiting began.

If I had been nervous hunting with Megan, I was terrified with Big Dog. If I so much as belched he was going to knock me to kingdom come. We waited more than half an hour and the darkness crept around us. I dared pull up my sleeve to look at my watch: forty-five minutes. I stifled a cough and a yawn. I wanted to yell from a lightning cramp in a calf. I held a finger under my nose to stave off a sneeze. And all the while I was perfectly still.

Then Glenn stood up. Not to shoot anything; just to stretch his legs! The noise seemed deafening. He sat down and rustled in his pocket, holding out a small chocolate bar.

'Want one?' he said.

I couldn't believe it. Beneath my balaclava I felt a rising indignation. I shook my head, thinking that at least one of us had to uphold the silent traditions of deer hunting.

After a time, Glenn reached into his pocket and again I heard the rustle of another chocolate bar being opened.

'Sure you won't have one? They're real good.'

My sense of outrage was almost complete when I heard Big Dog fart.

It wasn't until I heard the noise again, by which time I was apoplectic with the hypocrisy of it all, that I realised it had been two branches rubbing together.

And then Glenn became completely still. It had been too early for the deer to come out. He knew it but I was too inexperienced to understand. I felt foolish and was relieved that I hadn't said anything to him. I pulled my hood tight around my head.

Again, I could see nothing and without Glenn my night would have been empty. Over and over again, he carefully pointed to bucks, does and fawns that I would have missed. Big Dog added to the lessons Megan had taught me until my eyes were trained and ready, not to look for deer but to look for the shapes and lines of movement that could not be trees or bushes. You hardly ever saw a complete creature. You saw its flank or the curve of its neck, and then the electrical pathways in your brain filled in the missing pixels. We had five or six sightings, which was a good tally.

Just as it was becoming too dark to see, there was a rustling below and Glenn rose up with an agility that surprised me. He pulled back his bow and I heard a voice in my head shouting, 'Shoot! Shoot!' He stood like that for five minutes, an age in the deepening night, and then he sat down.

'I had a shot, but I couldn't see if it was a buck or a doe,' he said. 'And that means you don't shoot.'

We climbed down and, released from our vow of silence, we talked excitedly about what we had seen – about the ones that got away and whether I had spotted this or he had tracked that. I hadn't let him down and for a moment I thought he might even slap me on the back. I felt something like friendship radiating from him and silently basked in that warmth for the rest of the evening.

Glenn was going home the next day, Saturday 30 October, which meant I would have a chance to see Detroit if he didn't spend the money before he reached home. That night Jim, Glenn, Jim's nephew Mike and I went to the American Legion for a fish supper. Glenn and I told the others about our sightings and I checked an urge to exaggerate the number and the size of the beasts (how long, I wondered, before the temptation bested the hunter? Four outings? Five?). Mike, a high-school principal, insisted on picking up the tab. The ten-dollar bill stayed in Big Dog's wallet. We went back to the cabin, cracked open some beers and played Texas hold 'em for pennies.

'I've been watching this for years,' said Mike, dealing a hand. 'Deer hunters spend two hours a day hunting and about ten drinking beer, talking about their equipment and playing poker.'

Jim and Glenn chuckled. I looked around the table. I couldn't have been made more welcome; I couldn't have had more interesting company. But I also wondered how much better it would have been if Megan had been there. I bet Jim thought the same thing every day.

I woke on day 29 with senses of elation and loss. I had almost finished following the money, which in itself was nothing. Inside the thing, though, was something tiny but with great mass, something made powerful and intrinsic from experience. I thought of Kay and Rick and their love for each other, a sense of giving that I felt had rubbed off on me though only now was I willing to believe it. The characters who oiled my way and made me smile: Paul, Ray, Ron, Glenn, Megan and Jim. And Mr One-and-Only, Dean. The people who shoved my lumpen will to places outside my comfort zone and made me look at things differently – Paul Huning, Jennifer and Nathan Walker, and Darrell Mikulencak. There were the bit-part players: Margaret and Randall LaDow, Chuck Patel, Nicole Kilgore, Byron France, Elisabeth Fox, K.K. Snyder, Syd Rodway, Deneva Elvins, Judith Hunt, Laverda Puyear, Paula Morriss and Adam Antonucci. And there were those who didn't receive the ten-dollar bill but without whose presence my journey would have been poorer: John Brenneman, Connie Bisett, Clarence Hicks, Majick and Nacho, Ernie Schlatter and Phyllis Bell, Stacey, Rachel and Sarah, Wayne and, of course, the members of Crash Meadows.

My sleeping bag was damp and I peeled myself from it, went outside and splashed mineral water on my face. I was filthy again. There were beads of dew on the grass and I left footsteps on it as I made a circuit of the compound, mentally and foolishly saying goodbye to the silver trailer, the flagpole, the privy and the Australian pines. Charlie followed, sniffing at my ankles, and I petted him for the last time. I made coffee for Jim, Mike and Glenn and sat down with a cigarette. I would be giving up again tomorrow.

'What are your plans?' I asked the Big Dog.

'Got none,' he grunted. 'I'm heading home later. And before you ask, I ain't buying nothing. Don't need nothing.'

I thought of London, where people needed things all the time, spent their lives working for them and never seemed to amass as much as Glenn had. I decided to go on, make my journey in daylight, and the fact that I would be ahead of the money didn't bother me. I took Glenn's address and phone number and said I would call later. It was Halloween weekend, a time when people in America partied hard, but Glenn was planning to go home and stay there. I half hoped that he would be attending a wild party where I would celebrate with champagne and new friends, but I knew – had always known – that the end of the journey wouldn't come with fireworks, harps or bells.

I seriously doubted that Jim had ever hugged a man, but I forced one on him anyway and shook his hand long and hard. His eyes were red when I drove out of the compound, but not as red as mine.

I stopped for breakfast by the lake in Morley and watched migrating geese splash-landing like clumsy waterskiers. There was a weak sunshine and a silent peace blanketed the town and fell across my shoulders. I walked out into an icy wind and climbed back into the car. The mileage read 2,998.9.

I headed south, skirted Grand Rapids and then took the I-96 south-east. This would take me through Lansing and all the way to Detroit. The sun melted behind grey clouds. Woods gave way to farmland and the landscape became increasingly industrial the nearer I came to Motor City. It had suffered from a massive shift in population similar to that of St Louis. In the years between 2000 and 2010, 25 per cent of its residents had left the city for the suburbs. The motor industry still had a serious presence, but it was not what it had been in the 1950s and unemployment was running at 20 per cent. Some of its inner-city areas were run-down and abandoned. It had been hit particularly hard by the housing-market crash and crime and drugs had become endemic in the most deprived areas.

Glenn lived in Southgate, south-west of the city, and I treated myself to a room at a Holiday Inn. I ran a bath, ordered room service and fell asleep. Later, I found it had a laundry room and I washed all of my clothes, save what I stood in. I called Glenn and he repeated what he had already told me. He was going nowhere. We agreed I would visit him the next day.

Show Me the Money
(42° 13.024' N, 083° 13.019' W)

If I hadn't dreamed all night, I felt as if I were in one when I woke up. Soon, I would have to make decisions for myself and I wasn't sure that was something I would be able to adjust to very quickly. I had breakfast and drove aimlessly around Detroit until Glenn called and invited me over. He had five grown-up children, twelve grandchildren and a great-grandchild but now he lived only with his wife, Lois, in a large, modern house with a spectacular veranda and a broad sweep of garden. He had been a maintenance welder at the Rouge Ford plant in Dearborn, which was once the largest industrial complex in the world. He said he had been lucky, working at a time when the company paid well and provided good benefits. Today, younger workers were taken on and paid half what their older colleagues earned, and that was a source of resentment.

'The unions are weaker now and there's a global market,' he said. 'For a long time, the Japs simply made better cars than we did, and they made 'em cheaper. There was a time when Americans only bought American cars, but that changed around twenty years ago and people started buying Toyota and Honda.

The industry is still the biggest employer in the city, but it's nowhere near as big as it used to be.'

So what of the future?

'I don't work in the industry any more, but what I'm hearing is optimism. We've learned our lessons and we're making good cars again.'

We were drinking coffee on stools in Glenn's kitchen and on an island to his right was his wallet. He caught me looking at it and smiled. He reached over and picked it up.

'You looking for this?' he said. And he pulled out IA74407937A.

I felt bashful but he knew what I wanted.

'What time does this thing finish?' he asked.

'7.30.' It was just after 4 p.m.

'Well, I ain't going nowhere, so you might as well have it.'

I could have kissed him, but that might have led to a swift right hook, so I just nodded and took out a replacement from my pocket. He gave me my ten-dollar bill and laughed out loud.

'You happy now?'

I was. I was very happy.

Lois came in and I gave her some flowers I had bought earlier, then we said goodbye. Glenn smiled at me as I drove off and I felt like a dog with a bone. I listened for the sound of harps or bells – looked up and saw no fireworks – but decided it wasn't over. I had three hours left and I was going to use them.

There are two ways to enter Canada from Detroit, either over the Ambassador Bridge or via the Detroit–Windsor tunnel, counter-intuitively heading south into Windsor. I decided to take Alexander Hamilton for a little drive with the time remaining. I could say his journey had encompassed six states, 3,000 miles and two countries, and I liked the sound of that.

For once, I had not had to pack, so I had no luggage with me.

It was at the hotel. I drove into the tunnel and was stopped before its actual entrance, which was on the American side but staffed by Canadians, in much the same way as British immigration officers monitor Channel Tunnel arrivals into the UK from French soil.

I handed over my passport and car rental papers to a cheery man in a well-pressed uniform. I was feeling very pleased with myself. I had the ten-dollar bill, I had almost completed my mission and would explore Windsor before driving back for a celebratory meal.

'What's your destination?' asked the official.

'Windsor,' I replied.

'And what's your business there?'

'Oh, I'm just going to have a look around.'

'Can I inspect your luggage please?'

'Um, I don't have any.'

'Your rental has expired. Does the car rental company know you're leaving the country with this vehicle?'

'Ah, no.'

'So you have no luggage and you're leaving the country in an expired rental?'

He thought I was a car thief.

I had no choice but to tell him the unlikeliest story he was ever to hear, even if he found the elixir of youth and intended to stand guard at the Canadian border until the tunnel collapsed. But he believed me. He laughed and laughed and made me tell him everything. And the sound of his laughter was like harps and bells to me.

'Well, I'll let you in, but your insurance won't be valid. You want to risk it?'

I said I didn't. Only a fool would travel in North America without insurance. I would turn around and go back. But then, of course, I would have the same problem with American immigration.

'Am I in Canada?' I asked.

'Nope, you're in no-man's land.'

So I couldn't say Alexander Hamilton had travelled abroad?

'No, I'm afraid not.'

And then a broad smile broke out across his face.

'Oh, what the hell,' he said. And he stamped my passport.

I turned the car around and saw him laughing in my rear-view mirror. Then I went through the same thing at American immigration. No luggage, expired rental, no insurance. But they listened to my story and let me back in.

It was dark by the time I returned to my hotel and by now I was laughing too. Six states, I could say; 3,299.2 miles, I could say. And, with a light heart, a sense of achievement and a swollen chest, *two* countries, I could say.

Well . . .

. . . ish.

Epilogue

In quantum physics, scientists say that the act of merely observing an experiment affects its outcome. It is a difficult concept to grasp and one which infuriated even Albert Einstein, but it is a truth that must be accepted if trust is to be placed in the usefulness of the physics itself. That is where scientific faith is not so different from religious faith. I thought about this effect many times on my journey: my mere presence affected the ten-dollar bill's progress. So when people ask me whether anything can be taken from the movement of IA74407937A by economists or monetary planners, I have to be honest and say no. Was my ten-dollar bill's journey a true reflection of what happens to ten-dollar bills from month to month? I would have to say, probably not. The simple truth is that where people might have banked the bill or spent it at a K-Mart, where corporate reluctance would have stymied my efforts to follow it, they spent it some other way – they wanted to be kind to me and, at times, that must surely have involved them choosing something interesting to do with the money over something mundane or boring. At least that is what I suspect and if what I did amounted to an experiment, then its results said more about people than about money. That, on the whole, people are good. They will meet a stranger, feed him, give him a bed for the night and feel the need to send him away with good prospects. And I thank each and every one of them for that.

I must also make a qualification about mileage. The final mileage figure is mine, not the ten-dollar bill's, and it is inflated by two factors: most nights I drove for miles looking for accommodation and, naturally, I used the car to explore wherever I went. However, the bill also took on the mileage of each person who moved around whenever I wasn't with them. In Darrell Mikulencak's case, that involved a flight at 30,000 feet, which arguably made his journey longer than mine if you factored in the greater circumference of the stratosphere. We will never know, therefore, *exactly* how far IA74407937A travelled.

After Detroit, I drove to New York to catch a flight home. A friend lent me an apartment on the Upper West Side and I found myself again pointlessly comparing New York with Chicago.

The next day, with only two hours before I was due to leave for the airport, I received a call from another friend in London who had been monitoring my progress.

'You know that guy on the ten-dollar bill?'

'Alexander Hamilton?'

'Did you know that his portrait, the one that is actually used on the ten dollars, is hanging in the Mayor's Office in New York City?'

I did not know this but resolved to do something about it.

I called Michael Bloomberg's office and explained that I needed to see one of the portraits hanging on the walls. There were tours of the office, where people could admire the mayor's art for themselves, and there had been one that day, but I had missed it. Would they let me come and take a look? There was a long silence on the line, but then a promise that Andrew Brent, Mayor Bloomberg's deputy press secretary, would call me back.

I made my way downtown but with little hope. I had ninety minutes left when Andrew called me.

'You've done *what*?' he asked incredulously. And, as burdened as he must have been with more pressing matters, he arranged to meet me.

He was young and smart and high-powered and I think he thought me more than a little odd. He was dressed in a slim tailored suit and I was in my torn jeans. He led me through the opulence of the Mayor's Office and up two elegant flights of stairs to the Blue Room. The portrait, by John Turnbull, used to reside in the actual office occupied by Mayor Bloomberg, but now it was here, the room in which Andrew and the mayor gave daily briefings to the American media. It was eight feet by five and it hung above an impressive fireplace directly behind the lectern from which all important announcements were made. Hamilton was still at the heart of American politics. I manoeuvred myself, crab-like, in front of Andrew so he couldn't see my underwear, and handed him the ten-dollar bill. I felt in awe of the portrait. Andrew held up the bill and looked from it to the painting and back again.

'Well, I'll be . . .' he said. 'I had no idea.'

I stood in front of the picture and looked into the wise eyes of Alexander Hamilton.

It seemed a fitting way to end my journey and, under my breath and embarrassed, I found myself saying *thank you* to the elder statesman, then to Andrew, and I left the building.

Acknowledgements

I received no financial backing for my journey, but I would like to thank several people and organisations who helped me travel to the United States and get around once I was there, in particular Anna Streatfeild and Travelbag; Alamo/National car rental; British Airways; Jonathan Sloan and all at Hills Balfour; and Garmin, without whose equipment I would have become hopelessly lost.

I would also have become lost once I returned to England had it not been for my agent, Laura Longrigg at MBA, and Rosalind Porter and Alex Clark at Union Books. Thank you all for your wise advice and support.

For their patience with my endless boring rambling on a regular basis, I need not say thank you to my friends Jonathan Callery and Steve Redmond, but I will.

To my readers, Jan Owen, David Felton, Bill Scannell and Mike Dolan, I would like to extend my gratitude for their kind observations and valid criticisms. Also, for their unstinting support, I would like to thank my mother, Pat, sister, Marie, nephew, Ben, and nieces, Nicola and Laura.

But most of all, for bearing with me through this and all the time, all my love goes to my partner, Suzanne.